*The Cambridge Introduction to*
## *Literature and Philosophy*

Literature and philosophy have long shared an interest in questions of truth, value, and form. And yet, from ancient times to the present, they have often sharply diverged, both in their approach to these questions and in their relationship to one another. Moreover, the vast differences among individual writers, historical periods, and languages pose challenges for anyone wishing to understand the relationship between them. This *Introduction* provides a synthetic and original guide to this vast terrain. It uncovers the deep interests that literature and philosophy share while offering a lucid account of their differences. It sheds new light on many standing debates and offers students and scholars of literary criticism, literary theory, and philosophy a chance to think freshly about questions that have preoccupied the Western tradition from its very beginnings up until the present.

Anthony J. Cascardi is Dean of Arts and Humanities at the University of California, Berkeley, where he also holds the Sidney and Margaret Ancker Chair in Comparative Literature, Rhetoric, and Spanish. His many publications across the fields of literature and philosophy include *The Subject of Modernity* (Cambridge 1992); *Consequences of Enlightenment* (Cambridge 1998); and *Cervantes, Literature, and the Discourse of Politics* (2012), which was awarded the Phyllis Goodhart Gordon Prize by the Renaissance Society of America.

# The Cambridge Introduction to Literature and Philosophy

ANTHONY J. CASCARDI
*University of California, Berkeley*

Shaftesbury Road, Cambridge CB2 8EA, United Kingdom

One Liberty Plaza, 20th Floor, New York, NY 10006, USA

477 Williamstown Road, Port Melbourne, VIC 3207, Australia

314–321, 3rd Floor, Plot 3, Splendor Forum, Jasola District Centre, New Delhi – 110025, India

103 Penang Road, #05–06/07, Visioncrest Commercial, Singapore 238467

Cambridge University Press is part of Cambridge University Press & Assessment, a department of the University of Cambridge.

We share the University's mission to contribute to society through the pursuit of education, learning and research at the highest international levels of excellence.

www.cambridge.org
Information on this title: www.cambridge.org/9780521281232



First published 2014

*A catalogue record for this publication is available from the British Library*

*Library of Congress Cataloging-in-Publication data*
Cascardi, Anthony J., 1953–
The Cambridge introduction to literature and philosophy / Anthony J. Cascardi.
pages cm. – (Cambridge introductions to literature)
Includes bibliographical references and index.
ISBN 978-1-107-01054-3 (hardback) – ISBN 978-0-521-28123-2 (paperback)
1. Literature – Philosophy. 2. Philosophy in literature. 3. Truth in literature. 4. Values in literature. 5. Literary form. 6. Criticism. 7. Literature – History and criticism – Theory, etc. I. Title.
PN45.C3388 2014
801–dc23 2013042665

ISBN 978-1-107-01054-3 Hardback
ISBN 978-0-521-28123-2 Paperback

# Contents

# Acknowledgments

This book would never have been written had it not been for the persistent persuading, cajoling, and encouragement of my editor at Cambridge University Press, Ray Ryan. With steadfast good sense he succeeded in convincing me that it was not only possible to write an introduction to a set of subjects as seemingly vast and ungainly as the relations between literature and philosophy, but that the experience could be a rewarding one. In that he was certainly right. I can only add that by the time I did agree to write this book I was in quite a better position to carry it off than when his persuading first began.

What insights I have gained into the relations between literature and philosophy are owed to a train of colleagues and friends who have shared an interest in these subjects over many years. At Berkeley, Charles Altieri has been a constant intellectual companion. Conversations with Judith Butler, Hans Sluga, Rob Kaufman, Dorothea Frede, Ramona Naddaff, and Tony Long, among many others, provided some of the intellectual energy that helped sustain this project in direct or indirect ways. The same could be said for many other colleagues, far and wide, including Richard Eldridge, Alexander Nehamas, Bernie Rhie, Fred Rush, Stanley Rosen, Jay M. Bernstein, Aleš Erjavec, and Stanley Cavell. I am grateful to Christopher Patrick Miller for his help preparing the Index.

# Introduction

Literature and philosophy are very much like two family members: sometimes they quarrel furiously, and other times they get along quite well, either by ignoring one another's existence or by believing that they share every possible interest. This book is an introduction to the kinship that lies at the root of their relationship and their quarrels. It begins by explaining that, like the members of most every family, they share a history that bears upon all their dealings. That history is at least as old as Plato, who refers to it as "ancient." Its implications for the present are numerous. The literary challenges to philosophy, no less than some philosophical resistances to literature, persist in part because their respective proponents believe that there is something of essential value that the other fails to see. But the subject of this book is not just their differences. The affinities between philosophy and literature are substantial and deep; indeed, the differences in question would scarcely matter except for the fact that literature and philosophy share some essential concerns. Matters of truth, of value, and of form – which I adopt as the organizing categories of this *Introduction* – are not the exclusive province of either one. Yet literature and philosophy nonetheless tend to proceed in very different ways (and sometimes with different consequences) in their approach to these issues. This *Introduction* offers a way to make sense of the affinities and the differences that seem most consequential between them. It gives a broad picture of a field that is sometimes quite contested but, beyond that it explains why literature and philosophy ought to matter to one another, even when they do not always recognize this need.

"Literature" and "philosophy" name vast domains, and this Introduction is relatively short. To begin by defining these terms would be to set out on a fool's errand. Is a television series a work of literature? (*The Wire* has been regarded as such.) Is a graphic novel? Was Cicero a philosopher? Was Coleridge? Such matters may not be decidable in any conclusive way. I say this in full acknowledgement of the fact that the issues raised by such questions call for as much sharpening as possible. One might be tempted, for instance, to think that literature cultivates the use of fictions whereas philosophy's commitment to truth censures them. But this turns out to be roundly false; there is as much use of fiction in some kinds of philosophy as there is in literature. Likewise, there is a literature of fact, but also a literary interest in truth that may not depend on a fidelity to matters of fact. Or, one might be tempted to say that philosophy is interested in making valid arguments, and that literature does not share this interest and relies instead on plausibility to make its claims. There is a history of thinking about literature in these terms that goes back at least to Aristotle. But this is an equally unreliable way to distinguish them. Much of the European sonnet tradition is, for example, structured around some form of argument. But what *kind* of arguments, and addressed to whom? One might rightly ask. Milton's *Aeropagitica* is manifestly an argument about education – but it is also literature. We would likely find ourselves in a similar quandary with virtually any attempt to approach the relations between literature and philosophy by establishing watertight definitions, including those that might invoke notions of aesthetic value, historical specificity, or universal validity. Philosophy is, after all, a historically specific enterprise, and one that has undergone considerable change over time. Try to imagine the works of Descartes without the science of Galileo on the heavens – we might not have had *Meditations on First Philosophy* or *Discourse on the Method*. Kant and Hegel would likely have regarded questions of progress and history very differently had it not been for the French Revolution. Wittgenstein's writings, early and late, are tied to the worlds of Vienna and Cambridge. Philosophy is also aesthetic, which is to say that it is responsive to matters of form (including the shape of its own writing) and to the idea of beauty (think of Plato, Aquinas, and Kant). It is important to understand why Hume uses both the treatise and the dialogue (e.g., "Dialogues Concerning Natural Religion"), why Nietzsche prefaces *The Gay Science* with a series of German rhymes, and why Rousseau writes in the genre of the confession and Voltaire in the form of the "philosophical tale" or *conte philosophique* in works such as *Zadig* and *L'Ingénu*. In short, the issues of greatest concern in the sometimes vexed relations between literature and philosophy are rarely ones that can be settled by defining them as wholly different kinds of writing. This is an introduction to a set of relations, not to a set of neatly defined things. It is an inquiry into what Stanley Cavell described as an "open-ended thematics."[1]

We also need to recognize that each of these terms (literature and philosophy) has evolved considerably over time. These terms do not mean the same thing across all cultural and historical contexts because the practices to which they refer are the products of cultures in the process of change. In some historical contexts, for instance, the designation "literature" had little to do with things of special artistic value; the term simply indicated a kind of writing.

"Poetry" once meant virtually all of literature. The philosophical notion of "virtue," and likewise conceptions of the *specific* virtues indicate very different things in classical antiquity and in the modern Christian world. To speak as if literature and philosophy were fixed and unchanging would be to misrepresent the case. That said, each has come over time to attach particular value to its identity, often construed in opposition to the other.

Rather than work from definitions, I proceed by suggesting that literature and philosophy form parts of intersecting traditions. Traditions matter. Writers call into memory, build on, and struggle against their predecessors, sometimes repeating their efforts and sometimes displacing them. They take up old questions, try new answers, repeat or invent forms and styles, and inevitably think and write under the influence of those who have preceded them in what we may construe as traditions of discourse.[2] They cast glances at the writings from adjacent discourses – from religion, politics, and the law, among others. Traditions of discourse, like all traditions, create allegiances and also invite resistance. For the most part, literature and philosophy in the West have conceived themselves as part of distinct traditions. To be sure, there have been some significant points of convergence, as when Aristotle treats tragedy in the *Poetics*, when Jacques Derrida takes up questions of the law through Kafka's *The Trial* ("Before the Law"), or when Jorge Luis Borges reflects on time, identity, and chance in the stories collected in *Ficciones* (e.g., "Tlön Uqbar, Orbis Tertius" and "The Circular Ruins"). But because literature and philosophy have often conceived their identities in contrast to one another, the points of intersection between them are often flashpoints – the places when their divergent orientations and interests have sparked fierce battles.

This *Introduction* is designed to give an account of these flashpoints but beyond that to bring to light the interests that literature and philosophy share. It explains their sometimes sharp differences, but it also presents a vision of how literature and philosophy might each be able to acknowledge the other's claim on the things it holds of greatest value. Proceeding in this way leads to a series of further questions. How exactly does literature work philosophically (if it does)? In what ways can philosophy be thought of as incorporating the values that literature holds dear (e.g., style, expressiveness)? To say that literature and philosophy are different kinds of writing or different discourses says both too much and too little. The further question to be asked is what do these differences matter to the questions of truth, of value, and of form?

Chapter 1 takes up questions that center on notions of truth. "What is truth?" said jesting Pilate (John 18:38), declining to answer. Does truth lie in the propositions of language? In the correspondence of ideas to reality? Does it lie in the representation of verifiable facts or states of affairs in the world?

To what extent is truth established by consensus or agreement? Plato famously wished to reject literature because he regarded it as a form of untruth, and that because he defined truth in terms of faithfulness to immutable "forms." Is it possible for a work of literature to be true even though it makes no reference to anything that exists, either in this world or in any transcendental sphere? If so, what kind of truth would this be? Much of Chapter 1 will be devoted to different conceptions of truth, and to an investigation of the various sorts of truth-claims that literature and philosophy make. While I make no pretense to a historical coverage of shifting notions of truth, I do nonetheless take into account the role that Plato and a few crucial others (Aristotle, Descartes, Kant, Hegel, and Wittgenstein among them) have played in defining it for much of Western culture.

Truth intersects with a much larger field of concerns, including value and form. Truth may well have a value in itself; it may involve a commitment and require pursuit. There are also those who claim, roughly following Nietzsche, that any notion of truth implies some value, and that truth-seeking must also involve a critique of values. Hilary Putnam argued that the fact-value distinction cannot stand. Value can of course be thought of as something in and of itself, as context-free and independent of anything we might say or do. Plato's notion of the good might be thought of in this category. But that leaves out the question of how we pursue value, or are drawn to it, which for Plato was a matter of *eros* (desire). The work of Part II is to concentrate on the domain of value as including the powers (including the passions and the will) that revolve around the *activity of valuing*. This allows us to broach a much wider range of concerns about human action, interest, and freedom – concerns about what we ought to do (and why), about what and who we regard as worthy (and why), about the commitments we make, and about the sometimes different responses that works of literature and philosophy offer to these questions. One view of morality suggests that we should only regard as binding obligations those imperatives that we could imagine being accepted universally – agreed to and owned in principle by everyone. But how, then, might we account for conflicts of values (or conflicts among frames of value) of the kind we see in Sophocles' *Antigone*, for example, where kinship and the state command very different obligations, and thus are starkly opposed?

The terms "literature" and "philosophy" suggest not just a set of different allegiances, traditions, and interests, but a different set of forms and different ways of writing. Indeed, they often diverge in the role they ascribe to form in relation to thought, truth, and value. This is the subject of Part III. There are specific "forms," and then there is the more general notion of "form." Think of the former (forms) as aligned with genres and with other similar modes of speech and writing (e.g., the dialogue, drama, essay, treatise, novel, allegory). Think of the latter (form) as pointing to the quality that anything said or written has by virtue of the fact that it must inevitably be given some form or other. "Form" not only names things as seemingly diverse as the specific arrangement of words on a page, as in the case of "concrete" poetry or the narrative arc of a novel, but also the shaping of philosophical arguments in the form of dialogue, or as set of fragments, a treatise, or a meandering essay. A caricature of philosophy, which some would argue contains some kernel of truth, is that it regards matters of truth and of value as independent of the forms in which they are expressed. For literature it would seem to be otherwise, since the form of any literary work makes a definitive contribution to the way it frames value and truth. Questions of truth and value engaged by works like *Othello* and *King Lear* begin in what the characters say (sometimes quite literally, as Stanley Cavell has shown), and reach to every dimension of their form, including the fact that they are presented in concrete theatrical situations where we are held from responding directly to what is said. How far these differences reach is a question we will deal with in due course.

I hope it will be clear from what has been said thus far that each of these terms (truth, value, and form) needs to be construed broadly, although I hope without a sacrifice of clarity, to capture the wide array of stances that literature and philosophy have adopted toward them over a great expanse of time. As we proceed, a series of specific examples will help make the issues in question substantially more concrete than they might otherwise be. "Truth" needs to embrace something beyond the notion of a correspondence between ideas in the mind and things or states of affairs in the world, although the so-called correspondence theory of truth needs to be acknowledged as being of crucial importance, alongside the dialectical, pragmatic, and edifying accounts of truth that seem more congenial to works of literature. The notion of "truthfulness" put forward by Bernard Williams needs to be recognized alongside more skeptical views of the very idea of truth itself.[3] We must also probe the relationship between truth and rationality, and between the rational and the real (along with its potentially false cognate, "realism"). "Value" embraces questions of morality and ethics as well as questions of aesthetic value in literature. Whether value is absolute or constructed, given or made, and if so how, are deeply contentious matters that create very different allegiances among their partisans. "Form" in turn needs to be understood broadly enough so that the ancient dyad of form and content (and its implications for literary thinking) won't preclude considering the way in which forms are rooted in the historical and material conditions of life. What is the relationship between made forms and the forces that go into their making? This is a matter of equal importance for Hegel (e.g., in the opening sections of *Phenomenology of Spirit*) and for Nietzsche (e.g., in *The Birth of Tragedy*) as it is for writers like Melville and Whitman, and for Marxist philosophers like Georg Lukács and Louis Althusser.

While each of these three terms – truth, value, and form – names a set of contested issues, they also provide occasions to indicate how they matter to *specific* works of literature and philosophy, not just to a general dialogue between them. While this book is indeed an introduction and covers a relatively large amount of ground, it would hardly make sense to proceed as if these questions were wholly abstract. On the contrary, traditions are formed and are altered as the result of specific arguments, specific works, and the subsequent engagements and responses they provoke. Recognizing the impossibility of an encyclopedic treatment, my hope is that readers will add to the examples offered here many more drawn from their own experience, some of which will no doubt raise further questions.

One final note before proceeding. To consider the areas of similarity and difference, of conjuncture and divergence between literature and philosophy also lets us see the places where each discovers its own limits. The very notion of a discourse implies that there are things that cannot be said within it. Exposure to what lies outside a given discourse can generate an awareness of those limits and, with that, the invention of new forms of language and thought. I reserve the question of limits for the Afterword of this book, noting there that the project of philosophy has frequently been marked by the wish to honor the bounds of what can or cannot be said, known, and conceived. It would be too simplistic to think that an appeal to literature could or ought to liberate philosophy from an obligation to stay within its bounds. Indeed, literature has also found it important to be bound by truth and value, albeit in sometimes different ways and often through different forms than its philosophical twin.

## Suggestions for Further Reading

Gerald Bruns, *On the Anarchy of Poetry and Philosophy* (New York: Fordham University Press, 2006).

Anthony J. Cascardi, ed., *Literature and the Question of Philosophy* (Baltimore, MD: Johns Hopkins University Press, 1987).

Mark Edmundson, *Literature against Philosophy, Plato to Derrida: A Defense of Poetry* (Cambridge: Cambridge University Press, 1995).

Richard Eldridge, ed., *The Oxford Handbook of Philosophy and Literature* (Oxford: Oxford University Press, 2009).

*An Introduction to the Philosophy of Art* (Cambridge: Cambridge University Press, 2003).

Gary Hagberg and Walter Jost, eds., *A Companion to the Philosophy of Literature* (Chichester: Wiley-Blackwell, 2010).
Simon Haines, *Poetry and Philosophy from Homer to Rousseau* (New York: Palgrave-Macmillan, 2005).
Peter Lamarque, *A Philosophy of Literature* (Malden, MA: Blackwell, 2009).
David Rudrum, ed., *Literature and Philosophy: A Guide to Contemporary Debates* (Basingstoke: Palgrave-MacMillan, 2006).
Christopher New, *Philosophy of Literature: An Introduction* (New York: Routledge, 2001).
Ole Martin Skilleås, *Philosophy and Literature: An Introduction* (Edinburgh: Edinburgh University Press, 2001).

# Part I

## *Questions of Truth and Knowledge*

Chapter 1

# The "Ancient Quarrel"

In one of the most famous passages of the *Republic*, Plato refers to the relations between literature and philosophy as reflecting an "ancient quarrel":

> [T]here is an old quarrel between philosophy and poetry. One can quote many examples of this ancient antagonism: remarks about the "bitch that growls and snarls at her master," and "a reputation among empty-headed fools," or "the crowd of heads that knows too much" and the "subtle thinkers" who are "beggars" nonetheless.[1]

One of Plato's aims in the *Republic*, we are led to understand, is to intervene in this ancient dispute in order to determine whether literature ("poetry" in Plato's terms) can earn a rightful place in the ideal republic. To qualify for inclusion in the republic, literature will have to be judged to be both a source of truth and a conduit of virtue; at the very least, the proponents of literature will have to show that the poets are not the source of lies and do not encourage vices in the citizens of the state. In spite of the fact that Plato's treatment of literature has sometimes been misconstrued, Plato's answers to these questions have set the stage for much of the subsequent thinking about the relations between literature and philosophy in the Western tradition. This is especially so regarding what Plato has to say about literature's relationship to the overarching concern of this section: truth. Ever since Plato, literature has been cast in a defensive position with respect to philosophical claims about the nature of truth. The recurrent complaints are that literature is bound to distort the truth about the real nature of things, or at best has nothing to do with truth at all – that it is a form of speech whose purpose lies elsewhere: in the cultivation of pleasure, or in the creation of beautiful things for their own sake, or in preserving memories from the past. To see what Plato may have been intending in addressing the ancient quarrel between literature and philosophy, and to grasp the larger significance of the terms he set in motion, it is necessary to understand something about Plato's conception of the truth and to explain its relation to the preexisting tradition.

Plato says things that are relevant to literature in some of his other dialogues. He addresses the question of the poet's "enthusiasm" in the early dialogue *Ion*; he takes up questions of artistic inspiration as a kind of divine madness in the *Phaedrus*; and he discusses the nature of true and false images in the *Sophist*. But the most encompassing – and certainly the most notorious – of Plato's claims about literature are found in the *Republic*. Much, though not all, of what Plato says there through the mouth of Socrates bears specifically on the question of truth, and what does not bear directly on truth pertains to questions of value and form that are equally central to the larger purposes of the *Republic* and to what most anyone might consider in assessing the importance of literature in human life. To be sure, this leaves to the side the question of whether the Platonic dialogues are themselves forms of literature, and it likewise sidesteps the question of whether Socrates is a reliable spokesperson for Plato and, if not, which of the two is the greater ironist. Is the *Republic* itself, as has been suggested, a "philosophical poem" written as a way of perfecting literature rather than disparaging it?[2] Is Socrates' proposal to have a censor serve as a judge of literature in the ideal state to be taken literally? I will return to some of these questions later in this chapter.

It is best to begin with a clear picture of what Socrates and the characters Glaucon and Adeimantus have to say in Plato's *Republic* about literature in relation to truth. This will help establish the degree to which Plato marks a difference from what came before him, and it will help underscore why the backlash against Plato has so often taken up the cause of literature. Plato's critique of literature revolves around an especially influential philosophical conception of the truth, a conception that differs significantly from many of the ideas that preceded it. Indeed, without Plato's version of the truth, the discipline of "philosophy" might never have come to regard itself as a distinct form of inquiry at all, or have built a sustained identity around specific criteria, methods of argument, and standards of validity.

Before Plato, the notion of truth was not linked to philosophy in any special way. There were, of course, philosophical thinkers of tremendous importance before Plato, including Miletus, Thales, Anaximander, and Heraclitus (see text box).

### Who Were the Sophists?

Among the philosophers working before Socrates (the pre-Socratic philosophers) was a group that included a number of figures who appear in Plato's dialogues: Thrasymachus, Gorgias, Protagoras, and Hippias of Elias. Plato characterizes them as charlatans who pretend to have knowledge when they do not, and who distort the sense of such crucial things as "truth" and "justice." In the *Republic*, for instance, Thrasymachus is made to argue that justice is the same thing as power. Plato's engagement with the Sophists set up another "ancient quarrel" – the quarrel between philosophy and rhetoric.

But it was only with Plato and then with Aristotle that the term "philosophy" acquired a precise and stable meaning. Before Plato, the ability to speak the truth was associated equally with the poets. The poet's speech in Archaic Greece was closely associated with two primary powers, both of which were grounded in religion and sustained as part of the social practices of a cultic society: the power of memory and the power of the muse. Poets were able to draw on these powers in order to interpret and sing the praises of the gods and to memorialize the great deeds of heroes. Poets, possessed by the muses, came to interpret the Titan goddess of memory, Mnēmonysnē, just as the prophets interpreted the god Apollo.[3] Classical scholars and anthropologists have suggested that the powers of memory associated with ancient songs of praise were not open to question or dispute. Moreover, the poet's memory offered access to truths that were not available directly in experience, either because they belonged to the distant past or because they were located in a realm beyond the reach of mortals.

**Poetry or Philosophy?**

"Tainted souls who try
To purify themselves with blood
are like the man
who steps in filth and thinks
to bathe in sewage."
– Heraclitus[4]

One of the terms associated with the "poetic" conception of the truth, a term that Heidegger invokes in some of his writings as early as *Being and Time*, is *alētheia*. *Alētheia* means bringing something out of concealment,[5] bringing it out of the oblivion associated with Lethe, one of the rivers of Hades. (In Classical Greek, *lēthē* meant "oblivion," "forgetfulness," or "concealment.") Early in *Being and Time*, Heidegger argues that truth is (or ought to be) a matter of taking entities out of their hiddenness, rather than disabusing us of mistaken ideas. Although Heidegger did not yet link this disclosive power with poetry in *Being and Time*, one can already see the two as adjacent: poetic speech was true speech insofar as it had the power to bring into the light and to preserve what memory might otherwise have left concealed or lost in oblivion. Marcel Detienne put it this way: "Early *Alētheia* meant neither agreement between a proposition and its object nor agreement between judgments. … The only meaningful opposition involved *Alētheia* and *Lēthē*. If the poet was truly inspired, if what he had to say was based on the gift of second sight, then his speech tended to be identified with 'truth'" (*Masters*, 50). By remembering things, and by passing this memory along to future generations, poetic speech also helped preserve an understanding of how the world had come to be the way it is. Poetry supported the explanatory function associated with myth because it could give an account of things in connected sequences of verse.

One example among many is Hesiod's *Theogony*. Aristotle spoke approvingly of Hesiod at the very beginning of the first book of the *Metaphysics* as among those who inquired into the origins of things, standing thus on a par with the philosopher Parmenides. Hesiod's poem is a synthesis of many different Greek traditions concerning the gods, organized in a way that tells how the gods came to establish control over the cosmos. Part of what characterizes *Theogony*'s claim to the truth lies in its scope: it attempts to explain reality as a whole, in part by establishing the preeminence of Zeus over the entire cosmos. The same is true when the epic poets ask the muse to tell them their stories from the very beginning, as in the opening verses of the *Iliad* where we start with Zeus and Apollo.

It has been said (Detienne, *Masters of Truth*) that by the time we reach the classical age in Greek thought, when Socrates and Plato came on the scene, the truth-bearing function of poetry was quite diminished, and the system of beliefs that privileged the powers of sung speech had come to seem somewhat anachronistic. Why then does Plato worry so specifically about the poets and their claims to the truth?

In addressing this question, we must take into account an additional factor of crucial importance – the role of tragic drama. Plato himself is known to have been a writer of tragedies before his "conversion" to philosophy by the teachings of Socrates. Ancient tragedy conserved some of the cultic functions of the earlier religious poetry. Nietzsche's remarkable account in *The Birth of Tragedy* – some of which is consistent with historical research, some attributable to the influence of Richard Wagner on the early Nietzsche, and some pure speculation on Nietzsche's part – reflects this feature. Nietzsche proposed that tragedy was originally linked to states of dream and intoxication, associated with the gods Apollo and Dionysus. His argument was that tragedy provided an experience of the truth of the world – a truth attached existentially to human suffering – that was made all but unrecognizable by Socrates. In *The Birth of Tragedy*, Socrates is Nietzsche's example of the rational optimist – indeed, not just an example, but the original type of this "new man." And yet, as Nietzsche also acknowledges, tragedy by Socrates' time had itself been transformed into something quite different from the choral performances of the Archaic period.

The plots of the Greek tragedies dramatize complex conflicts among the characters – conflicts that are tied to themes as well as to music, performance, and spectacle. In Sophocles' drama *Antigone*, for example, the question of which should prevail – Antigone's demand for an honorable burial for her deceased brother or Creon's allegiance to the laws of the state prohibiting the interment of enemies or traitors – is more highly developed than whatever might have been sung in a work comprised of a single chorus. Moreover, Sophocles makes no pretensions as a dramatic poet to have access to a truth that could only be revealed through muse-inspired, magico-religious powers.

Yet tremendous powers of insight also remain in evidence in Sophocles' play, such as the powers attributed to characters – like the blind Tiresias – who fill the roles of prophets or seers. Moreover, tragedies in the classical age continued to involve numerous elements (including music, actors, chorus, stage scenery, and the like) that made their engagement with these questions entirely different from a purely discursive consideration of the same issues. The tragic staging of a conflict – about such things as one's obligations to kin and one's duty to the state – was always something unlike the philosophical procedure of considering different arguments judged in terms of reasons. In spite of the fact that tragedy in Plato's day was already distanced from mantic knowledge, it was still and has remained a form of "poetry" in the broad sense: it involved a kind of making (*poiēsis*) that is not reducible to the ideas expressed in it.

The principal complaints against literature leveled in the *Republic* hinge on two overarching notions that take the poetry of Homer and Hesiod – as well as tragic drama – specifically into account. First is Plato's particular conception of what "truth" is, and second is his idea that literature is one among many forms of "mimesis" (customarily translated as "imitation" and sometimes as "representation"). But the discussion of literature in the *Republic* begins in prejudicial terms, as many subsequent such discussions would: "It is the poets who have always made up fictions and stories to tell to men," says Socrates to Adeimantus in a remark that specifically references Hesiod and Homer (*Republic* III, 377d). The sense is that literature is predisposed to the communication of falsehoods.

**Socrates's Challenge to Homer:**

"'My dear Homer ... if our definition of representation is wrong and you are not merely manufacturing copies at third remove from reality, but are a stage nearer the truth about human excellence, and really capable of judging what kind of conduct will make the individual or the community better or worse, tell us any state whose constitution you have reformed, as Lycurgus did at Sparta and others have done elsewhere .... What city attributes its benefits to your skill?'" (*Republic* X, 599d)

This remark follows very shortly after a comment about the difference between two kinds of stories, "true stories and fiction" (III, 367a). Poetry is false, and its fictions "ugly," because it misrepresents the gods and the heroes; the poet is thus "like a painter whose portraits bear no resemblance to their originals" (III, 377e). Plato's conviction that the gods are the source of only the good leads Socrates in turn to address some of the specific "untruths" communicated by the poets, including their gloomy account of the afterlife, their description of weaknesses in heroes like Achilles, and their suggestion that the gods Zeus and Apollo may act in unjust and wrathful ways. This is, to be sure, a moral critique of poetry precipitated by the question of how to educate the citizens of the ideal state. But the moral critique of literature is underpinned by a particular conception of the truth as the faithful resemblance to originals, just as the distinction between true and false stories would suggest. As I explain in Part II, the association of truth with virtue, and of error or falsehood with evil, is a crucial ingredient in the moral critique of literature, not to mention the response to it by figures like Nietzsche.

Here, a closer account of Plato's conception of truth as it bears on literature is in order. The centerpiece of this account is Plato's famous analysis of poetry as "imitation" in *Republic* X. Plato explains in considerable detail how truth, as faithful resemblance to originals, in fact consists in faithfulness to the ideal forms of things. This is Plato's version of what modern philosophers have come to call the "correspondence theory" of truth, which survives even within philosophical systems that dispense with Plato's notion of "ideas."[6] Plato's forms are immaterial, invisible, universal, and eternal. Literature, for its part, seems closest to the arts involved in making copies of things. Literature makes copies of things in words, not directly from the ideas, but from the things in the world that are already, in a certain sense, material copies of the ideas.

In a frequently cited passage, Socrates proposes the example of three different beds: the bed built of wood by a carpenter, the idea of "bed" to which the carpenter adheres in the course of his material making, and the painted image of a bed that the carpenter has made. The poet's speech is like the painted image, except that it is an image in words. The conclusion to which Socrates leads his interlocutor is that the Idea of the bed, which can only be made by a god, and of which there is one and only one, is the form that all other beds – including those made in words by poets – must try to approach. There are many particular beds but only one Form. The god who makes the form of bed is "the author of its nature," which Plato also calls the thing "in-itself" (*Republic* X, 595–597). This is the true thing, and the obligation of all representations is to adhere as closely as possible to this "true thing" (i.e., "Form"). As between the bed of the carpenter and the bed of the painter, and by extension the bed of the poet as imaged in speech, there is a clear hierarchy to be discerned. The image of the bed, whether in painting or in poetry, stands at the farthest remove from the ideal bed, hence is the most degraded. This was the very object of Nietzsche's ridicule in his critique of all metaphysical notions of the truth: "The thing in-itself," he wrote, "is worthy of Homeric laughter: that it appeared to be so much, indeed everything, and is actually empty, that is to say empty of significance."[7] It is nonetheless instructive to see how persistent something like Plato's Idea has been throughout the history of philosophy, including in much more recent attempts to fashion philosophy as a true science.

In the *Sophist*, Plato proposes a more nuanced account of some of the distinctions we see at work in the *Republic*. Thinking in terms of visual images, but understanding that the discussion applies to discourse as well as to "spoken images," Plato gives the name *eikastic* to the kind of art that respects the form of the original in the proportions of its length, width, depth, and so on. An *eikastic* image is a true semblance; its opposite is the false semblance or *phantasm* (*Sophist*, 235–236). There is no question that, if given the ability to choose between making the thing in-itself and a copy, one would choose to make the thing in-itself. But only a god can make the Forms. The poet must attempt to make *eikastic* (true) rather than *phantasmatic* (false) images. It is telling, then, that the *Republic* goes on to compare the poet to a craftsman who uses the device of a moving mirror to make a copy of the world and everything in it:

> [T]his same craftsman can not only make all artificial objects, but also create all plants and animals, himself included, and, in addition, earth and sky and gods, the heavenly bodies and everything in the underworld. … The quickest way is to take a mirror and turn it round in all directions; before long you will create sun and stars and earth, yourself and all other animals and plants, and furniture and the other objects we mentioned just now. (*Republic* X, 596c–596e)

The suggestion is that this clever trick makes the poet into a kind of false god.

But there are yet two further prongs to Plato's critique of literature in relation to truth. The first has to do with the appearance or "look" of given things, the second with the secular poets' claims to knowledge. As for the question of the look of a thing, Plato recognizes that there is a difference in the way that something appears to us when viewed from different angles: the look of a bed viewed sideways will not resemble the look of it when viewed endways, or from above, and so on. But he goes on to insist that these different looks make no difference to the thing itself. The bed is indifferent to them: it *looks* to be different without *being* different. With this formulation of the distinction between appearances and the truth, Plato effectively established the terms that many later theories of "perspectivism" would contest, often in the name of literature. Nietzsche's perspectivism is perhaps the best known. He refers to the perspectival nature of the truth succinctly in the "Attempt at Self-Criticism" that prefaces the 1886 edition of *The Birth of Tragedy*: "[A]ll of life is based on semblance, art, deception, point of view, and the necessity of perspectives and error."[8] In *Being and Nothingness*, Sartre explains that even as the object may disclose itself through a single perspective or view, the sole fact of there being an observer in relation to it implies the possibility of multiplying the points of view *on* that perspective; our grasp of the phenomenon is based on the possibility of infinite perspectives. "This suffices to multiply the *Abschattung* [perspective, appearance] under consideration. ... Let us say that our [modern] theory of the phenomenon has replaced the *reality* of the thing by the *objectivity* of the phenomenon and that it has based this on an appeal to infinity."[9]

José Ortega y Gasset's views on such matters were particularly influential for literary thinkers; they were developed in the *Meditations on Quixote*: Don Quixote sees giants while Sancho sees windmills, or an advancing enemy army when Sancho sees a flock of sheep. In what may be the most famous sequence of episodes revolving around this theme, Don Quixote and Sancho agree to a linguistic accommodation: the difference between a thing that looks to one to be a shaving basin and to the other to be the magical helmet of Mambrino leads to the invention of a new word, the literary object "basinhelmet" (*baciyelmo*), which says not so much that it is *both* things as that it is in-between. In the theory of hermeneutics – a form of the theory of interpretation – this process could be described as a "fusion of horizons" or *Horizontverschmelzung* rather than as a linguistic accommodation; the point from a hermeneutic standpoint is that the truth is neither objective and ideal nor subjective and relative, but *inter*-subjective. A second and very different example is Virginia Woolf's novel *Orlando*, in which Orlando travels across many centuries, and even changes gender, all the while remaining faithful to an oak tree and to an Elizabethan poem about it, the interpretation of which nonetheless changes over time.

Plato additionally objects that poets speak about many things of which they have no real knowledge. In this they resemble the Sophists, who are accused in many dialogues of making arguments and giving speeches for hire. Kierkegaard interprets the Sophists as ones who have knowledge of nothing real, but only of phenomena, and who act as they do out of egotism: "[S]ophistry is the perpetual life-and-death struggle of knowledge with the phenomena in the service of egotism, a struggle which can never be brought to victory because the phenomenon rises again as fast as it falls."[10] This prong of Plato's critique of literature reactivates the notion of "real knowledge" or "true understanding" (*Republic* X, 598c–599e) that had been suggested as one of the shortcomings of the poets in the very early dialogue *Ion*. Ion, a rhapsode who recites Homer, speaks about many things with apparent skill but is unable to explain to Socrates which of all the matters contained in what he recites he actually knows. Socrates concludes by offering Ion the backhanded praise of being inspired rather than knowledgeable, "not skilled but divine."[11]

As for knowledge (*epistēmē*), Plato gives an account of what it means as part of the simile of the "divided line" in *Republic* VI: knowledge is of the forms, of the intelligible realm (as opposed to the sensible realm), and is different from opinion, which is comprised of beliefs and mere illusions. He associates "knowledge" with the understanding that an expert would have. It involves knowing something firsthand and with an awareness of its consequences and implications, rather than merely knowing how to speak about or portray it. (In the *Statesman*, 300c, laws are the forms of the truth known by the expert.) There is a difference between knowing how to prescribe a medication and writing a poem about drugs.[12] In Plato's response to poetry, this demand for "real knowledge" is associated with the critique of representation that is part and parcel of the doctrine of the forms:

> The art of representation is … a long way removed from truth, and is able to reproduce everything because it has little grasp of anything, and that little is of a mere phenomenal appearance. For example, a painter can paint a portrait of a shoemaker or a carpenter or any other craftsman without understanding their crafts; yet, if he is skillful enough, his portrait of a carpenter may, at a distance, deceive children or simple people into thinking it is a real carpenter. (*Republic* X, 598b–598c)

The question of the truth, and the standing of literature with respect to the truth, is thus associated with a bundle of concerns that include knowledge, representation, fiction, image, and falsehood. The interlocutors in Plato's dialogues have ways of settling these questions by drawing on the difference between true and false images and by characterizing the philosopher as the one who knows (the Forms), in contrast to the Sophists and poets who merely *seem* to know. But this settlement leaves two important matters unresolved, both of which bear directly on the literary entanglements of Plato's philosophical texts. These entanglements need to be addressed before saying anything further about the responses to Plato's arguments, or their continuation in the philosophical tradition. The first is the question of how anyone might know the true Forms in order to represent them accurately in words or images. The second has to do with Plato's ongoing recourse to the language of myth and image in the course of his own dialogues.

Surprisingly, perhaps, no one has been able to identify the exact passages that Plato means to refer to in describing the "ancient quarrel" between literature and philosophy ("the bitch that's growls and snarls at her master," etc.).[13] Indeed, there is some speculation that Plato may have invented the very idea of an old quarrel as a way to position his own critique of literature as an intervention into an important dispute, when its real aim was to introduce an element of rather sophisticated irony into his construction of the ideal "city-in-words." We know, after all, that Plato had himself been a writer of tragedies before turning to philosophy; elements of dramatic form – including character, dialogue, and setting – are present throughout the dialogues. Plato's characters, including Socrates, Glaucon, and Adeimantus in the *Republic*, are not mere talking heads but complex characters of substantial ethical and psychological depth. As one commentator aptly wrote, "they have about them the smell of mortality, with their individual histories, personalities and commitments. It is not just a question of what arguments are made, but of what sort of man would make a particular argument, or accept it, or long for it."[14] Moreover, there are very direct and deep traces of Homer and Hesiod in what Plato writes, in spite of the fact that these are among the very poets he singles out for criticism in the *Republic* (X, XI, 600d, 612b). And yet at a deeper level their myths are quite strongly "rewritten" by Plato, sometimes in explicit terms and sometimes more covertly.

Plato's critique of truth in poetry must be understood in light of the fact that he himself writes in a poetic idiom and reworks some very familiar poetic myths. Which ones is not a trivial question, since they give Plato a way to say something about the truth that is not fully covered by the notion of language or of images corresponding to forms. Plato's famous allegory of the cave in *Republic* VI resonates with the Homeric narrative of the hero's mythical passage through the world of shades and eventual emergence up into the light. The "Myth of Er" that Plato introduces in the *Republic*'s final book takes up the related paradigm of a leader who conducts a novice to gaze upon a sudden vision of the truth.[15] Likewise, Diotima in the *Symposium* invokes the language of initiation by a guide into an intense and sudden visual experience. (In *The Clouds*, Aristophanes mocks Plato for leading human beings away from solid ground toward an existence in the clouds.) These passages and many others like them suggest that Plato takes quite seriously not just the question of the truth in-itself, but the larger question of an education into the truth. Truth may be "defined," so to speak, as faithfulness to the ideal (and invisible) Forms, but that definition cannot itself explain how anyone might come to recognize the Forms or transmit that insight. In the figurative language in which Plato's and many accounts are often framed, to see the truth requires being led, making a turn (turning away from the darkness and toward the light), and while seeing clearly, not being blinded by looking directly at the sun.

The inhabitants of the allegorical cave described in the *Republic* see shadows and flickers on the wall, not the ideal forms of things. The prisoners live in this condition until some of them are brought out of the cave and into the light above. It might seem that the philosopher ought to free the prisoners of the cave from their condition, and it might seem that the philosopher can do this because he has himself come to recognize the difference between the shadow-forms in the cave and the way things "truly are" when viewed in full sunlight. But why, then, is it said that the light of the sun is too bright – that its power is blinding rather than illuminating?

> Suppose one of [the prisoners] were let loose, and suddenly compelled to stand up and turn his head and look and walk toward the fire; all these actions would be painful and he would be too dazzled to see properly the objects of which he used to see the shadows. … And if he were made to look directly at the light of the fire, it would hurt his eyes and he would turn back and retreat to the things which he could see properly. … [If] he were forcibly dragged out into the sunlight, the process would be a painful one, to which he would much object, and when he emerged into the light his eyes would be so dazzled by the glare of it that he wouldn't be able to see a single one of the things he was now told were real. (*Republic*, VII, 515c–516a)

### *A Blinding Light*

Hölderlin may well have had Plato in mind when he wrote that the presence of the gods is too blinding for humans to tolerate:

> "Unperceived at first they come, and only the children
> Surge towards them, too bright, dazzling, this joy enters in,
> So that men are afraid, a demigod hardly can tell yet
> Who they are, and name those who approach him with gifts."[16]

If the fully illuminated world is simply too bright a place to stay, then there must be some fundamental adjustment in our bearing toward the truth. Plato suggests that it would require a basic change in attitude:

> [T]he organ by which man learns is like an eye which cannot be turned from the darkness to light unless the whole body is turned; in the same way the mind as a whole must be turned away from the world of change until its eye can bear to look straight at reality, and at the brightest of all realities which is what we call the good. (*Republic* VII, 518d)

The sense of this passage is that poetry, image, and myth are essential because most, if not all mortals are incapable of looking directly at the forms themselves. The novelist and philosopher Iris Murdoch proposed a view very much like this. "Plato's view of art as illusion is positive and complex," she wrote in *The Fire and the Sun*; "images are valuable aids to thought; we study what is higher first in images. … [I]mages must be kept within a fruitful hierarchy of spiritual endeavor."[17] Her wider argument is two-pronged: first, that the standard interpretation of Plato's critique of literature as the source of falsehoods and a distortion of the truth represents a shallow understanding of his larger philosophical project; second, that literature participates, through images, in the search for a truth that is aligned with the pursuit of beauty and the good.

**Truth Pre-Supposed?**

Slavoj Žižek offers a very different view of Plato's allegory of the cave. For Žižek, we are all cave-dwellers; there is no "outside" the cave. The best we can hope for is an understanding of this fact, which in turn would yield an enlightened self-consciousness:

> [A]ll of us are these people in the cave – so how can we, immersed in the cave's spectacle, step onto our own shoulder, as it were, and gain insight into true reality? … We, the cavemen, have to work hard to arrive at some idea of the "true reality" outside the cave – the true substance, the *presupposition*, of our world is in this sense *always-already posited*.[18]

## Resistances to Plato

Not surprisingly, some of the most powerful currents of thought around literature and its relation to philosophy have taken the form of a backlash against Plato. Virtually all the contemporary currents – called "anti-foundational," "pragmatist," "anti-metaphysical," "deconstructive," and "materialist" (including "historical materialism") – have in one way or another imagined themselves as doing battle with Plato: inverting, subverting, overturning, deconstructing, or trying to overcome Plato's metaphysics of truth. Their efforts have frequently been organized under the banner of "literature." There are, of course, many strands within philosophy itself that have done equally fierce battle with Plato, but here I want to concentrate on the currents that have had the deepest resonance for literature. An opportune place to begin is with Nietzsche. Numerous commentators have noted that it may be impossible to winnow a consistent and coherent set of ideas about literature and truth from the vast and uneven corpus of Nietzsche's writings. Nietzsche himself repudiated some of the claims advanced in his early works, including *The Birth of Tragedy*. In other instances, such as *Will to Power*, what we have are simply fragments. In *Thus Spoke Zarathustra*, by contrast, where we are dealing with a poem, we are obliged to apply to Nietzsche's own text a principle that he argued is fundamental for all truth, namely that there are no truths, only interpretations. The question here, however, is how Nietzsche's rethinking of the category of truth, including his many apparent disavowals of it, are rooted in his response to Plato. What might this mean for the way in which we regard literature and truth in relation to one another?

Among the central claims of *The Birth of Tragedy* is the notion that Socrates represents a new type of individual, someone who makes a break with the traditions of dramatic poetry that came before him. As mentioned previously, Nietzsche takes Socrates as the paradigm of the new "theoretical man," and moreover of the "theoretical optimist" who sees error as a form of evil and whose commitment to the truth is linked to a form of moral and political perfectionism (97). As Nietzsche saw things, Socrates was bent on the destruction of tragedy and myth in the interest of the truth. For Nietzsche, the philosophical practice that Socrates invented was linked to a theoretical view of life, and it was over and against this view that Nietzsche wanted to recover the truth of tragedy. The power of tragedy, closer to wisdom than to the truth narrowly conceived as knowledge or *ēpistemē*, is twofold. On the one hand, it delivers the insight that human life is essentially illusion and suffering; on the other, it demonstrates that art can serve as a protection against the potentially devastating consequences of this fact. This establishes tragedy as something higher than the "theoretical" truth offered by the rational Socrates. Indeed, one of the most important features of "tragic culture" according to Nietzsche is that it takes wisdom rather than science as the highest end: "wisdom, uninfluenced by the seductive distractions of the sciences, turns with unmoved eyes to a comprehensive view of the world, and seeks to grasp … the eternal suffering as its own" (112).

Nietzsche has been particularly influential because he offered a way to locate literature as a vehicle of "truth" in a universe where there are thought to be no truths but only, as he said, "interpretations."[19] To claim that there is no truth – or no final truth – and that Plato's forms are an illusion serving to support multiple layers of equally false truths, is meant to be both sobering and uplifting. Nietzsche's views about the truth have been identified as a form of nihilism, where "nihilism" is understood as the condition in which there is no difference between one thing and another (between truth and falsehood, or between good and evil, for example); Hegel described it as "the night in which all cows are black" (see text box).

**"The Night in Which All Cows are Black"**

This phrase is taken from the "Introduction" to Hegel's *Phenomenology of Spirit*.[20] Hegel uses it to ridicule Schelling's view of the "Absolute," in which "everything is the same." For Hegel, that view of the "Absolute" inevitably diminishes "the full body of articulated cognition" (9). It leads to nihilism, because in that proverbial "night," the difference between *this* and *that* disappears.

Nietzsche would hardly reject the charge of nihilism, but he championed a certain kind of creative nihilism as the appropriate response to the truth about life. This truth – and it is for Nietzsche a truth *about life* rather than about intelligible forms – recognizes error as inevitable, indeed as fundamental. This includes the error of believing that there are truths at all. In *The Gay Science*, for example, Nietzsche characterizes "truth" as a kind of error that culture cannot do without. He lays the groundwork for pragmatism by arguing that truth is "the weakest form of knowledge."[21] The suggestion is that we need a form of truth that *works*, that works *in the world*, and that does not disparage the world of appearances. The Platonic conception of the truth achieves its ends at the expense of the appearing world, Nietzsche suggests, and he wants us to see that once we recognize that the notion of a "true world" is useless, we then have nothing against which to contrast the "apparent world." The world of appearances, which is the world in which literature is inevitably situated, can be "saved" from Plato's condemnation if we release ourselves from the grip of the metaphysical notion of the truth. Nietzsche's call to arms takes untruth rather than truth as the condition of life; he regards life – and not the intelligible and immaterial forms "above" the world of appearances – as the only term by which to measure things. Insofar as there may be "truth" at all, it is bound to be something *created within* the world, a function of the will, rather than something to be *discovered beyond* the world.

Nietzsche's response to Plato anchors many of the anti-metaphysical notions of truth that have come to be associated with literature. His commitment to the view that existence is suffering and illusion was hardly lost on a number of existentialist writers of both fiction and philosophy, including Sartre and Camus. However, Nietzsche himself remained attached to the idea that Plato (not Socrates) was driven by an "artistic necessity" to create a kind of philosophy that was in the end related to the very art he repudiated (*BT*, 90). In Nietzsche's colorful phrasing, the Platonic dialogue was "the barge on which shipwrecked ancient poetry saved herself with all her children: crowded into a narrow space and timidly submitting to the single pilot, Socrates, they sailed into a new world, which never tired of looking at the fantastic spectacle of this procession" (90–91).

Increasingly, scholars have recognized that the question of truth in Plato's dialogues cannot so easily be separated from the fact that they are in fact dialogues, and that we cannot always be sure how the words of Socrates and his interlocutors are meant. One must also bear in mind that Socrates is a character in these dialogues – the real Socrates wrote nothing, and Plato wrote virtually nothing in his own voice.[22] Socrates is remarkably persistent in his procedures of inquiry, sometimes seeming to force his interlocutors to speak, sometimes pressing them simply to agree with the formulations he offers. In the last part of the *Symposium*, for example, Socrates forces Agathon and Aristophanes to say that the same person ought to be able to write both tragedy and comedy (in apparent contradiction to the *Republic*, in which tragedy and comedy are kept apart). Among the most significant methods Socrates deploys are those of dividing and separating things that seem to the non-analytical mind to be the same (the method of *diarēsis*).

There is an additional dimension to the dialogues that Nietzsche was among the first to draw attention to in modern times: like tragedy before it, the Platonic dialogues were zones of convergence for an especially wide range of preexisting forms of speech.

> If tragedy had absorbed into itself all the earlier types of art, the same might also be said in an eccentric sense of the Platonic dialogue which, a mixture of all extent styles and forms, hovers midway between narrative, lyric, and drama, between prose and poetry, and so has also broken the strict old law of the unity of linguistic form. (*BT*, 90)

Nietzsche went on to voice the view, no doubt intended to shock, that Plato was the inventor of the novel. "Plato has given to all posterity the model of a new art form, the model of the *novel* ... in which poetry holds the same rank in relation to dialectical philosophy as this same philosophy held for many centuries in relation to theology: namely the rank of *ancilla* [handmaid]" (91).[23]

What do these notions – which are indeed on one level matters of form, to be addressed in Part III of this book – have to do with questions of truth? Beyond already allowing us to glimpse the fact that truth and form cannot be separated any more than value can be kept out of the picture, it means that reading anything that is said about truth in Plato's dialogues involves an act of interpretation. One must be alert to inconsistencies among the voices, take care not to assume that Socrates is always a reliable spokesperson, and understand that not all the views attributed to him are necessarily those of Plato. There are times when it may be necessary to take what Socrates says ironically. Indeed, why assume Socrates speaks the truth at all? If he does, it is often by indirect means. Indeed, Socrates himself proposes telling the citizens of the state a "noble lie" about the origin of the differences among social classes. In one of the most famous passages of the *Symposium*, Alcibiades tries to turn Socrates's irony back on Socrates himself. Alcibiades' reliance on simile in the following passage is remarkable:

> I propose to praise Socrates, gentlemen, by using similes. He will perhaps think that I mean to make fun of him, but my object in employing them is truth, not ridicule. I declare that he bears a strong resemblance to those figures of Silenus in statuaries' shops, represented holding pipes or flutes; they are hollow inside, and when they are taken apart you see that they contain little figures of gods.[24]

The speech continues with the most fulsome praise for Socrates, and is meant to go "over the top": "One might find many remarkable qualities to praise in Socrates," Alcibiades says, but in the end "he is like no other human being, living or dead" (*Symposium*, 221d, p. 110). And yet it is duly noted that Alcibiades was at this same moment too drunk to speak reliably. The dialogues require the interpretation not just of figures, images, and myths, but of over-arching tropes and strategies, such as exaggeration (hyperbole) and irony. In this additional sense, then, we have to consider the dialogues both as works of philosophy and as works of literature. Not surprisingly, among later thinkers it was principally the more "literary" philosophers like Erasmus, Montaigne, and Kierkegaard who grasped this fact about them.

## Further Reading

Jonathan Barnes, *The Presocratic Philosophers* (Boston, MA: Routledge and Kegan Paul, 1982).

Miguel de Beistegui and Simon Sparks, eds., *Philosophy and Tragedy* (London: Routledge, 2000).
Pierre Destrée and Fritz-Gregor Herrmann, eds., *Plato and the Poets* (Leiden: Brill, 2011).
Marcel Detienne, *The Masters of Truth in Ancient Greece*, trans. Janet Lloyd (New York: Zone Books, 1996).
Rita Felski, ed., *Rethinking Tragedy* (Baltimore, MD: Johns Hopkins University Press, 2008).
G.R.F. Ferrari, ed., *The Cambridge Companion to Plato's Republic* (Cambridge: Cambridge University Press, 2007).
*Listening to the Cicadas* (Cambridge: Cambridge University Press, 1987).
Kathleen Freeman, *Ancilla to the Presocratic Philosophers* (Oxford: Blackwell, 1962).
Simon Goldhill, *Reading Greek Tragedy* (Cambridge: Cambridge University Press, 1986).
Jean-Joseph Goux, *Oedipus, Philosopher*, trans. Catherine Porter (Stanford, CA: Stanford University Press, 1994).
Martin Heidegger, *Parmenides*, trans. André Schuwer and Richard Rojcewicz (Bloomington: Indiana University Press, 1992).
David McNeill, *An Image of the Soul in Speech: Plato and the Problem of Socrates* (University Park: Pennsylvania State University Press, 2010).
Ramona Naddaff, *Exiling the Poets* (Chicago: University of Chicago Press, 2002).
Andrea Nightingale, *Genres in Dialogue: Plato and the Construct of Philosophy* (Cambridge: Cambridge University Press, 1995).
*Spectacles of Truth in Classical Greek Philosophy* (Cambridge: Cambridge University Press, 2004).
Martin Puchner, *The Drama of Ideas: Platonic Provocations in Literature and Philosophy* (Oxford: Oxford University Press, 2010).
Stanley Rosen, *The Quarrel between Philosophy and Poetry* (London: Routledge, 1988).
Gary Alan Scott, ed., *Philosophy in Dialogue: Plato's Many Devices* (Evanston, IL: Northwestern University Press, 2007).
Jean-Pierre Vernant, *Myth and Thought among the Greeks*, trans. Janet Lloyd and Jeff Fort (New York: Zone Books, 2006).
*The Origins of Greek Thought*, trans. Janet Lloyd (Ithaca, NY: Cornell University Press, 1982).

*Chapter 2*

# Action, Imitations, Conventions of Make-Believe

It would be hard to think of two philosophers so close to one another in so many ways whose ideas about literature – and especially whose ideas about truth in relation to literature – are nonetheless more different than Plato and Aristotle. Likewise, it would be hard to imagine two philosophers more divergent in their approach to the vexing question of mimesis, which is almost always, it seems, a neighbor to questions of truth when literature is involved. While Aristotle was a student of Plato's and ultimately something of a Platonist when it comes to the difference between sense-perception and true "scientific" knowledge, he was also clear to distinguish his thinking from that of his teacher. Likewise, Aristotle's way of writing is strikingly different from Plato's. Unlike Plato, who wrote through the multiple voices of characters in dialogue form, Aristotle produced what are for all intents and purposes philosophical tracts originating mostly in lectures transcribed by others. His works are – in the words of one modern commentator – dry and formal: "His language bristles with technicalities, makes little appeal to the emotions, disdains graces of style, and frequently defies the simplest rules of composition."[1] Reading Plato, we think we may be reading a kind of literature, and in fact we are. The hyperbolic speeches in parts of *Symposium*, the description of the "descent" to the port of Piraeus to celebrate the cult of a goddess at the very beginning of the *Republic*, the motif of the cicadas in *Phaedrus*, and many more are all clear signs of a discourse that is as literary as it is philosophical. Literature is part of the fabric of the *Republic* even if Plato proposes excluding it from the ideal state.

With Aristotle, we are in a very different world. Reading his works, we know we are reading philosophy. He is methodical and systematic in the way he thinks and writes. The different subjects of philosophy are parceled out among his works in ways that correspond to its subdisciplines, many of which we still recognize today (ethics, politics, metaphysics, logic, etc.). Literature's place within this corpus is in *Poetics*. Although *Poetics* is probably the most influential single work any philosopher has ever written about literature, Aristotle's way of philosophizing did not help successive generations identify all the common questions and ground that literature and philosophy share. As a philosopher writing about literature, his work is closer to what we might describe as the "philosophy of literature." As such, its aims are to explain, justify, and establish norms for tragedy from within a framework that understands literature and philosophy as separate and distinct enterprises. And yet, many of the concerns of his *Poetics* are of great importance for any understanding of the deeper relations between literature and philosophy. Such is especially the case with the subject of truth in relation to Aristotle's interpretation of mimesis in tragedy.

The primary question is this: How does literature (tragedy in particular) as a kind of mimetic activity offer access to the truth – if indeed it does? What does literature contribute to knowledge – if indeed it does make such a contribution – given the fact that it is a mimetic practice? We may learn many things from literature, to be sure – things about history, manners, geography, society, and so forth. Literature is clearly a cognitive activity at some level, but it is more than simply cognitive. Is the concept of truth warranted in relation to it, and if so how? What if instead we were to say that literature gives a truth-*like* picture of things, or the picture of a world that *seems* to be true?

We can begin sorting these things out by recognizing that knowledge and truth are closely connected. If we regard knowledge as "justified true belief" or as the relationship between a proposition in language and a thing or state of affairs in the world, then knowledge embeds truth within it. "True" in turn implies something like correspondence to the way things actually are. But what happens when one attaches this to works of the imagination or to "imitations." Holding aside for now the question of how the "real" may be fashioned in part by the work of the imagination, the basic answer is not immediately clear. At the very least, we will need to distinguish what we know *about* works of literature and their imaginary worlds (such as the Macondo of *One Hundred Years of Solitude*, where truly marvelous things happen) from what they *allow us to know*, and to know as true. In addition, we will have to understand the special status of fictional worlds. What role do they play in the work of truth and knowledge, if they do so at all?

Aristotle did not have a theory about the logic of fiction as such; his understanding of tragic drama as a kind of imitation did not require it.[2] His ideas about imitation are best understood in the context of what can be known in the domain of human action. Aristotle was clear in explaining that not all kinds of knowledge or reason are the same – that there is a difference, for example, between theoretical knowledge and practical knowledge. Recognizing such differences is for Aristotle part of what wisdom requires. One can't expect to know how to govern, for example, in the same way that one knows the propositions of geometry. Likewise, what is true or valid in these realms is bound to differ. As Aristotle explains in *Nicomachean Ethics*, it is wrong to expect the same kind of certainty from practical reasoning that we can expect from theoretical reasoning. This idea is repeated in *Poetics*, where he says that poetry and politics (or poetry and any other art, for that matter) do not have the same standards of "correctness."[3]

Practical reason deals with circumstances that are by their nature in flux; it requires knowing what to do at a particular moment. Accordingly, it does not allow for the kind of certainty that one would expect in mathematics or physics. Theoretical reason involves truths about things that are not subject to such variability (e.g., the nature of entities in themselves, or the basic principles of mathematics). This latter kind of knowledge is what constitutes a science, and it is within the framework of a science that the most familiar kinds of truth have their place. For something to be a science there must first be a specific class of things about which it inquires. In addition, there must be principles, axioms, or postulates from which its demonstrations of truths begin. The most general of these are the ones Aristotle sets out in *Metaphysics*. The principle of non-contradiction is one example: we can't say "A is B" *and* "A is not B." To say "A *is and is not* B" makes no sense, at least in this way of thinking.[4] Finally, a science must allow for conclusions to be drawn about the objects under consideration: in the field of a science, it can be shown that the characteristics of the objects in question *follow from* the initial suppositions.[5]

This all too brief outline of some of what Aristotle means by knowledge and science may help explain why he associates literature (poetry) not with truth qua science but with probability and verisimilitude, and why his approach to poetry is descriptive and normative. Aristotle thinks that mimesis originates in a basic impulse of human nature; indeed, he begins by explaining mimesis in what we would call "naturalistic" terms. It originates in the inclination of all human beings to mimic things. All the many different kinds of poetry (*poiēsis*, making) involve imitative processes of some kind. (We will see later in this section how Aristotle's ideas overlap with contemporary theories of mimesis as "make-believe.") Aristotle's concerns in the extant sections of *Poetics* revolve around the hows, whys, and wherefores of imitation in tragic drama. *Poetics* offers an account based on examples such as Sophocles' *King Oedipus* of what works best in tragedy – of what best serves its aims (the purgation of the emotions of pity and fear) – through the imitation of an action compellingly presented.

It would be a terrible distortion to suggest that Aristotle's *main* purpose in *Poetics* is to address questions of truth. Matters of form are more important in his mind because these involve character and action directly. Likewise, in his account of mimesis Aristotle was not intending to address the things we commonly think of when speaking about fiction, representation, or expression. It makes no fundamental difference for Aristotle's theory of mimesis whether the events represented are fictional in the way we understand that term or not. And yet for Aristotle and many thinkers after him, the object of mimesis can be purely fictional and still show something true. "A feigned example hath as much force to teach as a true example," is the way Philip Sidney put it in his *Defence of Poetry*.[6] For Aristotle, the "truth" of tragedy is not the truth of Ideas, as Plato believed, but the truth pertaining to character and action. Aristotle offered many later thinkers a way of describing literature's relationship to the truth not by attempting to justify it against the complaint that it is but a pale copy of the true form or ideas of things, but on the grounds that it shows something about "the way things generally are" as regards the particular dimension of human nature revealed in action (i.e., character). For Aristotle, imitation in tragedy was necessarily of action. Only later did it come to be taken as the imitation of "nature." Sidney's *Defence* is representative of that current of thought: "There is no art delivered to mankind that hath not the works of nature for his principal object, without which they could not consist, and on which they so depend, as they become actors and players, as it were, of what nature will have set forth" (23). On this view, the kind of knowledge that literature is meant to provide does not involve the demonstration of epistemological certainty or a priori truths, but is designed with insight into virtuous action in mind. We can cite Sidney again, here in a passage closer to Aristotle, describing the purpose of poetry as "the knowledge of a man's self, in the ethic and politic consideration, with the end of well-doing and not of well-knowing only" (29). This puts us within striking distance of questions about the ethical links between literature and philosophy, which we will discuss in Part II.

As hinted at previously, what Aristotle has to say in *Poetics* about matters of truth is related to what can seem to be a puzzling distinction between poetry and history. Aristotle says that the historian speaks of what has happened; the poet speaks of what is likely to happen, of what may be expected to happen. Poetry in the sense Aristotle means it involves universals, while history involves particulars. Hence, Aristotle concludes that "poetry is a more philosophical and serious business than history" (*Poetics*, 1451b, 33). But by "universal" Aristotle does not mean anything like the universal forms that Plato calls "Ideas." He simply means the kind of thing a certain type of person is likely to say or do, according to either probability or necessity.

The meaning of "probability" and "necessity" in this context must be clarified. These terms indicate what one would naturally do, as for example by eating when one is hungry, or fleeing from a fire. They do not involve questions of moral obligation, such as when Antigone commits herself to seeking an honorable burial for her brother. "Probability" refers not to some relative degree of likelihood, or to the degree to which something might occur according to the laws of chance. Rather, it refers to what is general, to that which happens "for the most part,"[7] as when a mother (with all probability) weeps at the loss of a son, or a father responds with grief and rage at the murder of a daughter, or a brother with a mixture of joy and apprehension at the prospect of being reunited with a long lost sibling. When Hamlet remarks that his mother has too quickly shed her grief at the death of her husband, he means to draw attention to something that is *im*probable and *im*plausible (i.e., out of character). It is Hamlet's response that counts as "probable" in this context, not Gertrude's behavior. When Aristotle suggests that dramatic characters ought to bear "a likeness to human nature in general" (43), this is the kind of thing he means. Jane Austen opens *Pride and Prejudice* with the statement of a "universal" truth that can likewise be understood, for her, as drawing on this Aristotelian sense of probability: "It is a truth universally acknowledged, that a single man in possession of a good fortune, must be in want of a wife."[8] Such "probable" truths change.

There are truths that pertain to action and character, and these are of the "general" sort just discussed. Aristotle also acknowledges that even while some representations may be of purely fictional events, they are not necessarily deceptions, but can show something true about human action and character. Finally, we need to remember that for Aristotle, character and action go together hand in glove: character has no meaning aside from the ways it is established in the course of action. It is not, for instance, the case that the heroine of Brecht's *Mother Courage* is pre-endowed with a persevering character that allows her to slog on and on during the Thirty Years' War, but rather that in her resolve and through the slogging she assumes the character of a doggedly courageous human being. As Aristotle says, "the persons will have character if … their speech or their action reveals the moral quality of some choice" (*Poetics*, 1454a, 43). We will return to this matter when discussing Alasdair MacIntyre's work on character, action, and the moral virtues.

Not surprisingly given what Aristotle says about probability and necessity, he wishes to place limits on – but not to rule out – what are characterized as "irrationalities," by which he means preposterous or impossible events (*Poetics*, 1460a, 59). Irrationalities can provide a context for character to exhibit itself in ways that may reflect what is true about human action. Indeed, Aristotle says that "persuasive impossibilities" are preferable to those that are "possible but unpersuasive" (*Poetics*, 61b, 72). One should prefer events that may be impossible but are contextually plausible to ones that are possible but implausible (1460a, 71). These things must be presented vividly.

The matter of "vividness" is far from a mere detail; it is a point that links *Poetics* to *Rhetoric*. Although Aristotle addresses questions of the imagination (*phantasia*) in *Poetics* only implicitly, it is clear that his views about it played a significant role in his thoughts about how tragedy might best convey the truth. "In constructing one's plots and working them out in language one should put them directly before one's eyes as much as possible … seeing most vividly" (*Poetics*, 1455a, 47). In its etymology, vividness suggests liveliness. The interest in vividness reminds us that verisimilitude requires not just faithfulness to character, or the depiction of a world that could plausibly pass as real, but imitations that seem animated and lifelike.

Not surprisingly, what Aristotle says about imitation in tragedy has many implications for more modern genres such as the novel. An especially clear and eloquent statement of just such a position comes from contemporary America writer Joyce Carol Oates:

> Works of the imagination tend to begin with images. You find yourself "haunted" by something you've seen, or believe you have seen; you begin to create, with varying degrees of consciousness and volition, an entire world surrounding this image, a world or more precisely an atmospheric equivalent of a world, to contain it, nurture it, enhance it, "reveal" it. … As a fiction writer I'm unable to write, nor even wish to write, without a vividly evoked visual world. … Writing is transmitting by way of language a kind of reportage of emotion, and emotion must be linked to its specific place, time, and drama. Otherwise it's merely notional, and can't move us.[9]

The sense of her words is consistent with the idea that literature makes its claims to truth through the imagination and the emotions, and not directly by ideas and arguments – or, we may infer, by just making statements that conform to facts. Whereas arguments may lead to cognitive states of belief, literature works through the imagination and the emotions to produce effects that may include more than belief, including recognition and emotional transformation through the pity and fear that Aristotle associates with tragedy.

For Oates, as for many others, the writer must be able to transpose deeply felt emotions into words that create a world vividly conceived in the imagination and articulately rendered, populated by characters who seem to live and breathe and act as if they were real. If the writer's insights into character are true, and if the imagined world is convincingly drawn, then literature may have the power to move its readers emotionally to *recognize* what is true, rather than simply to *know that* it is true. The hope is that the reader will thus be drawn to see and feel things that might not otherwise be evident, to understand things that propositions about truth may not be able to capture, or that discursive arguments may not be able to show convincingly. Feeling plays a role in this work much as "seeing" does. Consider the advice of the Roman poet Horace, who wrote in a letter that became known as "Art of Poetry" that the mimesis of emotions would be the best way to make convincing appeals: "If you wish me to weep, you yourself / Must first feel grief" ("*Si vis me flere, dolendum est / primum ipsi tibi*").[10] Shakespeare's Hamlet echoes this in his speech to the players. For Sidney, poetry was a "speaking picture," designed to present with a special vividness and color what philosophy could only hope to approach in the abstract:

> [W]hatsoever the philosopher saith should be done [the poet] giveth a perfect picture of it in someone by whom he presupposeth it was done, so as he coupled the general notion with the particular example. A perfect picture, I say, for he yieldeth to the powers of the mind an image of that whereof the philosopher bestoweth a wordish description, which doth neither strike, pierce, nor possess the sight of the soul so much as [poetry] doth. (*Defence of Poetry*, 32)

These elements are as crucial to the production of tragedy's effects as are the various elements of plot that Aristotle signals. Aristotle speaks about the reversal of the hero's fortune and the recognition of guilt because these contribute to the purgation (catharsis) of pity and fear in the audience.

## Tragedy and Truth

*King Oedipus* is also a tragedy about knowledge, with some surprising connections to philosophy. Jean-Joseph Goux proposed that the paradigm of the philosopher is the figure of Oedipus. The Oedipus myth, he argued, set something of tremendous importance in place as a model for philosophical inquiry into the truth: not the truth conceived as a formal relation between a paradigm of ideas and what we say or represent (which is the Platonic model), but as a process of bringing out the truth by a process of insistent, sometimes forceful questioning.[11] The further suggestion is that Socrates, the principal interlocutor of Plato's dialogues, is modeled on the truth-seeking figure of Oedipus, who operates by forcing speech from his interlocutors. On this view, the philosophical search for truth is always either in tension with, dependent upon, or achieved through the power of a figure involved in interrogation. Part of what Nietzsche meant to indicate about Socrates as an "authority" is reflected in this idea. So too are Heidegger's later efforts to displace what he deemed to be the aggressive willfulness of philosophical thinking.[12]

The question of truth at stake in *King Oedipus* is initially posed in this way: Who among the citizens of Thebes was the murderer of King Laius? Finding this out is crucial because Thebes is bound to suffer from a plague for as long as Laius' murderer lives concealed within its borders. On the throne is Laius' son Oedipus, who shares power with Jocasta and Creon. Acting out of duty, Oedipus aims to investigate the matter in order to bring relief to the suffering city. But how are we to understand the aggressiveness of Oedipus' truth-seeking, and what are we to make of the consequences that follow from it? Oedipus' fate is related not just to what he knows but to his *demand* to know. Even at the bitter end, Jocasta's brother Creon reminds Oedipus that his posture remains stubborn and willful, and that he therefore remains ignorant: "You're still presuming to do as you please? / Never in your life were you free to choose."[13] The demanding nature of Oedipus' pursuit of the truth is in fact part of what blinds him to the very things that he ought to be able to see.

Oedipus' pursuit of the truth is conducted in full view of what seem to be very obvious clues offered to him by others in the play. The blind seer Tiresias tells him all but directly that he is guilty of the crime in question. Oedipus is known as a master of riddles for having deciphered the riddle of the sphinx, and yet he is unable to fathom the meaning of Tiresias' words, "he shall be shown to be a brother / to his own children, and to his mother / not only a son, but a husband too" (vv. 509–511). This makes his forceful inquest of others seem all the more cruel. At one point he presses for information from an innocent shepherd, using thinly veiled threats of torture: "If kind words won't work, pain can make you talk" (v. 1278.) Moreover, the answer to the question about the murder of Laius turns out to involve something other than an idea or a fact. As I will discuss further in Chapter 3, it involves the *relationship* between Oedipus (the one who seeks to know) and the object of his knowledge. Consequently, it raises the question of Oedipus' subject position, a position that involves a tragically ironic relationship between blindness and insight: blind Tiresias offers Oedipus keys to the truth, while Oedipus blinds himself when he comes to possess it. The blinding of Lear and of Gloucester in Shakespeare's *King Lear* lies not far away.

In Plato's *Republic*, Socrates defines truth as correspondence between the original forms and the various kinds of copies we make of them. Beyond the question of truth are the questions of self-knowledge and wisdom. Indeed, even if the truth is conceived to be everywhere and always the same, one's discovery of it is bound to be a contingent matter. Oedipus sets out to answer a much more limited question – the question about the identity of the murderer of Laius – but the matters of self-knowledge and wisdom are near at hand. What emerges is a tragedy about knowledge, rather than the narrative of a quest for enlightenment or a philosophical treatise on the truth, because in *King Oedipus* the self-knowledge that wisdom requires arrives too late. At the very conclusion of the play the Chorus voices a version of the insight that one cannot truly be declared happy until one's life is over: "Not one of us among the living here / should be regarded fortunate unless / our death has come before we ever learn / just what it is to suffer human grief" (vv. 1700–1703).

## Make-Believe, Conventions

The foregoing considerations raise some questions about the conventions that enable literature to speak truthfully and effectively even while making representations, images, or fictional worlds. But how is it possible that the imitation of an action can do this? That question is made no easier to answer when we recognize that the audience of the play would have known the myth of Oedipus before the play began. What they witness is the "imitation of an action" that is also the reenactment of a myth. While the audience feels pity and fear, they also know that it would be pointless to try to avert Oedipus' actions. Moreover, the conventions of theatre require that they not do so. What is it that we know that such conventions show? We know full well that Anna Karenina is a fictional character, but is it then a fictional grief we feel in relation to her? When we flinch at the torture suffered by the Magistrate in J. M. Coetzee's *Waiting for the Barbarians*, we are flinching at the representation, not the torture itself.[14] These questions have a way of spinning rapidly out of control. They seem to point out paradoxes that, while puzzling, hardly threaten to undermine our understanding of how these things work. To make matters manageable, I take up the suggestion advanced by Kendall Walton that fictional worlds are forms of make-believe, understanding that this is the beginning of an explanation, not the end of the story.

### A Game of "Pretend" Becomes Real Fiction:

The story of how Diderot's novel *The Nun* came about involves a story of pretend gone out of control, though ultimately to great success. The "game" began in 1760 as an elaborate practical joke, when Diderot sent a series of extremely convincing letters to a friend, the Marquis de Croismare, pretending to be from an escaped nun (but actually penned by Diderot himself). The marquis had earlier come to the aid of the real nun, Suzanne Simonin, and with the phony letters

Diderot hoped to entice him to return to Paris from his country estate in order to help the afflicted Sister. To accompany the letters, Diderot also wrote a series of journal entries, supposedly Suzanne's also, in which she describes her cruel treatment in the convent where her parents had sent her.

Finding an exceptionally believing reader in the Marquis, Diderot parlayed the hoax into a novel, published in 1796 as the memoirs of Sister Suzanne Simonin, under the title *La Religieuse* (*The Nun*).

Walton's *Mimesis as Make-Believe* is offered in the context of a general theory of the representational arts. Literature shares with all the other arts of make-believe a basis in pretend, and "the activities in which representational works of art are embedded and which give them their point are best seen as continuous with children's games of make-believe."[15] But who is pretending? Certainly the actors on a stage are, but what about the author? The playgoers? The readers of a novel (whose characters are not pretending in the way that actors on a stage are)? Thinking in terms of make-believe and pretend can help answer some questions about the difference between truths that hold within a fictional world and truths that hold outside it. When some hypothetical Anne pretends that she is having a tea party with imaginary friends, the proposition that she is entertaining her friends is fictional, and the fact that it is fictional makes it a *fictional truth*, or "true in some fictional world" (*Mimesis*, 35). To say that there is a land in which people are only six inches tall is not just fictional but, more specifically, fictional within *Gulliver's Travels*. Lilliput will never be found on a world map. Understood as a "prop" in Walton's sense, the work creates a world in which fictional truths can and do hold. It is by mandating the imagining of propositions (e.g., that there are people six inches in height) that props generate fictional truths.

That said, it is hardly the case that we don't ordinarily understand what fictions are, or that we are unsure of what our attitude toward them ought to be. It may seem that these theories are trying to define things that we ought to (and mostly do) accept as matters of convention and common sense. That would nonetheless be missing several points. For one, philosophy wishes not simply to point to what we know but to explain and justify that (and how) we know it. These explanations help satisfy that wish. However, they miss an appreciation of the depth of agreements at work in our common sense understanding of the conventions that we take mostly for granted. In ordinary language philosophy and in some of the work related to it (that of Ludwig Wittgenstein and Stanley Cavell in particular), by contrast, there is an appreciation of the unacknowledged depth of the agreements and conventions that comprise what we might think of as falling within the domain of "what we know." I will say more about these approaches later. Here I proceed to examples meant to highlight what it means to know some of the things we accept as conventions by showing what it might look like to forget them.

At one point in *Don Quixote* the hero rushes up to a puppet stage and destroys the Turkish soldier puppets he sees before him in order to free a puppet-damsel (Melisendra) from the tower in which she has been imprisoned. We know exactly what Don Quixote's mistake is here, and why it has come about. It is an instance of the very broad set of category mistakes that form the basis of his approach to the world. But what "everyone knows" (i.e., that these are "just puppets") also suppresses a set of historical facts (e.g., about religion and race) that Don Quixote refuses to disown. The episode is not unlike the joke retold by Stanley Cavell, in which some local yokel in a southern United States town rushes up to the stage during a performance of *Othello*, hoping to save a young white woman from the murderous advances of a black man.[16] We know exactly what convention has been breached; we know what mutual understandings are being brought into relief by it; and by seeing the terrible consequences of breaching conventions, we appreciate what our "ordinary" acceptance of them may conceal.

Cavell's reflections on *Othello* are not about matters of history or race; they engage a different but equally broad range of reflections about what our common understanding of conventions implies. The conventions of theatre are instances of pretend, and in that sense they are like games, including the "language games" and "forms of life" that Wittgenstein writes about in *Philosophical Investigations*.[17] I will say more about those questions in Part III. What is important to see here is that these various "games" involve us in situations where an effort to discern the clear difference between "true" and "false," or "reality" and "imitation" leads us astray. What happens on a stage is neither credible nor incredible, and in ways that apply to ordinary conduct equally well. Cavell writes: "That couple over there, drinking coffee, talking, laughing. Do I believe they are passing the time of day, or testing out the field for a flirtation, or something else? In usual cases, not one thing or another; I neither believe nor disbelieve." ("Avoidance," 329).

The conventions of theatre help illuminate what we (tacitly) understand about belief in "ordinary" circumstances. But there is more to the matter. One of Cavell's arguments in "The Avoidance of Love" proposes that the conditions of theatre "literalize the conditions we exact for existence outside … hence make that existence plain" (333). This is because in the context of a play there is a peculiar asymmetry between the world of the audience and that of the characters, an asymmetry that points out certain truths about our relationship to others, specifically about our inability to make good on the demand that we acknowledge others and not simply know them as one would know an object or a fact:

> [A] character cannot become aware of us; we are not in their presence. They are in our presence – we are acknowledging them (or failing to). The acknowledgment cannot be completed, and this shows not just what acknowledgment in a theatre is, but what acknowledgment in actuality is. (332)

I will say considerably more about the particular question of "acknowledgment" in discussing questions of value and form in Parts II and III. I conclude this chapter with a set of brief observations on the depth of agreements embedded in certain conventions, particularly those of the theatre as they pertain to tragedy. We should not allow the notions of a "fictional world" or a "stage world" to tempt us to ignore the significance of our acceptance of those conventions. Rather, we need to attend to each of them, not least by noticing what a breach of convention might imply, as in the case of the joke mentioned earlier in this chapter. On Cavell's account, the conventions of theatre are significant because of the way in which they demonstrate the tragic condition of our outsideness to one another. At the same time, these tragic conditions show what might be required for us to express acknowledgment:

> Whether or not we acknowledge others is not a matter of choice, any more than accepting the presence of the world is a matter of choosing to see it or not to see it. … Tragedy shows that we are responsible for the death of others even when we have not murdered them, and even when we have not manslaughtered them innocently. … [I]t is a question how acknowledgment is to be expressed, that is, how we are to put ourselves in another's presence. In terms which have so far come out, we can say: We must learn to reveal ourselves, to allow ourselves to be seen. (*MWM*, 332–333)

## Suggestions for Further Reading

Daniel Ahern, *The Smile of Tragedy: Nietzsche and the Art of Virtue* (University Park: Pennsylvania State University Press, 2012).
Gregory Currie, *The Nature of Fiction* (Cambridge: Cambridge University Press, 2008).
Stephen Halliwell, *Aristotle's Poetics* (Chicago: University of Chicago Press, 1988).
Suzanne Keen, *Empathy and the Novel* (Oxford: Oxford University Press, 2007).
John Lyons, ed., *Mimesis: From Mirror to Method* (Hanover, NH: University Press of New England, 1982).

David Marshall, *The Surprising Effects of Sympathy* (Chicago: University of Chicago Press, 1988).

Peter McCormick, *Fictions, Philosophies, and the Problems of Poetics* (Ithaca, NY: Cornell University Press, 1988).

Elder Olson, ed., *Aristotle's Poetics and English Literature* (Chicago: University of Chicago Press, 1965).

Amélie Oksenberg Rorty, ed., *Essays on Aristotle's Poetics* (Princeton, NJ: Princeton University Press, 1992).

Viktor Shklovsky, *Theory of Prose*, trans. Benjamin Sher (Normal, IL: Dalkey Archive Press, 1990).

Theodor Sider, *Writing the Book of the World* (Oxford: Oxford University Press, 2012).

M.S. Silk and J. P. Stern, *Nietzsche on Tragedy* (Cambridge: Cambridge University Press, 1981).

Amie Thomasson, *Fiction and Metaphysics* (Cambridge: Cambridge University Press, 2008).

*Chapter 3*

# The Single Observer Standpoint and Its Limits

Alongside Plato's theory of Forms and Aristotle's writings on mimesis, there is perhaps no more powerful set of views on questions of truth in philosophy than those that revolve around the modern conception of the "single observer standpoint." In epistemology, this underlies the notion of truth as seen from an objective position; in moral philosophy, it underlies the notion of judgment from an impartial perspective. The stance of the distanced and impartial observer underlies the conviction that the world is as it is, can be known as it is, and can be represented as it is known independent of our conceptual frames, linguistic practices, historical conditions, and conventional agreements. What is also important to notice is how readily the "ideal" and "impartial" standpoints are thought of in relation to the activity of observation. Observation is understood as a form of impartial looking, which is why it has served as such a powerful metaphor for knowledge and judgment.

In beginning to speak about conventions and agreements in Chapter 2, we have already begun to explore some views that offer alternatives to such ideas. But before we go further in exploring alternatives, we need to explain how the attempt to find a ground for truth and a similarly universal standpoint for morality came to rely on vision, and specifically how these efforts came to rely on vision as modeled on the sight of the "punctual" individual. Observation is modeled as we have come to imagine human vision is: it involves the "sight" of an individual who regards the world from a punctual standpoint but impersonally. To understand how these metaphors became so powerful, and to understand how the idea of vision in the punctual, individual sense could serve to support so many ideas underlying conceptions of truth and value, we need to invoke a third notion. This is the notion of the subject. Heidegger described subjectivity through its Latin and Greek roots (*subiectum, hypokeimenon*), which point to the idea of an "underlying ground" for everything that is. Beginning with Descartes, subjectivity was not just one world view among others, or a realm of competing world views, and it certainly was not a synonym for relativism. Rather, it became the position from which we set the world before us as if it were a representation to be viewed. Heidegger explained that "world picture" means "the structured image that is the creature of man's producing which represents and sets before."[1]

Whatever is viewed by a subject is an object; the notion of objectivity in turn carries with it the suggestion of impartiality in matters of truth and morality. The relationship between subject and object, as between representation and truth, establishes what would seem to be an unbreakable bond, at least for much of the modern age. What is true in this framework is objective, can be known with certainty, and can be calculated and measured in reliable ways. Heidegger writes:

> This objectifying of whatever is, is accomplished in a setting-before, a representing, that aims at bringing each particular being before it in such a way that man who calculates can be sure, and that means be certain, of that being. (127)

With this, the world is itself conceived and grasped as having the form of a picture. This was not always so; "the fact that the world becomes picture at all is what distinguishes the modern age" (130).

Heidegger bases much of what he has to say about these things on the writings of Descartes. In turn, much of what Descartes says about vision in his scientific writings (especially *Optics* and *Treatise on the World*) aligns with his philosophical views. Moving from optics to philosophy, "external" sight corresponds to the "internal" operation of seeing ideas imprinted in the mind's eye. The intellect inspects entities modeled in retinal impressions.[2] Self-consciousness is a matter of self-reflexivity, of seeing oneself as if reflected in a mirror. But this seeing is not otherwise conscious of its thinking *as* seeing; mental "seeing" is conceived as a transparent activity. For Descartes, certainty is a matter of eliminating distortions (typically those introduced by the senses). Under ideal conditions, the mind makes a perfect copy of what it sees.

There is nonetheless a tension between "seeing" and "saying," where a crucial dimension of saying involves telling. These tensions emerge within Descartes's writings. Descartes wrote that his aim in *Discourse on the Method* was to present his life "as in a picture." The visual bias in this is clear. So too when he describes man as "the spectator of all."[3] He also said that, rather than *teach* a method that everyone should follow, he only wanted to *show* his own method. The problem, however, is to explain how one can move from showing to a general philosophical method: how can a picture become a general frame (i.e., become the "world view" that Heidegger described)? In explaining how Descartes established the idea of representation as basic to subjectivity, we need to recognize that his texts draw support from fables, history writing, autobiography, and other forms of telling. Across all these forms are several interlinked questions that relate to the one just mentioned. How can one establish the basis of truth by recourse to fables? How can the general foundations of knowledge be established through a form of writing that is styled autobiographically, as a *self-portrait*? In raising these questions, the point is not to show that Descartes wrote literature rather than philosophy, but rather to learn something about the role of literary forms in the construction of the Cartesian subject.

Consider first the question of fables and histories. Histories are subject to error in part because they ask us to rely on what others have said and seen; we have not established for ourselves what they report. Philosophy, according to Descartes, must establish itself independently. Descartes also says that we can read the works of the ancients, including those of Plato and Aristotle – but from them we will learn history, not philosophy. There is a further critique of histories and fables in *Discourse on the Method*, and alongside it a critique of novels or "romances" (*romans*):

> Fables make one imagine many events possible which are not, and even the most accurate histories, if they do not exactly misrepresent or exaggerate the value of things in order to render them more worthy of being read, at least omit in them all the circumstances which are basest and least notable; and from this fact it follows that what is retained is not portrayed as it really is, and that those who regulate their conduct from examples which they derive from such a source, are liable to fall into the extravagances of the knights-errant of Romance, and form projects beyond their power of performance. (I, 84–85)

But there is also a moment in *Discourse* just preceding this one where Descartes says that he is himself writing a work that should be understood as a kind of history or fable. This is surprising, to say the least.

> By regarding this Treatise simply as a history, or, if you prefer, a fable in which, amongst certain things which may be imitated, there are possibly others also which it would not be right to follow, I hope that it will be of use to some, and that all will thank me for my frankness. (I, 83)

What we are faced with here is an apparent set of contradictions: there would seem to be true fables and false ones, examples worthy of imitation and ones that are not, histories (and stories) that are reliable, and ones that are not.

**Philosophy and Fables**

Descartes's critique of fables does not deter him from availing himself of them quite liberally. These often take the form of outlandishly fictional questions. "How do I know that I am not a brain in a vat?" That is a question posed by

Thomas Nagel in an essay on consciousness ("What Is It Like to be a Bat?" in *Mortal Questions*). Descartes wonders whether (and how) we can tell we are not merely dreaming ourselves and the world, and proposes a fable-like thought experiment to help him find an answer:

> "suppose then that I am dreaming, and that these particulars – that my eyes are open, that I am moving my head and stretching out my hands – are not true. Perhaps, indeed, I do not even have such hands or such a body at all."[4]

How we can truly know whether others are in fact human beings? "If I look out of the window and see men crossing the square ... do I really see any more than hats and coats which could conceal automatons?" (II, 21).

Some contemporary philosophical fables have even more of a science-fiction flavor, as in the case of the "total flight simulator" proposed by Thomas Metzinger: "A total flight simulator is a self-modeling airplane that has always flown without a pilot and has generated a complex internal image of itself within its own internal flight simulator. The image is transparent. The information that it is an internally generated image is not yet available to the system as a whole."[5]

These contradictions can be explained if we bear in mind that there is more than one "I" in Descartes's texts. There is the autobiographical "I" of René Descartes, who tells his own story of reading, learning, travels, disillusionment, and philosophical resolve in a way that is recognizable from conventional autobiographies. On this level, *Meditations* and *Discourse* recount the story of Descartes's personal search for the foundations of truth. The "I" who speaks is the "I" of the thinker proposing to tell of his own experiences. For example, Descartes recounts in *Discourse* that he was "nourished on letters" in his childhood and then subsequently realized that much of what he learned was untrue. But Descartes's interest in recounting the experiences of this autobiographical "I" is to give an account of how he came to arrive at the arguments and conclusions that should be valid for *any* "I." We can think of Descartes's autobiographical "I" as the self; we can think of the generalized or transcendental "I" has having the form of the subject. The broadest and best known philosophical conclusions that Descartes reached are ones that are meant to be valid independent of his own experiences, even if those experiences led him to general ideas such as the independence of the body and the mind, the refutation of skepticism that rests on the primacy of thinking (i.e., the irreducibility of the *cogito*, the "I think"), and the connection between thinking and existence. When Descartes asks what he is, he answers "a thing that thinks" (*Meditations*, II, 19).

**Is the "Subject" Gendered?**

Consider these lines from "Myth" by Muriel Rukeyser:

> Long afterward, Oedipus, old and blinded, walked the roads. He smelled a familiar smell. It was the Sphinx.
> Oedipus said, "I want to ask one question. Why didn't I recognize my mother?"
> "You gave me the wrong answer," the Sphinx replied.
> "But that was what made everything possible," said Oedipus.
> "No," she said. "When I asked, What walks on four legs in the morning, two at noon, and three in the morning, you answered, Man. You didn't say anything about Woman."
> "When you say Man," said Oedipus, "you include women too. Everyone knows that."
> She said, "That's what you think."[6]

## Correspondence Theories

The idea of knowing things from the standpoint of the single observer was closely aligned with the correspondence theory of truth. The notion that truth involves a correspondence between ideas in the mind and things or states of affairs in the world became part of epistemology beginning in the seventeenth and eighteenth centuries. In addition to Descartes, the key figures who developed these ideas were Locke and Hume. The antecedents of this line of thinking – which includes Aristotle's explanation of truth in *Metaphysics*: "to deny what is or to affirm what is not is false, whereas to affirm what is and to deny what is not are true"[7]– saw truth as a general form of relationality between knowledge and the real. Aristotle's notion of the "mind" was closer to what we would call the intellect (which he called *nous*). The conception of truth that Thomas Aquinas developed based on the Aristotelian model was similar but considerably more explicit. For Aquinas, truth involved "the equation of thing and intellect" (*Veritas est adaequatio rei et intellectus*). Likewise, for Aquinas, the mind can itself know the truth because it can know its own conformity to the thing it knows.[8]

The emergence of the notion of truth as a kind of "correspondence" to reality involved a new conception of the mind as a kind of inner "mental theatre." This mental theatre was regarded as separate from the body, non-spatial, and immaterial in nature. What is represented in the mind are ideas. It was not entirely clear just what "ideas" were, although Descartes refers to them as the "form" of thoughts – forms that are perceived directly. Ideas represented in this inner mental theater are true when they correspond to things or states of affairs in the world, which – it is supposed in this context – *really are* one way or another.

As many later thinkers (Richard Rorty most notable among them) have pointed out, there are numerous difficulties with the notion of truth as the correspondence between ideas in the mind and realities in the world. They begin with the empiricist responses to Descartes and continue with the entanglements in which the empiricists in turn found themselves. In *An Essay Concerning Human Understanding*, Locke challenged Descartes by asserting that ideas themselves must come either from internal reflection or from sensation. To invoke sensation implied that ideas came to be in the mind through a kind of "imprinting" mechanism. Likewise, Hume advanced what has been called a "copy principle" of knowledge.

**Goodman on the "Copy Theory" of Representation**

The notion of "world-versions" displaces the "copy theory" of representation:

> The most neutral eye and the most biased are merely sophisticated in different ways. ... The copy theory of representation, then, is stopped at the start by inability to specify what it is to be copied. Not an object the way it is, nor all the ways it looks to the mindless eye. ... For an aspect is not just the object-from-a-given-distance-and-angle-and-in-a-given-light; it is the object as we look upon or conceive it, a version or construal of the object. In representing an object, we do not copy such a construal or interpretation – we achieve it.[9]

But "impressions" were not themselves regarded as material elements of sensation, but rather as representations whose basis in turn lay in the senses. For this reason, Locke needed to introduce the notion of a mental capacity, a "faculty" able to make true-false judgments *about* representations. But his theory about the mind had no room for any such faculty. He was, as Richard Rorty suggested, caught "balancing awkwardly between knowledge-as-identity-with-object and knowledge-as-true-judgment-about-object."[10] In *Critique of Pure Reason*, Kant associated this with empirical psychology.[11] The project of moral philosophy as a new "science of man" was established on this precarious and uncertain ground.

## Implications for Moral Philosophy

There are other equally influential reasons why the Enlightenment project of justifying morality was unlikely to succeed – and perhaps, in retrospect, bound to fail. One dilemma is captured by Hume's dictum that no moral conclusions (statements about what one ought to do) can be drawn from statements of fact (i.e., from "is" statements). There has to be some mechanism to bind oneself to what ought to be done on the basis of what one knows to be true. Alasdair MacIntyre proposed that:

> these writers share in the project of constructing valid arguments which will move from premises concerning human nature as they understand it to be to conclusions about the authority of and precepts … [but] any project of this form was bound to fail, because of an ineradicable discrepancy between their shared conception of moral rules and precepts on the one hand and what was shared – despite much larger divergences – in their conception of human nature on the other.[12]

The precepts of ethics had traditionally been regarded as the means by which human beings could approach their full potential as moral beings – in MacIntyre's words, "man-as-he-could-be-if-he-realized-his-*telos*" (*After Virtue*, 53; emphasis in original). But one could not necessarily achieve this on the basis of knowing what is empirically true. Aristotelian and earlier Christian ideas about human nature relied on the idea of telos and moral purpose inherent in human nature itself, but this idea was no longer regarded as valid. With that underpinning gone, the Enlightenment attempt to bridge rational truth and the moral ends of man by means of an ethical system came to be regarded as invalid.

MacIntyre pointed to the need to revisit Aristotle's way of thinking about human nature as allied to moral purposes and ends. He argued that Jane Austen was Aristotle's truest heir in exemplifying what the virtues mean. Rorty, by contrast, took up the problem squarely from the perspective of truth, arguing not just that the Enlightenment conception of epistemology was flawed and inconsistent but that the commitment to the idea of truth as the basis for all other forms of philosophy (including moral philosophy) was misguided. This is a notion that Rorty extended to any form of philosophy that would appeal to a single, final framework to adjudicate knowledge claims and value judgments. He argued instead that these frameworks are all local and contingent. We can redescribe things when the need arises.

There are particular philosophers with whom Rorty was willing to forge an alliance because they reject the connection between truth and any final framework for establishing the way things truly are:

> Wittgenstein, Heidegger, and Dewey are in agreement that the notion of knowledge as accurate representation made possible by special mental processes, and intelligible through a general theory of representation,

> needs to be abandoned. For all three, the notions of "foundations of knowledge" and of philosophy as revolving around the Cartesian attempt to answer the epistemological skeptic are set aside. Further, they set aside the notion of "the mind" common to Descartes, Locke, and Kant – as a special subject of study, located in space, containing elements or processes that make knowledge possible. … They set aside epistemology and metaphysics as possible disciplines. (*PMN*, 6).

As this suggests, to set aside epistemology does not happen by virtue of argument, but rather as part of a "paradigm shift" in which the notion of the mind and of truth inherited from the seventeenth century would seem irrelevant, much in the way that medieval philosophy came to seem irrelevant for the thinkers of the Enlightenment. Truth for a pragmatist like Rorty is nothing special; it is simply "what works" in the way of ideas. What we require in order to see this, however, is a shift in framework that has to come from *outside* epistemology. We need to be ironists and pragmatists and to abandon the search for epistemological certainty. I turn to that subject next.

## Suggestions for Further Reading

Judith Butler, *Gender Trouble* (New York: Routledge, 1999).
Anthony J. Cascardi, *The Subject of Modernity* (Cambridge: Cambridge University Press, 1992).
John Dewey, *Art and Education* (New York: Capricorn, 1958).
*The Quest for Certainty* (New York: Putnam, 1960).
Jurgen Habermas, *The Philosophical Discourse of Modernity*, trans. Frederick Lawrence (Cambridge, MA: MIT Press, 1987).
Edmund Husserl, *Cartesian Meditations*, trans. Dorion Cairns (The Hague: M. Nijhoff, 1960).
Dalia Judovitz, *Subjectivity and Representation in Descartes* (Cambridge: Cambridge University Press, 1988).
Jean-Luc Nancy, "Larvatus Pro Deo," In *Glyph*, 2, trans. Daniel Brewer, (Baltimore, MD: Johns Hopkins University Press, 1977), pp. 14–36.
Robert Pippin, *The Persistence of Subjectivity* (Cambridge: Cambridge University Press, 2005).
Timothy Reiss, *The Discourse of Modernism* (Ithaca, NY: Cornell University Press, 1982).
John Richetti, *Philosophical Writing: Locke, Berkeley, Hume* (Cambridge, MA: Harvard University Press, 1983).
Dimitris Vardoulakis, *The Doppelgänger: Literature's Philosophy* (New York: Fordham University Press, 2010).

Chapter 4

# Contingency, Irony, Edification: Changing the Conversation about Truth

## Pragmatism

From a pragmatist standpoint, questions like "What is truth?" "What is consciousness?" and "What is reality?" that the Cartesian model was designed to answer could better be understood by watching how we actually use words like "truth" and "consciousness." This was the spirit in which Wittgenstein attempted to shift emphasis away from questions about essences and toward linguistic usage. His "therapeutic" approach to philosophy's fundamental problems was to ask questions about the place of an utterance within the give-and-take of "language games." This was the term that Wittgenstein adopted from Fritz Mauthner to describe the nature of language as a set of shared, rule-based practices. In his later work, Wittgenstein saw an utterance as more like a move in a game than an independently structured proposition. Whatever one says makes sense, if at all, in relation to other utterances, or as part of a web of contextual relations – but not as the manifestation of some deep-structure content. Similarly, Wittgenstein proposed that it was more fruitful to reframe questions about identity and essence in terms of "family resemblance." (Wittgenstein may have derived that notion from Nietzsche, who used it when talking about language families.) Wittgenstein's point was that things may be connected by overlapping similarities rather than by a single underlying feature.

Richard Rorty's work carried these ideas forward, specifically by insisting that "truth" and "value" do not have any particular form or underlying essence aside from the ways in which such terms are used. Rorty, like Wittgenstein, wanted to return them from philosophy to the forms of our everyday practices. "Truth," he said "is not the sort of thing one should expect to have a philosophically interesting theory about."[1] So too with value: "[Pragmatists] see certain acts as good to perform, under the circumstances, but doubt that there is anything general and useful to say about what makes them all good" (xiii). It is worth noting that Voltaire's *Philosophical Dictionary* has no entry for "truth," although it does have one for "tolerance." "We are all steeped in weakness and error," writes Voltaire; "let us forgive one another's follies, it is the first law of nature."[2]

**Woody Allen's Wisdom**

"Can we actually 'know' the universe? My God, it's hard enough finding your way around in Chinatown. The point, however, is: Is there anything out there? And why? And must they be so noisy? Finally, there can be no doubt that the one characteristic of 'reality' is that it lacks essence. That is not to say it has no essence, but merely lacks it. (The reality I speak of here is the same one Hobbes described, but a little smaller.)"[3]

**Nelson Goodman on Woody Allen**

"The message, I take it, is simply this: never mind, essence is not essential, and matter doesn't matter. We do better to focus on versions rather than worlds. Of course, we want to distinguish between versions that do and those that do not refer, and to talk about things and worlds, if any, referred to; but these things and worlds and even the stuff they are made of – matter, anti-matter, mind, energy, or whatnot – are themselves fashioned by and along with the versions. … This does not mean, I must repeat, that right versions can be arrived at casually, or that worlds are built from scratch. We start, on any occasion, with some old version or world that we have on hand and that we are stuck with until we have the determination and skill to remake it into a new one. Some of the felt stubbornness of fact is the grip of habit: our firm foundation is indeed solid. Worldmaking begins with one version and ends with another." (*Ways of Worldmaking*, 96–97)

For a pragmatist and self-proclaimed ironist like Rorty, the question of truth in relation to the real is not, in the end, the right one to be asking. What novelists and others writing literature know is that, no matter how committed they may be to the truth-content of their work, it can never be defended as a representation of the way the world is *in-itself*. In fact, one of their most important tasks is to acknowledge that there is *not* any such "world in-itself," even if there may be very plausible versions of the world. This point echoes Nelson Goodman's notion of worldmaking. Rorty sees this project ultimately as an ironic one. As for ethical imperatives, the ironist is aligned with tolerance. Indeed, tolerance may well be the ethical stance that best captures the insights of the anti-foundational thinker whose main goal is to substitute irony for assertions about the "true" or the "good" or the "essences" of things as they really are.

One implication of this view is that the ironist's theories are likely to be narrative. Rorty explains that this is because "the ironist's nominalism and historicism will not permit him to think of his work as establishing a relation to real essence; he can only establish a relation to the past."[4] This does not preclude forward-looking projects, although for Rorty these have to be limited to the private sphere rather than to the pursuit of public goals. Theoretical projects are about the past; creative projects are about the self – and the project of the philosophical ironist is to know the difference between them and to respect the place of each one.

Two of Rorty's examples will help us grasp what "self-creation" means here: Proust and Nietzsche. Proust's *Remembrance of Things Past* is a web of contingencies. "The narrator might never have encountered the madeleine, the newly impoverished Prince de Guermantes did not have to marry Madame Verdurin. He might have found some other heiress. Such contingencies make sense only in retrospect" (*Contingency*, 100–101). Whereas a philosopher like Hegel thought he had mapped Absolute Knowing, Proust's ambitions were quite different: "At the end of his life and his novel, by showing what time had done to these other people, Proust showed what he had done with the time he had. He had written a book, and thus created a self – the author of that book – which these people could not have predicted or even envisaged. … Proust temporalized and finitized the authority figures he had met by seeing them as creatures of contingent circumstance" (102–103). As Proust says in *Time Regained*, "I understood that all these materials for a work of literature were simply my past life."[5]

Nietzsche presents a different but equally illuminating example. Among his main philosophical targets are "Spirit" and "Being," both of which had been understood as far more than accumulations of contingencies or the products of circumstances. Nietzsche's narrative does not describe persons, as in Proust, but instead engages the "vocabularies" for which certain famous terms serve as "abbreviations" (e.g., "Europe," "Being," "Spirit"). Proust's was a critique of authority, but in a local sense. Ultimately he became as much of an authority on the people he knew as his younger self had feared they might be an authority on him: "This enabled him to relinquish the very idea of authority, and with it the idea that there is a privileged perspective from which he, or anyone else, is to be described" (*Contingency*, 102–103). Nietzsche similarly liked to show that everything that has been said about man is "at bottom no more than a testimony as to the man of a *very limited* period of time."[6] Nietzsche believed that the pursuit of essences in relation to entities such as "man" or "human nature" had exhausted itself and that something else must take its place. He very much wanted to play a role in shaping that new project.

**Nietzsche's Force-Fields: "Winners" and "Losers"**

Nietzsche sets up a force-field of resistances for his readers, whom he fears were liable to be too comfortable merely joining with him in a chorus of opposition.

What might it mean to "follow" Nietzsche? "Nietzsche desperately needs readers, for otherwise his grandiose claims about the epochal significance of his philosophy cannot possibly be justified. But insofar as his readers passively accept his critique of earlier philosophy, they will hardly be the "monsters of courage and curiosity' needed to transmit his philosophy to the future," says Malcolm Bull, who proposes the strategy of "reading like a loser" as the best available option.[7]

Proust and Nietzsche stand n very different positions when it comes to the project of "overcoming" the past and to the worry that one might oneself be "overcome" in the future. (Rorty sometimes uses the term "redescription" as an alternative to overcoming.) Proust was successful in redescribing himself, but he was also the kind of writer who would not be troubled by the prospect that someone coming after him might in turn redescribe him. In literature, one cannot guard against one's successors. The ironist theorist by contrast (e.g., Nietzsche) cannot imagine any successors because "he is the prophet of a new age, one in which no terrain used in the past will have any application" (*Contingency*, 102). The only true end of such a project lies in the end of history. Hegel begins by overcoming his predecessors and ends the *Phenomenology* only when knowing has reached its final, absolute goal. What more would be left to say? In philosophy, by Rorty's account, it was Derrida who eventually stopped trying to bring any such project to a close. Derrida had learned from Heidegger, who had in turn learned from Nietzsche. But what he also learned was that "Heidegger's litany is just Heidegger's litany, not Being's or Europe's. His problem becomes … to think the fact that 'there is no unique name – or, more generally, no definitive litany without *nostalgia*, that is, outside the myth of a purely maternal or paternal language, a lost native country of thought'" (*Contingency*, 122; emphasis in original).[8]

**Literary History as a Challenge to "Overcoming"**

The histories of literature and the arts teach a healthy skepticism about the idea of "overtaking" as "overcoming." Why wasn't the novel overtaken by film? Film builds on the novel, in some ways, but does not overtake it in any ultimate sense – no more, at least, than film put an end to photography or to the theatre. We sometimes say that the novel "displaced" romance. If that is a statement about popularity or cultural dominance it may be useful. But the novel also carries romance inside it, as the example of *Don Quixote* suggests. The two forms remained in dialogue (and still do) even as one receded in prominence while the other enlarged its cultural profile.

Coming to terms with the past is a very different matter than pretending to have the last word by creating something that nobody could overtake. Writers and artists do sometimes attempt to do this, but history inevitably proves them wrong.

## Edification

Understanding what "edification" means is important for rounding out the picture of what Rorty means by redescription and self-creation. Edification is something slightly different than mere self-improvement, although that is certainly part of it. Drawing heavily on Gadamer's *Truth and Method*, Rorty situates edification in the general ambit of education and *Bildung*, but with a slightly different spin. The aim of the edifying philosopher is not to discover truth (much less anything like "absolute" truth or "objectivity") but rather, Rorty says, "to help their readers, or society as a whole, break free from outworn vocabularies and attitudes, rather than to provide 'grounding' for the intuitions and customs of the present."[9] Its aim is in one regard therapeutic. This is something that philosophers in quest of essence and the truth – in the tradition that Rorty identifies as running through Plato, Descartes, and Kant – never sought to pursue because they thought that any real and lasting benefits to individuals or to society would be possible only if philosophy could firmly establish itself by identifying the very foundations of truth, the good, being, and so forth.

Edifying philosophy also contrasts with "systematic" philosophy. Kierkegaard used the term to describe some of his writings (*Opbyggelige Taler*, "Edifying Addresses"). Systematic philosophy needs to start from the very beginning, whereas edifying philosophy knows that we always begin *in medias res* (in the middle of things). This means that we start from within established cultures and history and learn to discern what we are to jettison and what we are to keep. Here is Rorty offering a characteristically pithy contrast between the two:

> Great systematic philosophers, like great philosophers, build for eternity. Great edifying philosophers destroy for the sake of their own generation. Systematic philosophers want to put their subject on the secure path of a science. Edifying philosophers want to keep space open for the sense of wonder which poets can sometimes create – wonder that there is something new under the sun, something which is *not* an

> accurate representation of what was already there, something which (at least for the moment) cannot be explained and can barely be described. (*PMN*, 369–370; emphasis in original)

The goal of edifying philosophy is not truth or knowledge, but rather to generate new and more interesting descriptions of ourselves, to sustain new and more interesting conversations and, in the public realm, just to avoid cruelty rather than to aim at the creation of some grand system or an ideal and eternal republic. These might seem like modest goals, and they are. Modesty, along with irony, is part of the point – because the vocabularies we use, the descriptions we invoke, and the conversations we sustain, are what "we" really are.

This much having been said, it is important to add that there is no guarantee that the process of edification will be successful. There are novels, such as Flaubert's *Sentimental Education*, that focus on its disappointments and failures. The larger point is that there are no independent criteria for what success may look like. Because edification is not systematic, there is no method to guide or guarantee it. One of its goals is simply to enable us to participate in the conversations around us, although with a skeptical eye cast toward anyone who would wish to talk *beyond* those conversations to something "foundational." The project of edification must be recognized as infinite: "Edifying philosophers can never end philosophy, but they can help prevent it from attaining the path of a secure science" (*PMN*, 372). The difference is between the "infinite striving for truth" and the "striving for 'all of truth.'" In his advocacy of the former, Rorty aligns himself with Kierkegaard, who made this the choice for "subjectivity" over "system" in the *Concluding Unscientific Postscript* (*PMN*, 377). In this there may be wisdom. Indeed, Rorty is not at all too shy to speak of wisdom. Near the close of *Philosophy and the Mirror of Nature* he writes:

> One way of thinking of wisdom is as something of which the love is not the same as that of argument, and of which the achievement does not consist in finding the correct vocabulary for representing essence, is to think of it as the practical wisdom necessary to participate in a conversation. One way to see edifying philosophy *as* the love of wisdom is to see it as the attempt to prevent conversation from degenerating into inquiry, into a research program. (372; emphasis in original)

### The Genealogy of Pragmatism

In its current usage, the term "pragmatism" names a philosophical approach that originated with William James and John Dewey. In 1907, James published a series of lectures entitled *Pragmatism: A New Name for an Old Way of*

*Thinking*. He proposed that the answers to "grand" questions are to be found in practice rather than in a new grand theory:

> "The tangible fact at the root of all our thought-distinctions, however subtle, is that there is no one of them so fine as to consist in anything but a possible difference of practice. To attain perfect clearness in our thoughts of an object, then, we need only consider what conceivable effects of a practical kind the object may involve."[10]

Pragmatists like Rorty urge us to abandon the quest for essences, arguing that they do not exist and that we can redescribe the world as we need. In the domain of language, this shift in orientation corresponds to a shift away from the idea that truth is a matter of correspondence between words and things or ideas, but rather is a matter of taking part in a web of contextual relations, which Wittgenstein called "language games." Wittgenstein's notion of the language game says that utterances make sense as part of a shared set of practices, most of which remain in the background until we fail to make sense of them or when, as Wittgenstein puts it, language "goes on holiday"[11] – or when, as we have seen in the previous sections, conventions are breached. Thinking along these lines, Charles Taylor asked:

> how is it that these segments of a medium that we deploy, when we talk, make music, paint, make signals, build symbolic structures, *how is it that these say something?* How is it that we can complete sentences of the form 'What this means (to say) is …?' whereas we cannot say this of sticks, stones, stars, mountains, forests?[12]

His answer was intended to draw out the public space on which language depends. There is no private language: we make meaning only when and because there is a public, shareable context available to us – and what we do in making meaning also gives shape to this shared space.

Hannah Arendt's account of human practices is likewise crucial to an understanding of what the single observer standpoint excludes. In describing the "public space of appearance" within which practices are formed,[13] Arendt pointed out that this is the difference between Kant's first two critiques on the one hand (*Critique of Pure Reason* and *Critique of Practical Reason*), and the third critique (*Critique of Judgment*) on the other. The first and second critiques gives us a picture of man as a reasonable being, subject to the laws of practical reason that he gives to himself – autonomous, an end in himself, and participating in a community of intelligible beings. In the third critique, Arendt proposed, Kant gives us a picture of men as earthbound creatures, living in communities, endowed with common sense (*sensus communis*, a community of sense), and needing each other's company even for thinking.[14] Human beings are language-using animals individually and collectively; in order for us to be what Aristotle called "political animals" we must be rational animals – that is, having the capability of speech (*ratio*). These are insights that theories of truth based on the standpoint of a single observer are likely to miss:

> [Language] serves to found public space, that is, to place certain matters before *us*. The blindness to the public is another consequence of the epistemological tradition, which regards knowledge as a property of the individual… [language] creates the peculiarly human kind of rapport, or being together, that we are in conversation together. To express something, to formulate it, can be not only to get it in articulate focus, but also to place it in public space … given this human capacity to found public space, we can and do ring all sorts of changes on it.[15]

Examining the work of Henry James, Robert Pippin made a related claim with regard to morality: "The key issue in morality might not be the rational justifiability with which I treat others, but the proper acknowledgment of, and enactment of, a dependence on others without which the process of any justification (or any invocation of common normative criteria at all) could not begin."[16]

The shared, public space that all these accounts invoke is also called "intersubjective" space. By whatever name we may call it, it would be a mistake to suppose that we are transparent to one another within it. While Wittgenstein argued that there can never be a wholly private language, others have argued that the self and the other can never hold one another wholly in common because of the absolute and irreducible uniqueness of each. For a thinker like Emmanuel Lévinas, this is precisely where ethical obligation is located; we have a responsibility "to the other who, refusing to be owned, falls to my responsibility, that is, signifies in all the ethical excellence of the obligation toward the other, in fear for him or her, and love."[17] The outsideness of self and other are thus transformed into an ethical demand. "The proximity of the other showing me his or her face, in society with me, and the implications of that encounter overturn the logical and ontological play of the same and the other, transforming it into ethics."[18]

Stanley Cavell's treatment of Shakespeare's *Othello* moves in a similar direction. Cavell approaches *Othello* in the course of a long discussion of questions about skepticism and knowledge. Cavell's point all along is not to defeat skepticism, as has been the general tendency in philosophy. Rather, his aim is to recognize the "truth" of skepticism, to identify what it has to say that philosophy typically wishes to disown or repress by taking it as something that needs defeating. To recognize these things is not the same thing as being a skeptic. Rather, Cavell offers an interpretation of skepticism that aims to discern the truth behind it. Among the key truths of skepticism – one which philosophy has often had a role in concealing – is the fact that we *are* outsiders to one another. This outsideness describes a fundamental opacity that cannot be overcome by knowledge. On the contrary, many projects of knowledge end up intensifying rather than reducing it. The questions that skepticism raises are covers for the fact of the outsideness of the other, for the fact that the other is not knowable by me in the way that facts about the world may be knowable. Tragedy becomes the place where this cover is blown, "the place where we are not allowed to escape the consequences, or the price, of this cover."[19]

What more does this imply? For one thing, that our relationship to the other calls not for knowledge but for what Cavell consistently calls acknowledgment. (This is a subject I will discuss again in Part III). Othello strives assiduously to establish certain facts about Desdemona, facts based on suspicions that Iago has some role in planting in his mind, but which are equally of his own doing. The most important of these facts is of course Desdemona's faithfulness. In the process, however, Othello fails to recognize the limits of what can be known about Desdemona; better said, perhaps, in regarding her as an object of knowledge, he fails to acknowledge her. In regarding her as if she were a thing in the world to be known with epistemological certainty, he effectively transforms her into something inanimate, lifeless. The figurative language of the play, in which she is as if a stone (alabaster), becomes a dramatic reality in the moment of her murder.

The key lines in *Othello* are these, spoken by Othello in Act V, describing Desdemona: "whiter skin of hers than snow, / And smooth, as monumental alabaster."[20] Cavell comments that "the failure to acknowledge a best case of the other is a denial of that other, presaging the death of the other, say by stoning, or by hanging; and the death of our capacity to acknowledge as such, the turning of our hearts to stone" (*Disowning Knowledge*, 138). The tragedy is in this case a striking display of the limits of what can be verified by ocular proof. To recognize these limits, and to recognize as well the need for acknowledgment in human situations, is what this Shakespearean tragedy shows about the opacity of human beings to one another. Cavell concludes:

> So there they are, on their bridal and death sheets. A statue, a stone, is something whose existence is fundamentally open to the ocular proof. A human being is not. The two bodies lying together form an emblem of this fact, the truth of skepticism. What this man lacked was not

certainty. He knew everything, but he could not yield to what he knew, be commanded by it. He found out too much for his mind, not too little. Their differences from one another – the one everything the other is not – form an emblem of human separation, which can be accepted, and granted, or not. Like the separation from God; everything we are not. (141–142)

## Suggestions for Further Reading

Hans-Georg Gadamer, *Dialogue and Dialectic*, trans. P. Christopher Smith (New Haven, CT: Yale University Press, 1980).

*Truth and Method*, revised trans. Joel Weinsheimer and Donald G. Marshall (New York: Continuum, 1995).

Anthony A. Long, *Epictetus: A Stoic and Socratic Guide to Life* (Oxford: Oxford University Press, 2002).

Friedrich Schleiermacher, *Hermeneutics and Criticism*, trans. and ed. Andrew Bowie (Cambridge: Cambridge University Press, 1998).

Richard Shusterman, *Practicing Philosophy: Pragmatism and the Philosophical Life* (New York: Routledge, 1997).

J. David Velleman, *The Possibility of Practical Reason* (Ann Arbor: University of Michigan Library, 2000).

# Part II

## *Questions of Value*

Chapter 5

# Values, Contingencies, Conflicts

In considering questions of truth across the dual spans of literature and philosophy we've already come to see how truth is virtually impossible to discern without taking questions of value on board. The same holds true for questions of value, which are likewise entangled with truth. The combined insight of these positions resonates with an argument put forward by Hilary Putnam that "factual description and valuation can and must be entangled."[1] In crystallizing the fact-value *connection* Putnam was refuting the strong version of the fact-value *distinction*. We glimpsed the kernel of that distinction in the form of David Hume's assertion that there can be no way to move from the realm of facts ("is") to the realm of value ("ought"). But Putnam and others suggest that there is hardly a truth known to man that does not imply some kind of value (including the value of knowing it *as* a truth). The notion of "truthfulness" as explained by Bernard Williams articulates one form of the value of truth, but it is only one. Moreover, the kinds of value questions that span literature and philosophy are hardly limited to questions of truth. Questions of value don't require that we first ask about truth. Value questions emerge as prominent in their own right throughout the history of literature as well as in the work of philosophers as different as Plato, Aristotle, Kant, Schopenhauer, and Nietzsche. And yet none of them was inclined simply to relinquish their interest in matters of truth.

The single term "value" must cover an exceptionally wide range of subjects. It needs to be construed broadly enough to encompass questions of ethics (of how we ought to act for ourselves, towards others, and towards the nonhuman world), of morality and the good (of what it is and how it comes into being, how it might be pursued, whether it is one thing or many, and indeed whether it exists at all), as well as questions of judgment, of norms, of freedom, and of our passionate attachments to things, persons, and ideas. At bottom, all these questions share a concern that numerous philosophers have articulated as "How should a human being live?"[2] This is a question that is best regarded as having no *special* terrain, which is to say that it does not require marking off a value-zone of "ethical life" or "morality" as separate from "aesthetic life," or politics, or economic life. We will need to touch on instances in which value is attached to some*thing* (such as a work of art) or some*one* (of human beings as such), as well as instances in which value is carried by our experience of these attachments. Henry James's novel *The Golden Bowl*, for instance, raises questions about the value of persons and of things (of Maggie Verver and the Prince, for instance, and of the golden bowl itself); and as a work of art it occasions experiences of value by virtue of its language, its nuanced account of perceptions and motives, and its particular insights into human relations.

## Value: Made or Found?

To cover this much ground is daunting, and attempting to do so briefly will require leaving out many details. The compensation, I hope, will be a useful set of contrasts, which can serve as the basis for more nuanced and expansive work outside the confines of this book. One of the crucial distinctions is between those who regard value as something *given*, and as standing principally in need of discovery, and those who regard value as something constructed and *made* – a function of the will, of desire, of the passions, or of various forms of power. As we'll see in more detail later, the first group includes the followers of Plato, while the second is divided between romantic-"expressivist" writers on the one hand and the followers of Marx and Foucault on the other. Three contrastive philosophical stances corresponding to these broad divisions can help provide an orientation as we move across this terrain.

First is Plato's conception of the good as unchanging, eternal, and unitary. This involves an idea of perfection, which as an ideal is mediated through the appearances of the phenomenal world, including literature, art, and philosophical discourse itself. We have already seen something of this in Plato's treatment of images and imitation, which in large part involves a moral critique of literature. Second is the conception of value as a form of human expression, best exemplified in romantic philosophy and literature, where expressive*ness* is itself taken as a value for human beings. Thinkers ranging from Rousseau and Fichte to Schopenhauer and Nietzsche share a conception of value that is based on the activity of a consciousness whose center of gravity is located in desire and the will, and whose core project is self-actualization. Relevant literary figures here include Byron, the two Shelleys, Schiller, Goethe, Keats, Conrad, and Lawrence. They share the conviction, or at least the hope, that human beings can establish a link between beauty and truth through the power of imagination. Keats in fact says that this power enables human beings to establish the truth itself: "What the Imagination seizes as Beauty must be Truth – whether it existed before or not."[3] (What happens when the imagination conceives something horrible, ugly, disgusting, or deformed? That is a question to be addressed later.) The imagination is, roughly speaking, the power of forming concepts beyond those derived from external objects; it is, in the words of one recent thinker, "a power over external objects, or the transformation of the external into the internal through the work of subjective creation, a creation that is given sensuous form and is therefore rendered external in the work of art, the poem."[4] Third among these stances is the materialist (and post-materialist) philosophies of Marx, Freud, and Foucault. Here, the inherited notions of "value" are called into question either because they rely on metaphysical claims or because they depend more specifically on the metaphysics of the modern Western subject, wedded to the priority of conceptual thought over all other kinds of cognition. "Value" hardly disappears in these accounts, but it is nonetheless mapped along different axes: the axis of power for Foucault, the axis of the unconscious for Freud, and the axes of productive forces and class relations for Marx. Numerous thinkers have claimed that these views offer more than just new approaches to literary texts, but are in fact called for by literature itself. The upshot is a divergence between those who believe literature is exemplary or normative in relation to questions of value (sometimes described, inaccurately, as "humanists"), and those who take literature to be engaged in a critique of value, especially in its received forms (sometimes described, also inaccurately, as "postmodernists").

### A Defense of Values as not Made by Us

"It seems absurd to a great many philosophers – and to a great many other people as well – to suppose that there are values 'out there' in the universe awaiting discovery by human beings who have some mysterious faculty of value apprehension. We must understand value judgments, they say, in some wholly different way. We must accept that there is no objective truth about value that is independent of the beliefs or attitudes of people who judge value: we must understand their claims about what is just or unjust, right or wrong, saintly or wicked, as simply expressions of their attitudes or emotions, or recommendations for others to follow, or personal commitments they undertake, or proposed constructions of guides for their own lives. Most of the philosophers who take this view do not think themselves personally as nihilists. ... Their arguments and examples show that they have our private lives rather than our politics in mind. ... I think them wrong about private lives."[5]

## Orientations

I begin with the Platonic view, not because there are many purebred Platonists around today, but because there have been some very important ones in the past, and because a few today have in fact helped point out some of the errors in many of the "received" views of Plato's ideas. Iris Murdoch is perhaps foremost among them. She also stands in a special position as a serious philosopher and an important novelist, comparable in this respect to Sartre and Simone de Beauvoir, although quite opposed to their views. The character Max Lejour in *The Unicorn* might well be taken as a kind of Platonist in saying that the good is "the unimaginable object of our desire," and likewise as a Platonist in averring that such an idea is "vulgarized by existentialists and linguistic philosophers when they make good into a mere matter of personal choice."[6] For Plato, the good is able to instill desire when it is manifested as beauty; but the good is not itself the *product* of human desire. Likewise, for Plato it would be inconceivable to have an idea of the good and not a desire for it.[7]

But Murdoch's stance as a novelist and philosopher is not identical to the actions or the beliefs of any of her characters. When she writes fiction she writes novels, not novelistic expositions of Platonic ideas. And as a novelist she represents the struggles of flawed characters as they operate in an imperfect world. While her characters often do reflect in words or actions a sense that there exists a form of the good beyond what humans themselves create, they are seldom inclined to pursue "the good" as such. Indeed, the good in-itself is something that seems always to lie beyond the reach of her characters, no matter how vigorous their striving or how deep their thinking may be. Some of her best novels, such as *The Green Knight*, probe the moral consciousness of characters who act in the shadow of the good, rather than under its full illumination. The good, as she conceives it, can be imagined and pursued only within the dim and dirty affairs of human lives. One can indeed understand that while some have called her a Platonist, others have labeled her an existentialist. To invoke the Platonic myth of the cave, which she engages in *The Fire and the Sun*, she is aware that human beings can only see the flickers on the wall, not the sun itself.

Beyond her philosophical views about the nature of the good, Murdoch's work is important because she writes literature out of the conviction that it places philosophical ideas on the rough ground that is necessary if we are to grapple meaningfully with the things that truly matter to human beings. Her work also shows, without prejudice toward literature or philosophy, why there is a difference between a theory of the good and the pursuit of the good, or between a theory of morality and grappling with a moral dilemma. A similar distinction could be made in other areas, to be sure. Consider the difference between a cow and the idea of a cow: the latter can seem remarkably clear and distinct, but also relatively impoverished; the former is multi-faceted, irreducibly particular, and potentially quite messy. One can milk a cow, but not the idea of a cow. The admirable clarity of ideal views about the good, which may lead toward norms, may come at the cost of the "rough ground" of the good as approached by human beings. "Human" here implies finite, flawed, and imperfect. To take a related example, the character Charlotte Stant in Henry James's novel *The Golden Bowl*, pursues a course of action that is driven by genuine love, but that nonetheless has messy consequences; as she remarks to the Prince, "What else can we do, what in all the world else?"[8] And yet, as Murdoch argues in her philosophical essays, the moral and ethical dilemmas encountered in literary texts must offer some sense of what the good in-itself is, even if only to question it.

Another feature of the received view of Plato, which perforce incorporates many post- and neo-Platonic elements, revolves around an understanding of the good as something supremely attractive, no matter how elusive or transcendent it may be. There is an inclination to see the good directly in things and in persons, be they saints or relics, works of art or the things of nature, the beloved of the Petrarchan sonnet tradition or the (ultimately flawed) "golden bowl" of Henry James's novel. This can also lead to idolatry. Murdoch takes up some of these questions in *The Sovereignty of Good*. But she is not a mystic; her view is that the "real," and not the good in-itself, is the proper object of attention, and ultimately of love. The good in-itself cannot be made visible, hence cannot itself be the object of attention: "While it seems proper to represent the Good as a centre or focus of attention, yet it cannot quite be thought of as a 'visible' one in that it cannot be experienced or represented or defined."[9]

These views are articulated in contrast to a composite view of the moral life that is, by Murdoch's account, behaviorist, existentialist, and utilitarian.

> It is behaviourist in its connection of the meaning and being of action with the publicly observable, it is existentialist in its elimination of the substantial self and its emphasis on the solitary omnipotent will, and it is utilitarian in its assumption that morality is and can only be concerned with public acts. It is also incidentally what may be called a democratic view, in that it suggests that morality is not an esoteric achievement but a natural function of any normal man. This position represents, to put it another way, a happy and fruitful marriage of Kantian liberalism with Wittgensteinian logic solemnized by Freud. (*SG*, 8–9)

In sketching her alternative picture, Murdoch offers the hypothetical narrative of a mother who initially regards her new daughter-in-law as good-hearted but lacking in dignity and sometimes rather immature. The mother nonetheless always behaves respectfully toward the daughter-in-law. Over time, however, the mother learns to see the daughter-in-law more truly; she comes to reflect on the limitations of her own initial judgment, and comes to regard the daughter-in-law in a new moral light, "not vulgar but refreshingly simple, not undignified but spontaneous, not noisy but gay, not tiresomely juvenile but delightfully youthful" (*SG*, 17). The difference between what this view proposes and the pragmatist account of our "redescription" of objects lies in the fact that the object of the mother's attention, the daughter-in-law, is herself independent of anything the mother might believe, desire, or will about her. Indeed, the mother's changed view of the daughter-in-law would be little more than a delusion if it did not involve seeing qualities that truly are in the daughter-in-law.

A similar emphasis on moral attention, and in particular on the attention to details as they are rendered in literature, is central to Martha Nussbaum's work across literature and philosophy, especially in *Love's Knowledge*. She takes the example of Henry James as a paradigm for what literature can accomplish in this regard. Her account of James's close attention to particulars is coupled with an Aristotelian conception of ethical deliberation rather than with Plato's account of the good. She writes, for instance, that "fine attention and good deliberation require a highly complex, nuanced perception of, and emotional response to, the concrete features of one's own context, including particular persons and relationships. … It seems *prima facie* plausible to hold, as James does hold, that the terms of the novelist's art can state what James calls 'the projected morality' more adequately than any other available terms."[10] But the importance of Aristotle lies not just in the emphasis on seeing particulars, but also in the sense that there can be rational deliberation about things that are not in themselves subject to universal rules. As noted in Part I, this deliberation is carried out by what Aristotle calls "practical reason." It is not quantitative in its procedures but neither does it imply that choices can only be made blindly, in the manner of a Sartrean hero seeking to exercise radical freedom where only bad choices seem to be at hand.

Can we in fact reason and deliberate about values, desires, and the good? Plato would certainly believe so. There are dialogues that raise questions about the difference between noble and base desires, as well as about which parts of the soul ought to be encouraged and which ones tempered. This interest is consistent with Plato's overarching interest in the question of the good. Subsidiary inquiries follow from it. Where the state is at issue, for example, the question of justice is paramount, but justice is located equally in the soul and in the state. Plato thinks about both together, and believes that the ideal state is the best context for the just soul. Justice is the highest virtue in the *Republic* because it can help regulate the others. The just soul has all the virtues in appropriate measure and balance.

On one level, Socrates is convinced that there is, or ought to be, a fundamental connection between the rational discourse in which one speaks (the *logos*) and the way one lives. Michel Foucault made this very observation by way of remarking that Plato's dialogues always seem to exclude other kinds of self-accounting. They do not, for instance, ask for an examination of conscience or a confession of wrongs, which are certainly among some of the most prominent other ways of engaging questions of value. (I will say more about narrative and moral personhood later.) The dialogues are fixated on the *logos*. Foucault's larger point was that the Socratic ethical project is shaped in relation to a demand to speak the truth that comes from the "outside," either from an interlocutor or in relation to some public demand.[11]

**Foucault on the *Logos* and Giving an Account of Oneself**

"We never see Socrates requiring an examination of conscience or a confession of sins. Here, giving an account of your life, your *bios*, is also not to give a narrative of the historical events that have taken place in your life, but rather to demonstrate whether you are able to show that there is a relation between the rational discourse, the *logos*, you are able to use, and the way that you live. Socrates is inquiring into the way that *logos* gives form to a person's life" (*Fearless Speech*, 97).

## Some Uses of Irony

There is yet another way of regarding the way Plato's Socrates tries to lead his interlocutors strongly, and that is to recognize this activity as something that Plato wishes to distance himself from. The ironic reading of Plato's treatment of Socrates has implications for matters of value. While irony may be regarded as a rhetorical feature of the dialogues, and indeed of a vast literary tradition, and so as part of their *formal* dimension, irony also implies a particular ethical stance vis-à-vis the self and others. Rhetorically, irony involves saying one thing and meaning another, or speaking in one register while carrying meaning in another. It describes the serious remark that is undercut, or the foolish statement that turns out to be wise at its core. Because irony inserts an element of distance between what is said and what is meant, it requires that there be some distance between the subject and the force of his or her words. When applied to the self, irony is a trope of inversion that can prevent the self from taking itself too seriously. Little wonder, then, that it has come to play a crucial role in the work of literary-philosophical satirists, many of whom could in fact trace their roots to some of the ironic elements of Plato's dialogues.

To take but one example from a much later historical moment, consider Voltaire's *Candide* and its response to the Enlightenment's optimism about human nature. (The full title of the work is in fact *Candide, or Optimism.*) Framed in the terms proposed by Alexander Pope, an enlightened contemporary of Voltaire's, there would seem to be little reason not to think of human nature as perfectible, if not already perfect, and likewise little reason not to believe that human beings could aim at making the world perfect as well:

> All nature is but art, unknown to thee;
> All chance, direction which thou canst not see;
> All discord, harmony not understood;
> All partial evil, universal good;
> And, in spite of pride, in erring reason's spite,
> One truth is clear, Whatever is, is right.[12]

Voltaire, by contrast, believed that unchecked, un-ironized optimism may lead to scandalous consequences, not least of which would be a foreclosure of the possibility that human beings might in fact improve themselves and the world around them by recognizing their own shortcomings. Voltaire shuns grand philosophical argument and writes instead in the "minor" genre of the fable-like story (*conte*). His ironic stance is rooted in an aversion to over-confident forms of self-understanding, and especially to those encouraged by pride-filled optimism. That attitude is captured in his satiric portrayal of Candide's tutor, Pangloss, who couples optimism with an inclination toward universal knowledge and rational argumentation. The result of Pangloss's own stance has been described as a form of "logorrhea."[13] Indeed, the etymology of "Pangloss" (from the Green *pan*, meaning "all," and *glossa*, meaning "tongue") suggests that Pangloss is *nothing but* words. Eventually, his own words undo everything he pretends to stand for. But there is more. The second part of *Candide* brings this ironic project to bear on Voltaire himself, explored through the figures of the Savant and the Venetian nobleman, Procuranté. Through them, Voltaire expounds many of the views to which he was himself committed, while continuing to subject these "proto-Voltaires" to deep criticism.[14] One can't help but relate this practice to the irony of some of Plato's dialogues, especially the "middle period" ones like *Republic* and *Symposium*. In fact, one recent commentator aptly described their aim as "to subvert dogmatism, inspire critical self-reflection, and model the sort of philosophical activity capable of transforming the world of human community."[15] Part of the message here is that irony, rather than progressive optimism or systematic argument, may be necessary for the transformation of the self. For Voltaire, it seems, irony helps settle some things, although hardly everything, about the question "How should one live?" The ironic self that Voltaire envisions does not aspire to be perfect, or fully enlightened, only freed from the religious and philosophical fanaticism that over-confidence can breed.

Voltaire's search for an answer to the question "How should one live?" is a quest for what he calls *une raison d'exister*. We might understand this as both "reason for existence" and "rule for living." As mentioned previously, this question is central to ethics, which has long been thought to require the capacity of practical, not theoretical reason, a capacity that Aristotle calls *phronēsis*. It involves deliberation rather than calculation, judgment rather than measurement, weighing how best to act in circumstances that are subject to change rather than determining truths that are timeless. It falls within the broad scope of what Aristotle calls "politics," defined as the most encompassing "science of the good for man" (*EN* X.2, 1094a, 1–2).

While Aristotle clearly favors the contemplative life over any other kind (and is in this sense the clear heir of Plato), it must also be said that for Aristotle, the good is something that *can be* pursued by each and every being and that *must be* actively pursued. The good is the thing toward which we can and must aim if we are to have any hope of finding satisfaction ("happiness," *eudaimonia*) at all. Aristotle says these things at the very beginning of *Nicomachean Ethics*, where he also explains that each sort of inquiry also has its particular aim. "Every art and every inquiry, and similarly every action and pursuit, is thought to aim at some good; and for this reason the good has rightly been declared to be that at which all things aim" (1094a, 1). Inquiry into the nature of the good for human beings is not the same as inquiry into truths about the natural world.

Inquiry into human action requires deliberation. The meaning of "deliberation" can be brought into focus by means of a contrast with other kinds of reasoning. We do not, for instance, deliberate about mathematical formulas or the processes of the natural world. We deliberate about things that are in our power to do, about the things that can be done by dint of our own efforts (*NE*, 1112a, 55). Sometimes it is said that we deliberate about things that are contingent and in flux, but we don't deliberate about things that may happen by accident or that are otherwise out of our control. No amount of deliberation can influence the chances that a natural disaster will or will not occur, although we can deliberate about how we ought best respond to it. The potentially more problematic claim is that we do not deliberate about ends, but only about means. A doctor, for instance, does not ordinarily deliberate about whether or not to heal, only about the means to do so; similarly, a statesman does not ordinarily deliberate about the values of law and order, only about the best means to bring these about. If deliberation involves choosing the best means, then it does so, for Aristotle, where the end or purpose (*telos*) is not in doubt.

### *Phronēsis, Sophia, Eudaimonia*

*Phronēsis* is the capacity to consider action in order to bring about change, and especially change that will enhance the quality of life. Many commentators contend that Aristotle considers the desired end, *eudaimonia* ("happiness," "flourishing"), to be a given, hence *phronēsis* is merely the ability to determine the ways to achieve it. Happiness for human beings is nothing specific. It only must conform to man's rational nature (*EN*, X.7, 1778a, 266). And yet Aristotle also says that *phronēsis* is not simply a skill, as it involves not only the ability to decide how to achieve a certain end, but also the ability to determine that end through a process of reflection

In Geek mythology, Eudaimonia was a goddess, one of the "graces," standing for happiness and prosperity. *Sophia* (usually translated as "wisdom") is by contrast the ability to think well about the nature of the world, to discern why the world is the way it is. *Sophia* involves reason concerning universal truths, and is sometimes equated with "science."

But we know this is not *always* the case, and indeed it is often the place of literature to drive home this very point. In difficult end-of-life circumstances, for instance, a doctor's decision to "heal" may not be clear; the end is in question, not the means. In an oppressive political regime, the ends of "law" and "order" may need to be suspended, at least on a temporary basis.[16] Moreover, there may be instances in which two ends may compete with one another, making the question of means appear secondary. Imagine the dilemmas faced by the parents of conscientious objectors to the Vietnam War, whose sense of duty placed them on a collision course with the children they loved; and consider likewise the dilemmas of those children, bound equally to the opposite sides of those values. In each instance we can well imagine that the meaning of "patriotism" might itself be contested.

Such dilemmas are the very stuff of which classical tragedy is made, and to grasp some of the things that Plato and Aristotle were hoping to achieve in writing about the good we need to say some further things about tragedy. We must first recognize that there is a difference between tragic events and tragedy as a literary form. Second we must recognize that characters in classical tragedy often struggle not between good and evil but among goods of equal measure. They typically attempt to act within competing frames of value, each of which has some claim upon them. Finally we need to consider some of the ways in which tragedy deals with disproportion in the areas of responsibility, justice, and suffering.

When we speak of the destruction caused by an earthquake or a hurricane as "tragic," and likewise when we recognize the fact that the victims of those disasters scarcely bear any responsibility for the suffering they endure, we are talking about unfortunate events rather than about the genre of tragedy. The difference lies not only in the fact that the latter involves a set of literary or dramatic materials, but also because the victims of natural disasters are not ordinarily implicated in the structure of events that so adversely affect them. One might imagine a tragedy being set against the backdrop of a natural disaster, but to imagine a tragedy set in this context we would also have to imagine some space for decision or choice, and some conflict of values, not just a dramatization of suffering at the hands of an inhospitable natural world. To say this in other terms, *pathos* (suffering) is not enough for tragedy; tragedy also depends upon the conditions of agency, including the ones that Aristotle describes in *Poetics* (e.g., recognition, character flaw, reversal of fortune, etc.).

## Further Conflicts of Value

Tragic dramas sometimes emphasize the incommensurability of goods by heightening the disparity of the "spheres of life" around which fundamental human allegiances are established. Take, for example, the often-staged conflict between public duty (e.g., to state or country) and some private bond (filial or amorous). Sophocles' *Antigone* presents a powerful version of just such a conflict. Hegel took it as a model for tragedy because of the clarity of the commitments of each of the main characters.[17] Antigone's filial duty is to bury her brother Polynices, who has died in battle. But since he has died waging war against the state, his burial is forbidden by the law. Creon commands:

> I've reached the following decision regarding
> Oedipus' sons: Eteocles,
> who died fighting for his country, is
> to be buried with full military honors,
> as is usual for heroic casualties;

but his brother, Polynices, who returned
from exile to wage war against his homeland,
who was determined to wreak his vengeance
on his own people and against his father's gods
– no one is to bury him or mourn for him.
His corpse will lie out in the open and dogs and crows
will do with it what dogs and crows
do.
And this is a command.[18]

Antigone, moreover, is implicated in both these spheres, the sphere of kinship and the sphere of the state: she is implicated in the sphere of the polis insofar as Creon's law reaches to all who dwell within its borders; but kinship puts pressure on her and on her response to the state's authority as articulated by Creon's decree. It raises questions about whether the law is just or unjust, and about how to act in the face of a law that may reach too far.

*Antigone*: Some honors belong to all the dead.
*Creon*: You cannot
honor the wicked alongside the just.
*Antigone*: Creon,
Uncle, how can any of us presume
to know what God thinks is wrong.
*Creon*: A traitor
remains a traitor, even dead.
*Antigone*: Well, I
Can't help want to reconcile the dead
with the dead. (vv. 375–383, 212)

Antigone chooses to bury Polynices, acknowledges her decision, and is forced to accept her own death as a result. And yet there is a value beyond her suffering that she acknowledges as she prepares to meet this fate: "If I must die, at least I won't / die the worst of deaths – a death without honor" (vv. 83–85, 197).

**Tragedy and the Conflict of Values**

The idea that tragedy revolves around a conflict of values is part of Hegel's reading of *Antigone*. Is there also a "conflict of values" underlying the tragedy of Oedipus? Hegel argues that there is, although not an obviously ethical one. The tragedy of Oedipus is that he pursues his right to uncover the truth about the murder of Laius without ever considering that he himself might be responsible for the murder or, indeed, that there might be anything about him of which he is unaware.[19] The conflict is between two rights: the right of consciousness to accept responsibility only for what it knows it has done, and the right of the "unconscious" to be accorded respect.

If tragedy revolves around the split of ethical consciousness into opposing forces (divine against human, city against family, man against woman), then its resolution, for Hegel, requires that action yield to judgment. Perhaps this is why Hegel himself moves from a discussion of *Antigone* to a treatment of *King Oedipus*. As Paul Ricoeur pointed out in his discussion of these matters, *Oedipus* is a tragedy of ignorance and self-recognition concentrated within a single individual.[20]

## Commensurability and Incommensurability of Values

We can see the philosophical importance of value conflicts in tragedy if we bear in mind the fact that one of philosophy's goals was to determine how to live well and to offer some protection against the misfortunes to which human life is vulnerable. Philosophy has sometimes envisioned its task as buffering our exposure to tragedy by reducing the misery that may result from moral conflict or unexpected changes in fortune. This is no small task, for a reason that the messenger in *Antigone* expresses succinctly: "A man's fortune is never fixed; / it changes constantly, and no one knows / what his fate will be" (vv. 872–874, 236). If tragedy asks us to confront an ethical risk, then how specifically might philosophy be of assistance in reducing it? While the answer will differ for different philosophers (and for some will not pertain at all), there is one prominent strategy when it comes to misfortunes produced by a conflict of ends. This is to imagine a moral framework in which rational decisions about different ends can be reached by placing them within some common framework where they can be weighed and measured against one another. Indeed, the goal of "practical reasoning" as we see it in both Plato and Aristotle depends on the commensurability of values.

An important example of Plato's thinking on this matter is the *Protagoras*; for Aristotle, it is *Nicomachean Ethics*. In both instances the goal is to make human beings good at deliberation and thereby in control of their lives. The conception of what it means to be human for Protagoras means finding some standards for choosing among competing values. Philosophical inquiry provides some fixed pints of reference and a framework for assessing competing conceptions of what may for contingent reasons be regarded as the best way to act. But the *Protagoras* also recognizes that conflicts of values are made possible by the diversity of values, which is itself a feature of human nature. Moreover, this dialogue recognizes the tenacity of the human attachment to these values. If there is an art (*technē*) to be learned in order to negotiate one's way through this thicket of differences, it lies not in a grand synthesis of any sort but in learning to make judicious choices, knowing that there can never be a quantitative way of comparing all the different value-claims that may come into play during the course of a human life, but nonetheless believing that human beings can make rational (and therefore potentially happy) choices.

A question raised in the *Protagoras* is whether a person would be living well who lived in pain and vexation.[21] Since the obvious answer is no, two further questions follow from it. One is whether pleasure is to be regarded as standing at the root of a good life. The second is whether and how knowledge may be of use in determining which goods to pursue. What kind of knowledge would this be, and what kinds of "measurement" and "weighing" would it involve? To diminish the kind of suffering that tragedy shows would require a belief that radically different values are in the end part of an integrated whole, and that pursuing one of them ultimately involves at minimum the *possibility* of pursuing all the others. (On some accounts it may in fact *require* pursuing all the others.) Plato asks in the *Protagoras* whether the virtues are all part of one thing ("Virtue") or whether they name separate things. "Wisdom, temperance, courage, justice, and holiness are five terms. Do they stand for a single reality, or has each term a particular entity underlying it, a reality with its own separate function, each different from the other?" (349b). Wisdom (*sophia*) involves a form of self-mastery that leads to balance in the soul and, it is hoped, to happiness in a life lived well. It describes the ability to choose well for oneself in the face of opportunities to pursue both pleasure and the good. Plato takes up a related question in the *Republic*, where the task is to determine the characteristics of the perfectly good city. We have already seen how Plato wishes to exclude tragic poetry from the ideal state, but now we can also see that he wishes to design a city that would itself be free from tragic conflict. Hence he wants to envision harmony among the various classes of citizens, and balance among the virtues associated with each. This requires justice. But what is the relationship between justice and the virtues of wisdom, courage, and moderation? Plato suggests that justice includes the other virtues. If everyone in the city is just, the city as a whole will also be just.

Aristotle is in many regards Plato's heir when it comes to thinking about the virtues. *Nicomachean Ethics* makes rather more explicit and systematic the ideas we have just touched upon. Aristotle characterizes justice as the "complete virtue." He is also committed to the idea that the virtues must be lived if they are to have any meaning at all: "[justice] is complete virtue in its fullest sense because it is the actual exercise of complete virtue," (1130a, 108). The most difficult challenge here is to exercise justice toward *others*. In fact, Aristotle regards the "best person" – the one who is truly excellent (who possesses *arēte*) – as the one who exercises justice toward another and not just toward himself. This is the context in which Aristotle says that justice is not merely a part of virtue but is in fact "virtue entire" (1130a, 109).

Since justice involves equity and for Aristotle this means finding the mean or middle ground, one has reason to believe that it can provide some measure of defense against tragedy. Of course, there are many instances in which injuries may be done to others in the course of our dealings with them even where we seek to be just. Some of these incidents may involve mistakes, some accidents or "misadventures" that come from bad luck; others may involve weakness of the will (*akrasia*), in which we may well know what justice requires but decide nonetheless to do otherwise; still others involve acts of deliberate injustice. There is some potential for tragedy in all of these cases. But tragedy seems fundamentally to contravene the requirements of justice because of the disproportion between actions and consequences. The paradoxical sense in tragedy is that the protagonist may well suffer *necessarily*, but generally suffers *out of proportion* to what is deserved. In *Poetics*, Aristotle describes the case in which someone suffers because of a particular "flaw" in an otherwise noble character. But Aristotle's ethics is not tragic at all. The belief underlying his ethical philosophy is that one can in fact act justly, toward oneself and toward others, and that this is a key to happiness no matter how difficult it may be to achieve: "how actions must be done and distributions effected in order to be just, to know *this* is a greater achievement than knowing what is good for the health" (1137a, 131; emphasis in original). A flawless character would have no difficulty finding the best possible way to act in any given set of circumstances. But the tragic flaw in a character pinpoints one of the reasons why questions of value must be considered in the context of their application in the practical world, and not just from the perch of theoretical philosophy.

"Flaws" of character and judgment are hardly limited to tragic drama. Consider the case of Joseph Conrad's *Lord Jim*, in which there is genuine doubt as to whether the main character (Jim) is a coward, and if so whether he is capable of recovering from the cowardly act of abandoning ship. The doubt also exists for the reader because it is transmitted by the narrator, Marlow. Indeed, the scene in which Jim jumps from the *Patna* is shrouded in the veils of a prose that is designed to make a definitive moral interpretation of the matter virtually impossible. Moreover, the retrospective narrative breaks off just as the fateful incident occurs. We are allowed to assemble it piecemeal, after the fact, during an official investigation in which Jim is asked for the plain facts. About this, Jim (or the narrator, speaking for him in free indirect style) muses "Facts! They demanded facts from him, as if facts could explain anything!"[22] The moral interpretation of the events is hardly clear for Jim himself, although he needs to come to terms with them as part of his own self-understanding:

> The facts those men were so eager to know had been visible, tangible, open to the senses, occupying their place in space and time, requiring for their existence a fourteen-hundred-ton steamer and twenty-seven minutes by the watch; they made a whole that had features, shades of expression, a complicated aspect that could be remembered by the eye, and something else besides, something invisible, a directing spirit of perdition that dwelt within, like a malevolent soul in a detestable body. ... He wanted to go on talking for truth's sake, perhaps for his own sake also; and while his utterance was deliberate, his mind positively flew round and round the serried circle of facts that had surged up all about him to cut him off from the rest of his kind. ... This awful activity of mind made him hesitate at times in his speech. (19)

There are examples in this novel of other ethical selves whose deficiencies are far more clearly visible. The German captain, for instance, seeks an existence of ease and profit. The French lieutenant adheres to feudal honor in ways that make him seem relatively diminished, as well as less than fully relevant to his own historical circumstances. Jim is the only one who undertakes to question whether a person can possess moral autonomy and gain the level of dignity presumed to attach to it. He does so, moreover, by a process of self-questioning that involves an implicit critique of the alternatives sketched out in the other characters.

Characters like Lord Jim are categorically barred from what we might think of as the "transcendental" standpoint in which moral difficulties can be resolved by appeal to some higher authority. They instead rely on the resources of *this* world – including the resources of interpretation, reflection, and memory – many of which are provided by the narrative forms through which the novel investigates them. There is no guarantee of certainty or rightness about the values or judgments that these characters make. Writing of Henry James in a similar vein, Robert Pippin proposed that moral questions confronted by James's characters are not necessarily settled one way or the other. The moral complexity that results is linked to the unavailability of common moral assumptions, of "what we used to be able to rely on in interpreting and assessing each other."[23]

> The problem is not that we are too confused about what we dimly see must be done, or simply too weak to bring about what (we see) must be done. There is a much more fundamental and justified uncertainty

> about what must be done in itself; this uncertainty has a distinct historical ground, and threatens the very possibility of moral meaning – threatens, but, I want to suggest throughout, does not destroy or finally undermine it. (14–15)

Densher in *The Wings of the Dove* may not succeed in finding a firm moral compass, and in that he may fail in responding to the challenge presented in the figure of Kate Croy. But this does not amount to general failure, in the same way that fallibility is not a bar to improvement, moral or otherwise.

These examples help underscore some of the differences between a philosophical consideration of the good, or the virtues, and imagining these enacted by the characters in a drama or other literary work. Philosophy may wish to help us know the nature of the good, of obligations, of duties, and so on, and to help us live satisfying, happy lives, free from pain and vexation. By contrast, literature captures the *claims* that values make on human beings. What it presents is neither theoretical nor empirical. The characters and plots in tragedy and similar works are neither occasions to test the plausibility of different views against one another, nor attempts to resolve particular dilemmas at a theoretical level. Literature makes other affordances. It is not bound by the strictures of argumentation, but neither is it bound to be empirical. (We make a bad mistake if we look to it for empirical evidence, as with the joke about the researcher who attempted to find out what the weather was like during the "winter of our discontent" in Shakespeare's *Richard III*.) Literature stands between the general, overarching considerations about the nature of value that are characteristic of philosophical inquiry even at the level of practical reasoning, and the empirical questions that other forms of knowledge – other sciences or *epistēmē* – are equipped to address. In relation to questions of value (and no doubt others as well), it attempts to show not just what values *are* and how they might be reconciled, but to show our attachment to them. To borrow a phrase from Harry Frankfurt, its role is to show the *importance* of what we care about.[24] T.S. Eliot put the matter this way. "What poetry proves about any philosophy is merely its possibility for being lived."[25]

## Suggestions for Further Reading

Robert C. Bartlett and Susan D. Collins, "Interpretive Essay," In *Aristotle's Nicomachean Ethics* (Chicago: University of Chicago Press, 2011), pp. 237–316.

Daniel Boyarin, *Socrates and the Fat Rabbis* (Chicago: University of Chicago Press, 2009).

Elaine Scarry, *The Body in Pain: The Making and Unmaking of the World* (New York: Oxford University Press, 1985).
Max Scheler, *On Feeling, Knowing, and Valuing*, ed. Harold J. Bershady (Chicago: University of Chicago Press, 1992).
Gregory Vlastos, *Socrates: Ironist and Moral Philosopher* (Ithaca, NY: Cornell University Press, 1991).
Bernard Williams, *Shame and Necessity* (Berkeley: University of California Press, 1993).

*Chapter 6*

# Reason and Autonomy, Imagination and Feeling

The genre of the novel, glimpsed briefly in Chapter 5, places us squarely within the field of value as "made," not as found. This does not mean that novels do not involve various forms of seeking, striving, searching, or longing for some essential value. On the contrary, novels quite often involve some form of quest. But it does mean that they tend to place value in the activity of seeking itself, and in what it may yield for the seeker by way of growth in self-awareness, rather than in anything that might be discovered externally. But we have yet to say what it means for either philosophy or literature to think of value as itself the product of human activity. How do we locate human value in forms of life that we ourselves generate? From a modern perspective it might hardly seem possible that things could be otherwise, but the idea of value as "made" is so broad that we will have to parcel it into more manageable pieces. This will in turn provide the opportunity to add nuance to what might otherwise be a very clumsy concept.

Here are some questions we should bear in mind as a way of framing this discussion: (1) What does it mean to ground human value in autonomy and freedom, and what might be obstacles to their achievement? How can these be balanced with moral obligation? (2) What is the role of the many different human powers that come into play in various forms of value-making – powers such as desire, the imagination, the force of genius, and the will? We can recognize that much of the literature and philosophy roughly described as "romantic" makes large investments in these powers; the question (3) is whether they can be reconciled with reason and morality, and if so how? (4) How should we deal with theories that doubt the transparency of value and call into question our ability fully to know and determine it for ourselves? Among these are psychoanalysis (which grounds value in unconscious desire) and historical materialism (which grounds value in forms of material production and in the consciousness of class). Both are skeptical about the idea that we can ever be in full conscious control of what we do as value-making beings, and yet they lie very close to the work of literary interpretation and have been central to a number of interpretive procedures that have clear implications for philosophy.

The relations between literature and philosophy around this broad set of questions need to be ranged against the backdrop of their similarities and differences. To what extent do they converge on such matters, and where do they stand opposed? We need to guard against overgeneralizing in our response, but we can draw some provisional distinctions. If we think about value as involving principles that are universal and transcendent, even where they are the products of human activity, we are likely to foreground the universality of reason as itself a productive force. For Kant, as we will see, morality concerns "pure practical reason." It aims to balance freedom and autonomy with absolute (categorical) obligations. Such ideas about value strive to reach beyond what any particular instance, literary or otherwise, may show. And yet it turns out that many conceptions of value rely on the evidence of literature. Not even Kant could imagine such things as freedom, autonomy, and moral obligations apart from a series of narrative examples; his conception of morality rests on some fundamentally literary elements even where it might hope to reach beyond all examples and transcend all particulars.

That said, there remain some basic differences of approach to be reckoned with. Philosophy typically involves making arguments and proposing illustrations in relation to them. It asks for reflection both about the way things *are* and the way they *ought to be*, even where value is shaped by human beings. Where literature can be construed as philosophical, it offers imaginative investigations, explorations, and "essays" around questions of value – where an essay indicates a trial or an attempt put forward as provisional rather than as leading to a single conclusion. Stanley Cavell described the philosophical engagement with literature as involving "allegories, experiments, conceptual investigations."[1] To this we might add that literature can give expression to value in a way that purely conceptual investigations cannot. Literature tends to shape value around such things as the narrative of a life (however complete or partial, or filled with desires, hopes, and disappointments, as is often the case in the novel); or as concentrated in moments of affective intensity (as with lyric poetry); or as epitomized in the complex crossings of motives (as in drama), where meaning cannot be separated from the dramatic force of dialogue. It involves making works and performing expressive acts that are themselves instances of value and that in turn reflect certain basic capacities that are central to the ways in which we value ourselves.

## Autonomy and Freedom

It might seem strange to place the topics of autonomy and freedom under the umbrella of value as "made." But there is a reason for doing so. It goes to the heart of what autonomy means – literally, giving oneself (*auto*) the law (*nomos*). Autonomy suggests that our capacity to act as moral beings is essentially independent of anything that we do not determine for ourselves. Of course our actions will always have to be carried out in contexts where limiting factors may impinge on them; the "essential" part means that we do not want to think of them as originating in a will that cannot in principle act freely, or as incapable of being made transparent to itself because it is subject to some unknowable other power. Autonomy is connected with freedom – again, not to say that we will in fact be able to do anything we might wish to, but that, as a matter of principle, we are able to form intentions and to act in ways that emanate from our own will, which is not inherently constrained. When we act autonomously we exercise *transcendental freedom*; this is something Kant distinguishes from any empirical freedoms we might enjoy (i.e., acts that seem free just because they have no significant empirical constraints). He offers one of the most succinct formulations of his view of morality in *Foundations of the Metaphysics of Morals*, where he writes: "Reason must regard itself as the author of its principles, independent of foreign influences; consequently, as practical reason or as the will of a rational being, it must regard itself as free."[2]

The idea that human beings can act freely and, moreover, that moral action and our own moral worth depend upon this, is widespread in modernity. When Rousseau famously said in *The Social Contract* that "Man is born free, and everywhere he is in chains,"[3] he was asking why human beings should consent to social and political arrangements that do not honor their natural freedom. One of Rousseau's great tasks was to explain how there could be a truly "general will" that is not simply the sum of individual wills (the "will of all"). But it was Kant's version of this Rousseauean idea that became most closely associated with the modern notion of autonomy. The central Kantian idea of morality is so fundamental that it can be difficult to grasp. Its most succinct formulation is as follows: "Pure reason is practical in itself alone, and it gives (to man) a universal law, which we call the moral law."[4] What does this mean? We first have to clarify that Kant is *not* saying that pure reason is only practical; clearly that is not the case, since pure reason also has a cognitive role to play (understanding). What he is saying is that in its *practical nature* (i.e., as concerns matters of action and the will) reason can and must depend on itself and not on anything else. He is saying that *reason and nothing but reason* is the source of the moral law. This means that the moral law does not depend on desires, interests, or any other motivational source; and furthermore it means that since the moral law is indeed rational it is universal in scope: whatever it legislates carries with it the force of an "ought" that applies to everyone, to human beings in general.

The form of this universal "ought" is what Kant calls the "categorical imperative." Again, the notion can be difficult to grasp because it is so fundamental. The categorical imperative is the binding part of freedom, the part that tells us what we *must* do. Again, because it is the product of a rational and universal will, we know that it binds us in ways that are consistent with human freedom. Kant considers various candidates for the categorical imperative and finds only one. This is to act in such a way that whatever is willed could be imagined as binding for everyone, for oneself as well as for all others. "Categorical" means that there are no exceptions. Universality of scope lies at its heart, and this follows from the rational nature of human beings. However abstract, impersonal, and unrealistic all this may seem, it also suggests that, as human beings, we are able to ordain for ourselves in moral affairs on the basis of a faculty that is internal to our nature; we are not beholden to anything other than reason in determining the way we ought to act.

**The Basis of Freedom**

There are many disagreements among philosophers about some of the specifics involved in Kant's arguments about freedom, reason, and the moral law. Do we first experience ourselves as acting freely and without any prior cause except reason, and construe the principle of transcendental freedom on this basis? Or does the moral law first have to be conceived in order for it to be recognized in experience? These questions may not place the core of Kant's idea in jeopardy, but they do lead in quite different directions. In the first case, we experience a spontaneity in the course of representing empirical objects; spontaneity is just mysteriously "there," and is a basis for morality because it does not rest on anything prior. In the second, we recognize that we can and do deliberate. Freedom is just a presupposition of deliberation, and not something whose first principle requires a prior support in "spontaneity." The first of these lines has generally been associated with "Continental" philosophy; the second has often been followed by Anglo-American thinkers.[5]

A perennial question is whether this view of things does not create a problematic separation of two planes or "worlds" within experience. For Kant, "experience" is not just sense experience; it is sense experience, understanding, and reason – the phenomenal *and* noumenal worlds. It is something he considers necessarily to be a whole, but as divided nonetheless between two domains: the world of phenomena, which we know through the senses, and the world of "things in themselves" (*noumena*), which we can never know directly. Similarly, the domain of morality finds human beings divided between a world of pure, noumenal freedom and a world of contingent actions. In each case, Kant's way of responding to the "gap" between these two worlds reflects what has been called the "Copernican turn" in his thinking. In the matter of cognition, this means recognizing that, while we can never know things in themselves, the world must correspond to the faculties by which we know it. (The "turn" here lies in the reversal of the idea that our faculties must somehow "map" a world that is independent of them.) Similarly, the obligations we regard as binding in moral philosophy (the categorical imperative) must derive from our rational faculties, not from commandments issued by a higher authority or responsive to some imagined ideal.

This apparent division of worlds has sometimes been thought problematic. One reason is that it seems to subordinate the realm of phenomena to the transcendental (noumenal) realm. This has been especially worrisome for literary critics and aesthetic theorists, since literature and art fall within the phenomenal world. I will address these and related concerns later. For now, it's important to explain that Kant himself recognized a problem that was created by the separation of pure reason from practical reason, and likewise recognized that this separation was exaggerated by the initial division of his critical project into two parts, as reflected in *Critique of Pure Reason* and *Critique of Practical Reason*. Consequently, he wrote a critique of judgment (*Urteilskraft*) as a way to try to bridge this gap. Kant himself regarded *Critique of Judgment* as crucial to his philosophical ambition to be systematic and complete. It was the place where the nature of experience as a whole could be recaptured, but it was also the place where he discovered the difficulty of bridging the gap between these two worlds. He himself described there being a "great gulf" between the world of sensible nature (understanding) and the supersensible realm (reason), "just as if they were so many separate worlds."[6] The role of reflective judgment is to mediate between the two, but Kant also says that he could not derive its principles with all of the argumentative rigor he would have wished. When he wrote the "Preface" to *Critique of Judgment*, he admitted that "the difficulty of unraveling a problem so involved in its nature may serve as an excuse for a certain amount of hardly avoidable obscurity in its solution" (7).

### Skepticism and "Experience"

"Experience" is a term that Emerson invokes in the course of his oblique engagement with Kant. But Emerson also recognizes that experience has a long prior history, in which Montaigne figures as particularly important. Montaigne wrote an important essay entitled "On Experience," and Emerson chose Montaigne as one of his "representative men" in an essay subtitled "the skeptic." Montaigne is not a skeptic in the way that Descartes is. The skeptic in

Descartes works in the service of epistemology; skepticism is like a poison that Descartes introduces in order to see what can survive it. Montaigne's skepticism presents itself as a form of resistance to entrenched religious beliefs as a caution against unquestioned cultural practices. In prizing experience, Emerson wants to guard against a skepticism that dismisses the value of the ordinary world by seeking higher or deeper truths to support it.

*Critique of Judgment* nonetheless *does* propose a new way to look at the claims of reason that has many implications for literature, where particular instances (the work, the line, a given character, a particular turn of phrase, and our varying responses to them) need to be ascribed as much importance as general concepts or principles. *Critique of Judgment* proposes a form of rationality that begins from particulars. We do not start from general concepts (e.g., "red," "table," "uniformity") and "subsume" particulars under them. Rather, the particulars come first, and we then seek the concepts for them. (These "particulars" for Kant are subjective moments of feeling that accompany our cognitive representations of things.) In so doing, we also ascribe value to the particulars in question, a value that might otherwise be overlooked. Assertions about beauty are exemplary of this way of reasoning. They begin from what we feel alongside what we cognize, and then work toward universal agreement on the basis of those feelings by uncovering the principles that warrant the assent of everyone. I say "uncovering" the principles because it is not a matter of taking a public poll, canvassing great numbers of people, or reaching a threshold of actual agreement on a particular matter. Rather, it is a matter of discovering that we have the ability to reach agreement. For Kant this is because we share a "common aesthetic sense" (*sensus communis aestheticus*). This is not a common intellectual sense but a common basis of feeling, and in *Critique of Judgment* it is this shared feeling that is the basis for "generalizing" or "universalizing" our judgments. It is, in short, the basis for an *aesthetic* imperative that has also proved useful in thinking about questions of value that extend to morality. Here are his words:

> The judgment of taste exacts agreement from every one; and a person who describes something as beautiful insists that every one *ought* to give the object in question his approval. … We are suitors for agreement from every one else, because we are fortified with a ground common to all. … The judgment of taste, therefore, depends on our presupposing the existence of a common sense. (82–83; emphasis in original)

Such claims hope for universal validity and therefore universal bindingness, backed by an "ought" that is as powerful as that of any other kind of rational claim. But claims of taste will always be asserted provisionally because we are always in the position of soliciting the agreement of others. This means that while we may presuppose the existence of a common sense that binds us to others, we will always be in the position of forming communities of agreement and belief in relation to particular claims. Two further facts follow. One is that the work of criticism as we understand it in literature and the arts is central to the process of aesthetic judgment. The second is that this work is in-itself an expression of certain capacities that make us human – above all the capacities of feeling, imagination, and communication.

In addition to grounding judgments in feeling, this approach also speaks directly to the power of the imagination, to feelings of beauty and sublimity, and to the work of genius, all of which are central to literature and especially to the literary projects associated with romanticism. The imagination is certainly one of the most significant human powers, but does that mean it necessarily trumps reason? And what about feeling? We can hardly conceive of a human world without the range of feelings called up in us by works of literature, which we recognize to be tied to our feelings toward others and to the world in general. But does this mean that our hopes and our plans should be dictated by our emotional responses? We also recognize that there are powers, evident in nature, far greater than us; we stand in awe of them, but does this mean we must feel definitively diminished on such occasions?

Before embarking on an exploration of the terrain in which feeling, imagination, desire, genius, and will are regarded as standing in tension with reason – and recognizing the potential for unwarranted polarizations on those matters – it is useful to consider a brief outline of what Kant has to say about these key terms, in part because each one has a place in a larger project that is thought to be consistent with rationality.

*Imagination*: In one regard, Kant thinks of the imagination as the power of forming mental images: "the imagination, in a manner quite incomprehensible to us, is able on occasion, even after a long lapse of time, not alone to recall the signs for concepts," (*CJ*, 77). But clearly it is much more than that. The imagination is also *productive*; it works in conformity to a "law without a law" (*CJ*, "General Remark," 86), which is to say, in conformity with the rules established by the genius.

*Genius*: In Kant's words, genius is "the exemplary originality of the natural endowment of an individual in the *free* employment of his cognitive faculties" (*CJ*, 181; emphasis in original). The "freedom" he refers to here does not have to do with volition, but rather with the fact that its objects are not predetermined by concepts. Note also that Kant does not describe genius as anything outside the scope of the natural, but rather as having an *exemplary originality*. This means that the genius is able to set rules for art. Art must operate in an undetermined way but it also needs rules – rules that will not betray freedom. Genius is able to give the rule to art.

*The sublime*: "Sublime is the name given to what is *absolutely great* ... that is sublime in comparison with which all else is small"; "the sublime cannot be contained in any sensuous form" (*CJ*, 94, 97; emphasis in original). This means that there is no concept that can grasp the sublime. There are two forms of the sublime, one involving magnitudes of absolute greatness (Kant calls this the "mathematical" sublime), and one involving powers, energies, and forces of absolute greatness (the "dynamical" sublime). In both cases, the sublime occasions feelings of pain as much as of pleasure: initially there is a moment of pain, when we feel overwhelmed; but we nonetheless extract some pleasure from these experiences insofar as we are not actually undone by them. In the end, the sublime offers reassurance of the viability of our human powers when measured against that which is "absolutely great." This also suggests, as is sometimes said, that the sublime is a secularized form of transcendence.

## Wordsworthian Examples

These terms are as central to romanticism as they are to Kantian thinking. Yet it would be a mistake to think that all of romanticism involves the liberation of the imagination and the cultivation of passionate feelings as values in themselves unbound from (or opposed to) the work of reason and the central interests of philosophy. Wordsworth's poetry is a good place to explain some of this because he has allegiances both to the work of the imagination and to the role of the poet in providing access to forms of insight that might not be captured otherwise. Wordsworth might well seem to be contradictory in his views about poetry, saying both that it flows from powerful feelings and that it is a form of truth and knowledge. He makes assertions in support of both these views, and in this regard is representative of the divergent tendencies within romanticism. In "Preface" to *Lyrical Ballads*, for example, Wordsworth says both that "All good poetry is the spontaneous overflow of powerful feelings" and that "Poetry is the first and last of all knowledge."[7] Although the "Preface" is too long to be addressed in detail here, we can nonetheless look at two passages in which these apparent contradictions are resolved. They offer a sense of the balance between imagination, morality, and feeling. In them, Wordsworth explains that it is through feeling (and also through the use of ordinary language) that poetry is able to establish its claims to knowledge as truly general. The first is a gloss on Aristotle's statement that poetry is more "philosophical" than history. Wordsworth agrees "it is so: its object is truth, not individual and local, but general and operative; not standing upon external testimony, but carried alive into the heart by passion" (658). In this regard, his project is congruous with Kant's in *Critique of Judgment*; Kant, for his part, says that "we introduce this feeling not as private feeling, but as a public sense" (*CJ*, 84).

In the second passage, Wordsworth offers a definition of the poet and poetry. "What then does the Poet?" asks Wordsworth.

> He considers man and the objects that surround him as acting and re-acting upon each other, so as to produce an infinite complexity of pain and pleasure; he considers man in his own nature and in his ordinary life as contemplating this with a certain quantity of immediate knowledge, with certain convictions, intuitions, and deductions, which from habit acquire the quality of intuitions; he considers him as looking upon this complex scene of ideas and sensations, and finding everywhere objects that immediately excite in him sympathies which, from the necessities of his nature, are accompanied by an overbalance of enjoyment. … [T]hus the Poet, prompted by this feeling of pleasure, which accompanies him through the whole course of his studies, converses with general nature, with affections akin to those which, through labour and length of time, the Man of science has raised up in himself. (659–660)

This shows that Wordsworth does not want to *reduce* the activity of poetry to imagination or feeling. Rather, he insists that the poet's imagination produces effects of pleasure (and pain) and that these, in a reflective way, are the source of sympathies that can be shared generally.

### Sympathy, Pity, and Other "Moral Sentiments"

It has long been of interest to philosophers and others to identify the feelings that human beings hold in common, and which in turn hold them in common. These are the "moral sentiments" (Adam Smith). For this the term "sympathy" came to serve as a general designation. The idea was invoked as a counter to skeptical views about morality, such as Mandeville's notion that it is illusory or Hobbes's view that morality is only a form of self-interest.

> How selfish soever man may be supposed, there are evidently some principles in his nature, which interest him in the fortune of others, and render their happiness necessary to him, though he derives nothing from

> it, except the pleasure of seeing it. Of this kind is pity or compassion, the emotion which we feel for the misery of others. ... Pity and compassion are words appropriated to signify our fellow-feeling with the sorrow of others. Sympathy, though its meaning was, perhaps, originally the same, may now, however, without much impropriety, be made use of to denote our fellow-feeling with any passion whatever.[8]

Rousseau argued that pity required the imagination and not reason. "Pity is native to the human heart," but it is not awakened by reason. "[Pity] would remain entirely quiescent unless it were activated by the imagination."[9] Why in particular the imagination? The moral sentiments ask us to put ourselves in the place of another; but since the experience of others cannot be known by sense or by reason, we must rely on the work of the imagination. "By the imagination we place ourselves in [the other's] situation, we conceive ourselves enduring all the same torments, we enter into, as it were, his body, and become in some measure the same person with him" (*Moral Sentiments*, 48).

The imagination plays a central role in this project. Take as an example Wordsworth's poem "Michael" from 1800. On one level the poem is about the regrettable fate of a shepherd (Michael) and his son (Luke), who lose their ancestral farm because of mounting debts and the son's waywardness in London. But if this were all, then the poem might simply be presented as an example of lament over the loss of rural ways, the passage of time, and the squandering of opportunity, all mixed with sentiments about the hopes and regrets of parental nurturing. But the poem does something more by offering an image of what remains of the farm, the "straggling heap of unhewn stones" (v. 17; 415). These were the stones with which Michael began to build the sheepfold on the evening before his son's departure for the city, and it was this stonework that Michael continued, throughout Luke's absence, until his dying day.

> There, by the Sheepfold, sometimes was he seen
> Sitting alone, or with his faithful Dog,
> Then old, beside him, lying at his fey
> The length of full seven years, from time to time,
> He at the building of the Sheepfold wrought,
> And left the work unfinished when he died. (vv. 467–472, 427)

As one commentator has suggested, Michael's project is very much like the work of the poetic imagination, if not actually a stand-in for it:

> It is the work that [Michael's] imagination fashions from his life and that outlines him. In his own poem, Wordsworth does not therefore use

> reality as merely a pretext for the imagination. … On the contrary, his aim is to bring out what unites him and his subject, Michael – the role of the creative imagination in the constitution of reality itself, in the articulation of the meaning of our existence, and in the achievement, against life's changes and defeats, of whatever permanence we can enjoy.[10]

What is more powerful here, the work of building in stone or the work of imagining, hoping, and remembering? In "Michael," the work of the imagination and the work of building in stone are both subject to forces of time and forgetfulness that threaten to erode them. Wordsworth recognizes the fragility of the imagination's work, and is fully aware of just how precarious its products may be. The "work in stone" is also the intangible bond between father and son, which was established in their physical work together in building the sheepfold. Michael speaks to his son:

> Lay now the corner-stone,
> As I requested; and hereafter, Luke,
> When thou art gone away, should evil men
> Be thy companions, think of me, my Son,
> And of this moment; hither turn thy thoughts,
> And God will strengthen thee: amid all fear
> And all temptation, Luke, I pray for thou
> May'st bear in mind the life thy Fathers lived …
> When thou return'st, thou in this place wilt see
> A work which is not here: a covenant
> 'Twill be between us but, whatever fate
> Befall thee, I shall love thee to the past,
> And bear thy memory with me to the grave. (vv. 403–410, 413–417; 425)

There are numerous other places where Wordsworth describes what the poet does as a form of work and as a form of building. These are reminiscent of our discussion of *poiēsis* in Part I, except that here the task is to articulate the ways in which the power of the imagination can yield a work, in words, that is as durable as one made of stone. In "The Prelude," the poet's spiritual odyssey culminates in "building up a Work that shall endure" (XIV, v. 311; 376). The works made by the imagination serve in their turn to reveal the sympathies that bind human beings together as a community. In order to do this, however, the poet must clear away the false sentiments that pervade the social world; this can best occur in the solitude of nature:

> Far from the living and dead Wilderness
> Of the thronged world, Society is here

A true community – a genuine frame
Of many into one incorporate. (vv. 613–616; 396)

## Some Dangers of Sympathy

Attention to the common and the low as a way of gaining access to feelings that bind all human beings together runs the risk of turning into pathos. Wordsworth himself bordered on it from time to time. His poem "The Recluse" draws very near this range of sentiment as he tries to probe the connections between the most unfortunate human beings and the creatures of the animal world. At the same time, the poet risks overreaching in claiming sympathy for all:

Already hath sprung up within my heart
A liking for the small grey horse that bears
The paralytic man, and for the brute
In Scripture sanctified – the patient brute
On which the cripple, in the quarry maimed,
Rides to and fro: I know them and their ways.
The famous sheep-dog, first in all the vale,
Though yet to me a stranger, will not be
Stranger long; nor will the blind man's guide,
Meek and neglected thing, of no renown! (vv. 502–511; 393)

Wordsworth's sympathies for the most humble and unfortunate human beings, as well as for the creatures of the natural world, were no doubt amplified by his disillusionment with the French Revolution, the advent of modern science, and the beginnings of industrialization. He speaks explicitly of his involuntary return from France in "The Prelude." But there are a set of philosophical beliefs about nature at work in "The Prelude" that help explain why nature demands attention. For Wordsworth, the work involves an attention to nature that takes the form of love, and it is precisely a loving regard that enables the presence of a divine intellect to be discerned in nature. If the scientific revolution produced a "disenchanted" world (i.e., a world in which no spiritual animating presence could be found), romantic poetry of the kind Wordsworth represents seeks a re-enchantment of the world. Indeed, "The Prelude" presents the imagination as a form of divine power that supports the generous affinities (the "spiritual love") that the poet feels with the world as a whole:

This spiritual Love acts not nor can exist
Without Imagination, which, in truth,
Is but another name for absolute power

> And clearest insight, amplitude of mind,
> And Reason in her most exalted mood.
> This faculty has been the feeding source
> Of our long labour. (XIV, vv. 188–194; 372–373)

How does any of this translate into a vision of morality? In exploring this question, let's consider how Emerson's essays place the question of human powers in relation to Kant's ideas. The essays can be thought of as "crossover" texts because their philosophical insights are not derived from the procedures of argument conventionally thought of as "philosophical," but are instead generated by a prose that is expressive, imaginative, allusive, and self-aware in just the ways that literature tends to be. Their claims are at once suggestive and forceful, though hardly the result of any systematic plan. Their interest in perfectionism also moves the Kantian ideal of autonomy in a new direction. Perfectionism can be thought of as a call that the (higher) self makes to itself or, perhaps better, as a call that the self hears made by its better self. "Perfectionism" suggests that the ideal self is not out of reach, as a Platonic ideal might be, but is in fact attainable. Moreover, perfectionism in the way that Emerson approaches it is not the product of rational reflection, as in Kant; we have just said that it involves the "call" of a higher self, but that call is only heard as the voice of the self echoes with the texts and traditions of the past. (Their writings are in this sense highly inter-textual.) For Emerson, the inter-texts in question include those by Shakespeare and Montaigne, both of whom he regarded as "representative men" in a series of essays of that title. (For Thoreau in *Walden* it also means attending to the interplay of writing and the work of nature.)

**Emersonian Philosophical Interventions**

... responding to Kant's "division of worlds":
"Every fact is related on one side to sensation, and on the other, to morals. The game of thought is, on the appearance of one of the two sides, to find the other: given the upper, to find the under side" (*Essays*, 690).

...on skepticism:
"Who shall forbid a wise skepticism, seeing that there is no practical question on which any thing more than an approximate solution can be had?" (694).

... praising Montaigne:
"Montaigne is the frankest and honestest of all writers. ... [H]e anticipated all censure by the bounty of his own confessions" (698).

Stanley Cavell argued that we should regard Emerson and Thoreau both as philosophical writers, and in particular as the heirs of Kant. This is true, but it is more often Kant's epistemology rather than his moral philosophy or his aesthetics that resonates in their work. They tend to draw us in the direction of a life lived in the "middle realm" of experience, aware of the possibility of perfection, and driven by it, but careful not to dismiss the value of the ordinary world as a result. This value is a matter of concern from which one can draw philosophical implications about Emerson's commitment in his address "The American Scholar" to "the near, the low, the common."

> [T]hat, which had been negligently trodden under foot by those who were harnessing and provisioning themselves for long journeys into far countries, is suddenly found to be richer than all foreign parts. The literature of the poor, the feelings of the child, the philosophy of the street, the meaning of household life, are the topics of the time.[11]

So too in Wordsworth's commitment to a poetic diction and subject matter that are dissociated from the lofty (and pretentiously "poetic") and are instead adherent to the forms of ordinary speech. "To pipe a simple song for thinking hearts," is how Wordsworth describes it in the poem "Heart-Leap Well" (v. 4; 398). In writing about the *Lyrical Ballads*, which Coleridge and Wordsworth published together, Coleridge explained that Wordsworth's aim was "to give the charm of novelty to things of every day, and to excite a feeling analogous to the supernatural, by awakening the mind's attention from the lethargy of custom and directing it to the loveliness and the wonders of the world before us."[12] In the very important "Preface" to the second edition of *Lyrical Ballads* Wordsworth himself made it a point to explain that he has written in the "language really used by men" (651) and that he has chosen subjects in which ordinary things are presented in an unusual light. This is all part of a larger rationale, not so much a defense of poetry as the vision of a new kind of poetry. Its purpose, for Wordsworth, is a moral one; its resources lie in language and the imagination; and its strategies involve awakening human passions – but as much as a form of understanding and knowledge as a form of moral reflection. Wordsworth demonstrates how poetry can provide intelligently felt reflection on matters of general human concern. Indeed, given the association of romantic poetry with the imagination, it is remarkable to see how often Wordsworth refers to knowledge. His appeal to "ordinary language" rests in part on the belief that it is more "philosophical" than other kinds of poetic diction: "such a language [ordinary language], arising out of repeated experience and regular feelings, is a more permanent, and a far more philosophical language, than that which is frequently substituted for it by Poets" (651). The reason has in part to do with the fact that it allows the poet to demonstrate the power of what Wordsworth calls the "feeling intellect" ("The Prelude," XIV, v. 226; 370).

On one view, literature is the place where these powers are given tangible expression; indeed, literature can itself be regarded as something of value because, as expressive activity, it embodies some of the powers that make us human. Other views suggest that literature shows the fundamental opacity of these powers – fundamental because they cannot ever be made transparent, adding that this opacity is itself part of what being human involves. There are, as well, middle grounds to be considered: examples in which literature is committed to a demonstration of the value of human activity that is neither despairingly skeptical nor impossibly idealist in its orientation, and that is often set within the framework of a world that is "ordinary" rather than exceptional. Wordsworth is committed to such a position, relying as much on the powers of the imagination and on experiences of beauty and sublimity as on a belief in reason. The work of poetry involves collaboration of reason and the imagination to produce a "feeling intellect."

## Suggestions for Further Reading

M. H. Abrams, *Natural Supernaturalism* (New York: Norton, 1971).

Isaiah Berlin, *The Roots of Romanticism* (Princeton, NJ: Princeton University Press, 1999).

Harold Bloom, ed., *Romanticism and Consciousness* (New York: Norton, 1970).

Paul de Man, *The Rhetoric of Romanticism* (New York: Columbia University Press, 1984).

Morris Eaves and Michael Fischer, eds., *Romanticism and Contemporary Criticism* (Ithaca, NY: Cornell University Press, 1986).

Richard Eldridge, *On Moral Personhood* (Chicago: University of Chicago Press, 1989).

*The Persistence of Romanticism* (Cambridge: Cambridge University Press, 2001).

Julie Ellison, *Emerson's Romantic Style* (Princeton, NJ: Princeton University Press, 1984).

Paul Guyer, *Kant and the Experience of Freedom* (Cambridge: Cambridge University Press, (1996).

*Kant's System of Nature and Freedom* (Oxford: Oxford University Press, 2005).

Gertrude Himmelfarb, *The Moral Imagination: From Adam Smith to Lionel Trilling* (Lanham, MA: Roman and Littlefield, 2012).

Thomas McFarland, *Originality and Imagination* (Baltimore, MD: Johns Hopkins University Press, 1985).

Gene Ruoff, ed., *The Romantics and Us* (New Brunswick, NJ: Rutgers University Press, 1990).

Thomas Weiskel, *The Romantic Sublime* (Baltimore, MD: Johns Hopkins University Press, 1976).

## Chapter 7

# Forces and the Will

In the time since romanticism there have been efforts, both literary and philosophical, to sustain and enlarge the commitments reflected in Wordsworth's allegiance to the idea of a "feeling intellect," cited at the close of Chapter 6; but there have also been many efforts to call them into question. The works of Freud and Marx are examples of the latter, as are various versions of deconstruction. We will deal with some of those approaches in the next chapter. Perhaps most common in discussions of the relationship between literature and philosophy in this area is to point to Kant as one pillar of a tradition that places its faith in reason *as opposed to* other dimensions of human nature, including the passions and the affects. Contrastingly, it is not uncommon to point to literature, however vaguely defined, as a tradition in which the passions, the senses, the imagination, and the will, have pride of place. As we have already begun to see with regard to the imagination, moreover, these notions are at best schematic. They neglect the fact that many of the Enlightenment thinkers – rationalists, empiricists, and idealists alike – engaged in non-dismissive ways with the passions, the senses, and the will.

As we have just seen, however, Kant and many others like him were interested in finding a way to balance the powers of the imagination, the senses, and the will, with the rational side of human nature.[1] Thus, for example, Kant came to focus not on willfulness or on willing, but on the *rational will* as the key to morality. Similarly, the dynamics of taste and genius in Kant's *Critique of Judgment* strive to balance the creative powers of the imagination with the demand for universal agreement in aesthetic judgments. Both the creative powers and the possibility of agreement in judgments of taste are necessary. Kant says that taste "clips the wings" (i.e., regulates) genius; genius with clipped wings is not incapable of flight, it merely flies under the guidance of reason.

Kant is hardly the only philosopher to have hoped for a way to reconcile reason with the passions, the imagination, and the will. The attempt is in fact ancient. It lies at the heart of what Plato proposed in the *Phaedrus* by comparing the soul to a chariot drawn by two winged horses that pull forcefully in opposite directions. The white horse characterizes the soul's noble instincts; the dark one corresponds to its ignoble elements. The challenge lies in knowing what the charioteer should do to balance these forces. Plato's answer does not propose that the soul ought to disavow the passions or desires; but he certainly does suggest that the passions need to be guided. This is where reason in the soul has a role to play. And yet, not even reason, which concentrates on the eternal truth of ideas, is the highest power for Plato. Plato elsewhere describes a force of attraction, a force that is erotic rather than rational, which has the strongest power to draw human beings toward the good – specifically, toward the good as manifested in beauty. If we are indeed drawn by the force of eros toward an image of the good, then some of the problems we associate with the struggles of reason and the will to act rightly or with justice may be resolved with relative ease. Insofar as we fall under the sway of the erotic force of the good, we would hardly need to worry about finding a rational determination for the will. The will would be drawn toward the beautiful as a manifestation of whatever is true and good in-itself.

There are nonetheless some problems with this view. One of them lies in the recognition that we are not always in fact drawn to do what we might apprehend as good. Even beauty may not always have the power to ensure this. Moving from the sphere of eros to that of the intellect (*nous*), Aristotle and other ancient thinkers treat one form of this problem as what is called *akrasia*, or "weakness of the will": I look at the chocolate cake and know that eating a second piece of it would be bad for me, but I eat it anyway. A stronger, darker, version of this problem was formulated in "The Imp of the Perverse." Poe identified a "perverse" principle at the base of human action, according to which action is driven not by truth or goodness, but by an essential and irreducible force of error:

> [T]he assurance of the wrong or error of any action is often the one unconquerable force which impels us, and alone impels us to its prosecution. Nor will this overwhelming tendency to do wrong for the wrong's sake, admit of analysis, or resolution into ulterior elements. It is radical, a primitive impulse – elementary.[2]

A prose poem by Baudelaire, "The Bad Glazier," ranges this impulse across a variety of instances. In one, a friend sets fire to a forest

> to see, he explained, whether it were really as easy to start a fire as people said. Ten times in succession the experiment failed; but the eleventh time it succeeded only too well. … Some malicious Demon gets into us, forcing us, in spite of ourselves, to carry out his most absurd whims.[3]

**Flowers of Evil**

The notion of an erotic attraction toward beauty and the good has been challenged fiercely in modern times. Consider the attraction of the foul and the hideous in Baudelaire's "Carrion."

> Remember, my soul, the thing we saw
> that lovely summer day?
> On a pile of stones where the path turned off,
> the hideous carrion –
> legs in the air, like a whore – displayed,
> indifferent to the last,
> a belly sick with lethal sweat
> and swollen with foul gas.[4]

**Eros in Nietzsche**

Nietzsche makes the idea of erotic attraction the basis for one of his most stinging critiques of the discipline of philosophy. "Supposing truth to be a woman – what? Is the suspicion not well founded that all philosophers, when they have not been dogmatists, have had little understanding of women? that the gruesome earnestness, the clumsy importunity with which they have hitherto been in the habit of approaching truth have been inept and improper means for winning a wench?"[5] He means to say that philosophers have failed to respond to the playful, erotic enticement of the truth. As Robert Pippin comments, "Philosophers should be understood as inexpert, clumsy lovers."[6]

The inscrutability of such matters is something I will have more to say about in Chapter 8 when discussing various kinds of "opacity" that literature and philosophy confront. For now it is worth noting that one of the earliest formulations of the "opacity" of human action came not from a philosopher, but from Poe, a writer of essays and short stories. Philosophy is inclined to believe (although clearly does not always believe) that there are transparent motives for action, in part because it hopes to provide rational accounts of human action. The idea of a "rational agent" is presupposed by much philosophical discourse. Proponents of "reason" may well argue that some restraint of the passions and the will is necessary in order to achieve balance among our inclinations, or to harmonize forces in the soul, but advocates of the primacy of the passions and the will are liable to respond that this will inevitably diminish the sources of what makes us most human, not least among which may be our darker or unfathomable motives. Can the passions be fully acknowledged without simply inverting their relationship with reason? What is the fate of reason among thinkers who recognize the centrality of the passions and the will?

## Spirit, Value, Valuing

I proceed with a philosopher whose name is often linked to the ambitious effort to encompass all of human "spirit" in its entirety, an effort that is as much about the passions and the will as it is about reason: Hegel.

### Higher and Lower Powers

For Hegel, reason (*logos*) is *substantive* rather than merely formal; it is a driving power and not just a calculus; it operates through the "lower" and the "noncognitive" mental structures – imagination, recollection, emotion, desire, love, and so forth; as an implied consequence of all the above, reason is always embodied in empirical situations and entities; reason is impure rather than pure, contains unreason, contingency, and negativity as integral ingredients.[7]

Hegel was concerned with a dynamic of consciousness that involves the elements of force and desire, if not also the will, in an explicit way. Part of what Hegel meant by "Spirit" incudes the various forces that drive our meaningful connections with the world and with others in it. "Spirit" (or human consciousness, writ large) is not just a name for the intellectual mind and its activity; it is not simply a form of conceptual grasping; it is an active, striving, and historically embedded capacity. In the broad Hegelian scheme of things, Spirit and matter are not themselves fundamentally opposed. The activity of Spirit is expressive, and part of its task is to recognize as part of itself those things that it externalizes in (and as) the world. Though Hegel does not use the term "world" in this context, we can surmise that "Spirit" and "world" are not fundamentally distinct because "objective" and "subjective" are for Hegel two moments of consciousness itself. Consciousness may be divided and incomplete at any particular moment, but ultimately it is one. For Hegel, Spirit is the capacity of consciousness to enrich itself in the course of its own striving. Indeed, Hegel is committed to the belief that a truly enlarged form of reason – ultimately, reason as "Absolute Spirit" – must embrace both the dynamic, desiring component of human nature (as "force") and the more intellectual activity of reason. Together, these would lead toward fully self-reflective understanding. Spirit evolves through the activities of force and reason, taken together and made real in the development and expression of human consciousness throughout history.

Along with the will, desire is one of the most significant forces of Spirit. Desire goes beyond need. Human beings desire things that reach beyond their survival and pleasure, things that sometimes can be more valuable to them than the satisfaction of sensuous needs. In fact, the objects of human desire include many intangibles, such as recognition, autonomy, and freedom. Such things are not lying out there, like a buried treasure, waiting to be found. Literature sometimes symbolizes these things as treasure-like, as when in the genre of romance personal worth is verified by the discovery of a great treasure. But these are ultimately ways of representing value rather than of pursuing or creating it for ourselves. The modern view is that we participate in the creation of such values *as* we pursue them. The process is ongoing, because in the satisfaction of one desire we discover others; with every satisfaction we uncover new openings, hence new possibilities that may raise consciousness to higher levels. Absolute Knowing embraces all this.

**Negativity**

The activity of Spirit involves transformation by the force of *negativity*. What does this mean? For Hegel, any given thing or moment of consciousness establishes itself as what it is as much by an assertion or a positive determination as by *not being* something else, or by *being opposed to* and *going beyond* something else. "Value" is neither something that can be named as a distinct feature in this process, nor is it something pursued by choosing one thing over another; it is better understood as emergent from the activity of consciousness (Spirit), which is propelled forward by the forces of desire.

## Force, Life Force

Working partly in concert with Hegel, and partly in reaction to his views, many influential thinkers have wanted further to underscore the *force*ful elements of human nature, sometimes worrying that the powers at work in Hegel's "Spirit" – especially the ones associated with the "lower" forces – were in the end subordinated to more abstract forms of consciousness. Among the foremost thinkers in this line are Schopenhauer, Nietzsche, and Deleuze. On the literary side, we could mention Goethe, Shelley, and Shaw. In *The World as Will and Representation*, Schopenhauer argued that the will is not itself a force but is rather grounded in something else he calls "life force." He approaches this view by way of a stunning reworking of Kant's distinction between the sensuous and super-sensuous realms. The known world, the world represented to us, is only part of reality. It is not all of the world, only its external face: "the world has an entirely different side which is its innermost being, its kernel, the thing-in-itself."[8] For Schopenhauer, this "thing-in-itself" is not an ideal essence, as it was for Kant, but is rather the "Will." To say that the will expresses a life force that has no other, external ground also means that human beings must learn to act without any deeper or higher "principle" to guide them.

For Schopenhauer, life force is "transcendental" because it lies beyond any and every instance or expression of it. But it clearly has a manifestation in the world of empirical life; it shows up in the form of constant struggle, striving, suffering, and strife. Tragedy is an especially powerful representation of such struggles and of their most unfortunate consequences. Schopenhauer calls tragedy the "pinnacle" of the literary arts. This is because tragedy shows human beings subject to chance and error and the will in conflict with itself. Invoking examples that range from Shakespeare and Calderón to Goethe and Voltaire, he identifies tragedy as the place where noble individuals undergo a process of lengthy suffering only to find themselves defeated, "renouncing the purposes they had so intensely pursued" (*WWR*, III.55, 303). In tragedy, the world works as a "quieter" of the will. It brings forth "resignation, abandonment not merely of life but of the entire will to life itself" (ibid.). This, more than anything else, is the tragedy of tragedy.

The peculiar and unfortunate truth of tragedy can better be understood if we consider Schopenhauer's views about the affirmation and denial of the will. Schopenhauer outlines two directions from which we may engage the will. One is naively "affirmative." Imagine someone who had no idea that suffering is an unavoidable part of life, or who came simply to accept suffering in return for the promise of some other, perhaps greater pleasures. Such a person "would no more fear death than the sun the night" (*WWR*, IV.55, 186). We might imagine this affirmative posture to be a wonderful and welcome thing. But given the resistance that the will inevitably meets, this is an impossible fantasy. Quite the opposite would hold true of someone unable to overcome suffering at all, or who could only experience the will in relation to its limitations: such a person might well feel undone by a "denial of the will to life" (ibid.). Schopenhauer was not trying to recommend one or the other of these approaches; they are both real and are equally problematic. Rather, as he explains in *On the Freedom of the Will*, the highest human possibility lies in taking responsibility for our actions: "the accountability for our actions … rests on the unshakable certainty that we ourselves are the doers of our deeds."[9] Nietzsche saw in Schopenhauer an example of great courage for this very reason: "The Schopenhauerian man voluntarily takes upon himself the suffering involved in being truthful, and this suffering serves to destroy his own willfulness to prepare that complete overturning and conversion of his being, which it is the real meaning of life to lead up to."[10] His goal was to transform every "it was" into an "I willed it thus," "[t]o redeem the past of mankind and to transform every 'It was' until the will says: 'But I willed it thus! So I shall will it!' – this did I call redemption and this alone did I teach them to call redemption."[11]

## Strong Characters

George Bernard Shaw's *Man and Superman*, makes clear reference to Nietzsche's idea of the superman (*Übermensch*) in its title. The subject of the play, and a number of its characters, are drawn from the Don Juan myth, first presented as a drama by Tirso de Molina in 1630 (*The Trickster of Seville*). In Shaw's play, it is one of the women characters (Dona Ana) and not Don Juan who is identified with the "life force." As the passage below reveals, the devil remains skeptical about all talk of "life force." Why? It may be the role of evil to deny that force, or to resist its ability to bind things together in an organized way:

> *Don Juan*: Life is a force which has made innumerable experiments in organizing itself; that the mammoth and the man, the mouse and the megatherium, the flies and the fleas and the Fathers of the Church, are all more or less successful attempts to build up that raw force into higher and higher individuals, the ideal individual being omnipotent, omniscient, infallible, and withal completely, unilludedly self-conscious: in short, a god?
>
> *The Devil*: Wagner once drifted into Life Force worship, and invented a Superman called Siegfried. But he came to his senses afterwards.[12]

Many of the literary texts that foreground the will do so by presenting strong characters (Nietzsche referred to them as "individuals," Emerson as "representative men"), characters who seem to embody the will as a "determined phenomenon." This is in fact the very phrase that Schopenhauer invokes to describe the "person."[13] Strong-willed characters strive to choose freely, and in so doing distinguish themselves from others. Think of the strong and tragic characters of romantic literature in this regard – of Goethe's Faust, of Shelley's Beatrice Cenci, as well as Shaw's Dona Ana, to name but a few. In their power, strong characters foreground the attempt to resist the forces of accident, circumstance, or luck in the formation and the fate of the self. Schopenhauer himself recognized that any account of the affirmation or denial of the will expressed in a "general way" would be difficult if not impossible to grasp

(*WWR*, IV.55, 186). Ultimately, this would be a betrayal of the will itself. He saw ideas about the will as valid only insofar as they are attached to the context of life. His hope was to illustrate his own views by invoking "living knowledge" as expressed in action and behavior. And yet his own language and method did not allow him to do this. This is where the example from Shaw and so many others we might adduce are important. Literature is of course not life, but by the turn toward "life" Schopenhauer did not mean biological life. The will is a dynamic force, wholly engaged in the worldly contexts around it; but it is not a feature of biological life; it can hardly be understood by looking inside the human body. Rather, attention to "life" requires responding to instances in which the will is given both the compass and the particularity it requires, where freedom and openness come under the pressure of external limitations, and where we act and engage nonetheless.

This is easier said than done, not least because "character" is something more than what we may will or do. As one critic said of Shelley, "our actions … cannot shape our character; they can only 'express' it, or provide an occasion for us to express it."[14] In fact, the will may bind us to unhappiness and imperfection. We might dream otherwise and hope to be otherwise ("we might be all / We dream of happy, high, majestical"[15]). But that may lead to what Shelley called the "dark idolatry of self,"[16] where the will may chain us to "permitted ill" (v. 171). And if that is the case, then happiness might better be sought in the form of a release (specifically, a release of and from the will, or what Heidegger calls more broadly *Gelassenheit*). In Shelley's "Revolt of Islam," Cynthia's sermon to the sailors urges kindness: "Reproach not thine own soul, but know thyself / Nor hate another's crime, nor loathe thine own" (VIII.xxi, v. 11). Shelley's Prometheus is certainly a "strong character," sometimes compared to Milton's Satan; Shelley himself said that Satan was the only imaginary being resembling him in any degree. Yet Prometheus is by Shelley's own account also more tempered: "in addition to courage and majesty and firm and patient opposition to omnipotent force, he is susceptible of being described as exempt from the taints of ambition, envy, revenge, and a desire for personal aggrandizement."[17]

There is nonetheless beauty to be found in the suffering created by the "dark idolatry of self." Such beauty may not be enough to yield moral redemption, but it can be the source of value, and particularly so for anyone who regards the self as an aesthetic entity. Shelley says of his tragic protagonist Beatrice Cenci, for instance, that she "appears to have been one of those rare persons in whom energy and gentleness dwell together without destroying one another: her nature was simple and profound."[18] The fact that she is a literary character helps underscore the fact that the crimes and miseries in which she was involved are not revelations of her "core" self, but are rather "the mask and the mantle in which circumstances clothed her for her impersonation in the scene of the world" (ibid.)

## Suffering, Passivity: Werther's Sorrows

As a rule, assertive striving and active struggling tend to make themselves more noticeable than passivity or inaction. But we need also to remind ourselves of the literature that dwells on passivity, that concentrates on the weakness of the will, and that explores the smothering of desire by inaction. Consider Goethe's novella, *The Sufferings of Young Werther* (sufferings here meaning "sorrows," *Leiden*). It engages the will and its determination (or lack thereof) as questions rather than as assertions. *The Sufferings of Young Werther* draws our attention to the passions and the will in relation to a state of mind in which they appear to have been disempowered, rendered nearly inactive, all but incapacitated. But why? There are of course the basic elements of the plot, in which the object of Werther's desire, Lotte, marries another man and so deprives him of the will to act. But that hardly explains Werther's initial reticence, nor does it explain the world-negating and self-destructive consequences that his disappointment brings.

*The Sufferings of Young Werther* also posits a time before the will and desire were problematic. This is not a mythical time in universal history; rather, it is imagined as a time in each person's own narrative, conceived as the idea of childhood itself. Werther sits among Lotte's children at school and feels them close to him because they have no will. What Werther feels with Lotte, by contrast, is something strong and difficult to comprehend: "I never know what I feel when I am with her."[19] But neither feelings nor desire is able to move him to action. Not surprisingly, this leads to suffering of uncommon proportions, all the more so because what Werther feels is not something he recognizes as any ordinary passion, but love. Love is in principle able to make a person feel complete in interdependence. Better said, perhaps: in love the particularity of one person can meet the particularity of another, both in the spirit and in the flesh. Why then should the very thing that might bring happiness also be the source of such misery? Why should it bring a "sickness unto death"? (This pregnant phrase is one that Kierkegaard borrowed from Goethe's novel.) Curiously, this "sickness" first shows up as a loss of imaginative engagement. Werther takes no interest in the world. Even books fail to excite him.

It does not take Werther's suicide to reveal one of the fundamental issues that Goethe is dealing with in this work, which is hardly just about unrequited love. Passivity and suffering are the keys. There is a clue to this core issue in Goethe's two passing references to a play by Lessing, *Emilia Galotti*. Lessing was loath to accept a split between vision (or wishing) and action. Rather, he held that vision, feeling, and achievement ought to comprise a whole: the arc of a truly complete action must reach from its imaginative conception all the way through to its tangible projection in the world.[20] And yet there is nothing to guarantee that we will act at all, much less in the form of a complete arc.

## Nietzsche on Valuing and the Will

Perhaps more than any other modern thinker, it was Friedrich Nietzsche who brought the question of the will and its relation to value into the foreground. But because Nietzsche's ideas are so often mistaken or misinterpreted, we need to take care to attend to what he wrote. It is simply too easy to misrepresent his views by encapsulating them in slogans or set phrases (e.g., "will to power," "the superman," "nihilism," the "death of God," the "transvaluation of all values"). Also, if we take Nietzsche just as the source of these views, and if we also take him as always affirming, advocating, and defending them as literal truths, we will have missed a great deal about the way he thinks and writes, and we will have missed his deep affinity with literature. In Nietzsche we have a philosopher whose understanding of the world, and of the place of values and the will in it, are consistent with some of the fundamental premises often associated with literature.

Nietzsche's outline of the genealogy of modern moral psychology is rooted in his conception of the truth of appearances. This is a fundamentally aesthetic conception of the truth. For Nietzsche, the idea of a distinction between a superior, more valuable "true world" on the one hand and the lesser, "appearing world" on the other, such as Plato made, is simply false. Herein lies one prong of Nietzsche's "inversion" of Platonism (and of Christianity along with it). Every truth is one among many possible interpretations.[21] There are no independent facts against which these interpretations can be measured. Nor are there any neutral or objective standards against which they can be judged. Some may be better than others. Most importantly, some are *stronger* than others. But none is absolute.[22] In this sense "untruth" is a condition of life: "truth is … not something there, that might be found or discovered – but something that must be created" (*WP*, 552). Likewise, value is created, not found, because truth and the world are constructed. "There are no moral phenomena at all, only a moral interpretation of phenomena" (*BGE*, 108, p. 78). Moreover, value is constructed by the will (will to power). "Whatever has value in our world now does not have value in itself, according to its nature – nature is always value-less, but has been given value at some time, as a present – and it was we who gave and bestowed it" (*WP*, 302). So too for the individual: "The individual derives the values of its acts from itself; because it has to interpret in a quite individual way even the words it has inherited … as an interpreter the individual is still creative" (*WP*, 767). Life, as valuation, is best regarded in the ways we regard literature.

## Beyond Good and Evil

Nietzsche's views have such tremendous affinity with literature because what we intuitively understand, and sometimes take for granted, about fiction and other forms of literature resonates deeply with his understanding of a world constructed of values. It's not that literary texts always bear thematic support for his views about nihilism, the overcoming of all values, or the figure of the "superman." Rather, it is that most are committed to the principle that the world is an assemblage of perspectives. Literature knows that the world is always "seen" (hence interpreted, valued) from some particular standpoint. It cannot be presented or seen from all perspectives. Even when a narrator assumes an omniscient stance, this is the end only a stance, and furthermore only a stance about the characters and events in a fictional world. The commitment of literature – by virtue of its very existence *as* literature – is to the possibility that things might always be otherwise. Things are the way they are in one particular literary universe or "world version" (Nelson Goodman's term from *Ways of Worldmaking*), but there is never a reason to take that universe as the only one, much less as the true world. The same holds true with respect to characters. They have no essential qualities, from which it follows that they have no secondary or accidental qualities either. They are "appearances" in just the sense that there is nothing to be discovered by attempting to look "behind" them.

For Nietzsche, life is like literature in the sense that it requires self-creation. "Being" is becoming. The overarching form of this interpretive, creative activity is larger than literature itself: it is art. Heidegger made a point of explaining this in his 1936–1937 lecture course on Nietzsche (the part published as *Nietzsche: The Will to Power as Art*). Art is an affirmation of the sensuous, appearing world, which the "will to truth" wishes to deny by drawing us away from it, toward the "super-sensuous" world. In an inversion of Plato's views, Nietzsche writes that "The will to *semblance*, to illusion, to deception, to Becoming and change is deeper, more 'metaphysical,' than the will to *truth*, to reality, to being." Or, in one of Nietzsche's most famous sayings, "We have *art* in order *not to perish from the truth*"[23] (*WP*, 822; emphases in original).

Correspondingly, to accept the fact that the word has no value in-itself, only the values enacted or created within it, is to embrace nihilism. Value "itself" is nothing other than "a symptom of strength on the part of the value-positers" (*WP*, 14). The totality of value (if we should want to think of such a thing) is simply the totality of valuations, the strongest and most creative of which prevail. As it relates to questions of morality, this is a core idea of *Beyond Good and Evil*:

> The diversity of men is revealed not only in the diversity of their tables of what they find good, that is to say in the fact that they regard diverse goods worth striving for and also differ as to what is more or less valuable, as to the order of rank of the goods they all recognize – it is revealed in what they regard as actually *having* and *possessing* what they find good. (98; emphasis in original)

*Beyond Good and Evil* was the title of the last of Nietzsche's "books of aphorisms" (7). Nietzsche's idea of a stance "beyond good and evil" means two things. First, that we must learn to evaluate human actions, their value and their power, in terms that recognize the provisional, man-made nature of "good" and "evil." Second, that we must learn to interpret things (in literature as in life) by recognizing that the value-terms "good" and "evil" may be ways of concealing relations of power. We may be tempted to take Iago in Shakespeare's *Othello* as an example of evil in-itself (not least because he bears some resemblance to the character-type from medieval English drama known as the Vice). But Iago's moral quality is ultimately a function of the dynamics of power at work among all the characters of the play; these operate through the motives of jealousy, ambition, and revenge. "Good" and "evil" carry with them a set of implicit assumptions about the moral framework of the world, in terms of which human actions are in turn described as right or wrong, just or unjust, even when those ascriptions turn out to be problematic. But these are not absolute. Yet Nietzsche's claim is not just about moral or ethical ambiguity. His notion of a position "beyond" good and evil is that of a stance that would render these ethical and moral dilemmas irrelevant, and from which we could see them as conditioned by factors that are not ethical or moral at all, but rather as driven by power and the will. These forces can be creative, but creative forces are for Nietzsche also connected to an opposing, destructive force. He famously said that in order to create a new star one must begin from chaos. Indeed, creation and destruction are often paired, with destruction providing a necessary opening for creativity and with creativity eventually needing to turn destructively against itself in order to make way for new forms of creative activity.

## Suggestions for Further Reading

Charles Altieri, *Subjective Agency* (Oxford: Blackwell, 1994).
Malcolm Bull, *Anti Nietzsche* (London: Verso, 2011).
Gilles Deleuze and Felix Guattari, *Anti-Oedipus*, trans. Robert Hurley, Mark Seem, and Helen R. Lane (Minneapolis: University of Minnesota Press, 1983).
Harry G. Frankfurt, *The Reasons of Love* (Princeton, NJ: Princeton University Press, 2004).
Peter Jones, *Hume's Sentiments* (Edinburgh: Edinburgh University Press, 1982).
Michel Meyer, *Philosophy and the Passions*, trans. Robert F. Barsky (University Park: Pennsylvania State University Press, 2000).
Martha Nussbaum, *The Therapy of Desire* (Princeton, NJ: Princeton University Press, 1994).
Stanley Rosen, *The Mask of Enlightenment: Nietzsche's Zarathustra* (Cambridge: Cambridge University Press, 1995).
Elaine Scarry, *The Body in Pain: The Making and Unmaking of the World* (New York: Oxford University Press, 1985).
Georg Simmel, *Schopenhauer and Nietzsche*, trans. Helmut Loiskandl, Deena Weinstein, and Michael Weinstein (Amherst: University of Massachusetts Press, 1986).
Robert Solomon, *The Passions* (Notre Dame, IN: University of Notre Dame Press, 1983).
Roberto Mangabeira Unger, *Passion: An Essay on Personality* (New York: Free Press, 1984).

Chapter 8

# Opacity

In Chapter 7 we focused on questions of the will as they are arrayed across a number of philosophical and literary instances, some of them setting the will in contrast to reason, others arguing for a settlement between the two. But there nonetheless comes a point when neither reason nor the will seems able to lend itself to further scrutiny. Our actions and our values seem to be driven by something inscrutable or opaque. Poe's "Imp of the Perverse" gives us one insight into just that possibility.

In this chapter, we will look at three different ways in which opacity, rather than transparency, seems to govern questions of human action and value as they range across literature and philosophy. These views are anchored (1) in desire, (2) in ideology, and (3) in writing. In approaching these matters through the works of Freud, Marx, and Derrida (who will be our primary points of reference), we shall consider them as philosophers. We will take Marx as a philosopher of history and of ideology, Freud as a philosopher of the unconscious, and Derrida as a philosopher of writing. None of these categories corresponds to the more traditional domains of philosophy, in ways that have direct consequences for literature. Moreover, their own work is quite often literary in significant ways: Freud works through narrative accounts, Derrida focuses on texts, and Marx's view of history is narrative in its shape. The question of opacity is at issue in all their writings. Freud suggested that consciousness and the will are not fully in command of themselves, and that we are moved to act by motives that may be largely opaque to us – opaque because they are repressed rather than simply unknown. Marx took the true conditions of our existence as distorted by ideology; indeed, much contemporary Marxist thinking holds that there is no getting "outside" of ideology because there is no getting outside of the effects of power that are produced by the organization of productive forces in society. Derrida holds (in *La Carte Postale*) that there is no communication without miscommunication, that a condition for any message to be delivered is that it can and does go astray. Writing is, moreover, a system of tropes and deferrals in which there is no foundational or fundamental sense to be discovered ("White Mythology").

All of these positions raise questions about interpretation that have clear implications for literature and philosophy both. Psychoanalysis, for example, must reckon with the symptom, which demands interpretation. Freud developed a theory about the relationship between latent content and its representation as manifest content that parallels the "deep-structure" theories we will discuss in Part III. In Marxism there is a similar set of issues that revolve around the relationship between the economic base and the superstructure. Derrida follows Nietzsche in positing that there is nothing outside the text (language, interpretation). In all these instances, value still is of course something made rather than discovered; the important proviso is that it is not made in the ways we might intend or wish. As Marx famously said in *The Eighteenth Brumaire of Louis Bonaparte*, "men make their own history, but they do not make it as they please."[1]

In addition to an exploration of these views, and following our discussion of them, we will turn briefly to two thinkers who reckon with opacity in a very different way: Maurice Merleau-Ponty and Emmanuel Lévinas. For Merleau-Ponty, the question of the "other," the one who lies outside the first-person subject, is an outgrowth of the question of embodiment and transcendence – that is, of the fact that we are isolated from others and yet can transcend that condition insofar as we share the inter-subjective medium of language. For Lévinas, it roots in questions of finitude: ethical responsibility falls to us not because we grasp the other as *like* us; rather, ethical responsibility appears precisely *because* it comes from some place outside the subject, a place which is potentially infinite in its opportunities and its demands. Neither the opacity of the other, nor the potential infinity of ethical demands can be fundamentally reduced, but can (and must) be met by acts of responsibility.

## Interpretation and the Unconscious

We sometimes strive but fail to make sense of ourselves and others. Moreover, we sometimes act in ways that are contrary to our stated purposes, or that respond to motives that are concealed, including from our conscious selves. The first set of fundamental "opacities" we will consider root in unconscious forces, including the force of the instincts and the drives. They are "fundamental" in the sense that they are susceptible to interpretation or, for Freud, to therapeutic treatment, but not ultimately to full disclosure. While I said some things about force and desire in Chapter 7, now is the occasion to discuss them in relation to the unconscious. We will look at two particular areas where the topic of desire leads to questions about the meaning and the ends of action in light of the fact that not everything we do is transparent. The first involves the dynamics of the death drive, which has direct implications for ethics in narrative and elsewhere. The second revolves around Freud's interpretive method and therapeutic aims in relation to a variety of textual materials, including dreams, jokes, and slips of the tongue. In the first of these instances, the opacity in question is a function of the deeply counter-purposive current that Freud uncovered in the course of his investigation of the instincts that go "beyond" the pleasure principle. We will say more about it shortly. The second involves the ways in which the textual material of such things as dreams and patients' narratives are the (over)determined products of deeper forces, usually involving some kind of repression and transformation. In both cases, the demand for interpretation, the search for meaning, and the striving for satisfaction are pit against a series of countervailing forces – the instincts foremost among them – that are prior to, or deeper than meaning. As Paul Ricoeur explained, the interpretation of dreams and of symbols ordinarily asks for a hermeneutics, but Freud recognized that certain forces distort meaning and subvert conscious purposes, and these in turn require an energetics.[2] Moreover, Freud aimed at a therapeutic practice and not merely at interpretation. At the early stage of his thought, this involved something like catharsis. Later in his career he focused on the therapeutic transformation of material that, in its pathological form, was the cause of suffering.

A key Freudian text to deal with in relation to the first of these scenarios is *Beyond the Pleasure Principle*. The pleasure principle says that we naturally seek a lowering of the tensions caused by unpleasure. What lies "beyond" the principle of pleasure shows up in clinical cases where there is a return to or a repetition of some earlier, seemingly unpleasurable incident. For example, dreams reported by neurotic patients who have suffered some trauma seem to bring the patient repeatedly back to those traumatic circumstances.[3] Such patients would appear to be "fixated" on their trauma. Similarly, Freud says, patients will repeat repressed material rather than remember it, which would be preferable from a therapeutic standpoint. Indeed there seems to be a "compulsion to repeat" traumatic experiences that overrides the pleasure principle. How can this be explained? Freud answered by positing an entirely new interpretation of an instinct as "an urge inherent in organic life to restore an earlier state of things" (30). In their most radical form, instincts drive any organism toward an inanimate state. For this reason, they work in concert with the death drive.

But what then is to be said about the instinct of self-preservation? How does the conflict between the death drive and self-preservation work out? What Freud says is that the self-preservation instincts ensure that the organism will follow *its own path* to death: "The organism wishes to die only in its own fashion. … Hence arises the paradoxical situation that the living organism struggles most energetically against events (dangers, in fact) which might help it attain its life's aim rapidly – by a kind of short-circuit" (*BPP*, 33).

This has created an especially important opening for a critique of ethical systems that rely on the ideal of progress toward a human goal that can be characterized as "happiness" or "satisfaction." Foremost among these is Aristotle's notion of *eudaimonia*, built around the teleology of human beings. Aristotle begins *Nicomachean Ethics* with the statement that "every action and pursuit is thought to aim at some good" (1094a, 1). Freud saw grounds in biology, in the dreams of trauma victims, and in the neuroses of his other patients, to question these teleological principles deeply. He is explicit about this in *Beyond the Pleasure Principle*:

> It may be difficult for many of us to abandon the belief that there is an instinct towards perfection at work in human beings, which has brought them to their present high level of intellectual achievement and ethical sublimation and which may be expected to watch over their development into supermen. I have no faith, however, in the existence of any such internal instinct and I cannot see how this benevolent illusion is to be preserved. What appears in a minority of human individuals as an untiring impulsion towards further perfection can easily be explained as a result of the instinctual repression upon which is based all that is most precious in human civilization. (36)

As far as his critique of desire is concerned, Freud proposed that a basic human drive toward pleasure also worked in the service of death. Pleasure, for Freud, involved the reduction of excitation; but the reduction of excitation would ultimately lead to stasis and finally to death. Hence the pleasure principle was tied to its converse, the death drive. This paradoxical conjuncture has provided one important basis for the reevaluation of the role of narrative in the project of ethics. Instead of thinking that life involves a quest for fulfillment to be achieved through a process of "improvement" or "education," the suggestion here is that life is ordered by an instinctual un-doing of the very possibility of satisfaction.

In an influential essay ("Freud's Masterplot"), Peter Brooks took the counter-purposiveness of the death drive and the short-circuiting of the instinct of self-preservation as the basis for the interpretation of narrative plots.[4] According to this view, narratives involve the striving toward a goal (e.g., happiness, the satisfaction of desire) that undermines its own success. Accordingly, there is an attempt to defer the satisfaction of that self-undermining goal by avoiding too rapid a conclusion. This short-circuiting in turn opens the space in which narrative "development" can occur – the space that encompasses everything between the beginning of the plot and the end. Freud says something closely related about dreams, namely that they are "detours" by which repression can be evaded.[5] This is consistent with Freud's thinking that an "end" is also, inevitably, a return to origins; it is not the production of anything "new," and not the moment of fulfillment, satisfaction, growth, or progress, but rather a form of repetition that impels us to question the meaning of all such values.

Balzac's novel, *The Wild Ass's Skin* (*La Peau de chagrin*) is a paradigmatic case for these matters. It turns on the following premise: The protagonist, Raphael, wanders into a curiosity shop and purchases a kind of talisman – the skin of a mythical wild beast, the chagreen (*chagrin*). The magical skin has the power to grant his every desire. But the stipulation is that the size of the skin is tied to his life-span – as each wish is granted, the skin shrinks and his life is correspondingly shortened. His initial desire is for an orgy, which instantly arrives. Toward the end of this night of excess Raphael begins to tell his life story to his friend, Emile, who is unable to stay awake to the end. In the second part of the novel, Raphael presents the story of his life under the interdiction of his father's prohibition against gambling, his assiduous studies in Paris, and his ill-fated love for Feodora, the "woman without a heart."[6] In the final section, Raphael remembers the talisman and its effect on his life just as he learns that he has inherited a fortune of six million francs. Thereafter, he proceeds to attempt the impossible: to cease desiring altogether, in an attempt to prolong his life. The end of the novel, "The Agony," is about the impossibility of resisting the desire that is destined to bring about death.[7]

But there are more than just structural correspondences between narrative and the death drive to be reckoned with in Freud's work. There is the broader issue of the incorporation of death into life that Freud approached from a number of different angles, involving the interpretation of literary materials and myth. Prominent among them is his interpretation of various versions of a myth in which a protagonist – typically a suitor – is asked to choose from among three caskets, sometimes three women, as a test. Among Freud's many references to the myth of the "Three Caskets" is Shakespeare's *Merchant of Venice*, in which Bassanio and two other suitors have to choose among three caskets in order to win Portia as a bride. The caskets are of gold, silver, and lead; the right one is the one that contains her portrait. Two other suitors choose gold and silver, so Bassanio chooses the leaden casket, which does indeed contain Portia's portrait; and while this confirms their love, it leaves Bassanio all but silent ("Thy paleness moves me more than eloquence"[8]). These words are reminiscent of the episode at the beginning of *King Lear* when Lear opts *not* to choose the third daughter (Cordelia), the one who "loves and is silent."[9] An aged man, Lear is bound to die, yet he insists on being told how much he is loved.[10] In his interpretation of Freud, Paul Ricoeur suggests that the figure of the "third woman" introduces a form of fate that begins with some not fully conscious choice and ends in death. The question he poses is whether one comes to accept death or not. If Lear does, then it comes too late, since Cordelia precedes him.

Much of Freud's work involved the interpretation of textual materials, including slips of the tongue, jokes, and the case histories of patients such as Dora and Little Hans. For Freud, dreams were also texts, not least because they are only accessible through their retelling. However, the task is not just to uncover some opacity lying *beneath* texts that are otherwise transparent. Certain dreams are puzzling and enigmatic at *every* level. Freud describes them as appearing to be "*disconnected, confused,* and *meaningless.*"[11] For this reason, it is not so much a statement of the "essential meaning" of the dream that Freud hopes to find, but rather an understanding of how the dream works. The outcome of interpretation is framed in pragmatic terms; it aims at the therapeutic goal of a relief from symptoms.

There are four principal mechanisms involved in the work of the dream. First is condensation: while each element in the content of a dream is overdetermined by material in the dream thoughts, "it is not derived from a *single* element in the dream thoughts but may be traced back to any number. … [A] dream element is, in the strictest sense of the word, the 'representative' of this disparate material in the content of the dream" (*OD*, 154). Second is dramatization, which Freud also associates with the pictorial arrangement of psychical material in the dream. Third, there is displacement. Dream thoughts are often expressed in an unusual form, not in prosaic language but, as Freud says, "represented symbolically by means of similes and metaphors, in images resembling those of poetic speech" (*OD*, 157). Recognizing this displacement allows the dream thoughts to be separated from the "poetic" language of the dream. Finally, there is the "master trope" of repression. Here Freud suggests that adult dreams are often instances of repressed wishes, which manifest themselves as if in disguise (*OD*, chapter 9).

The interpretation of dreams thus requires an understanding of the mechanisms that transpose some ultimately unknowable latent content into a manifest form. Though there is much more involved in both, Freud's interpretative framework is not unlike how one branch of Marxist thought saw the relationship between the economic base and the superstructure of cultural forms. Slavoj Žižek in fact argued that Marx "invented" the symptom by virtue of his approach to the relationship between these two levels (see text box).

**"How Did Marx Invent the Symptom?"**

This is the title of a provocative essay by Slavoj Žižek, who attributes the idea to the French psychoanalyst Jacques Lacan. The answer turns on the similarity between the interpretive procedures of Freudian psychoanalysis and Marxist historical materialism, especially as they involve the dream (Freud) and the commodity (Marx):

> The theoretical intelligence of the form of dreams does not consist in penetrating from the manifest content to its "hidden kernel," to the latent dream-thoughts; it consists in the answer to the question: why have the latent dream-thoughts assumed such a form, why were they transposed into the form of the dream? It is the same with commodities: the real problem is not to penetrate to the "hidden kernel" of the commodity – the determination of its value by the quantity of the work consumed in its production – but to explain why work assumed the form of the value of a commodity, why it can affirm its social character only in the commodity-form of its product.[12]

The question nonetheless arises: what role might the interpretation of the dream content and of patients' neuroses play as part of a therapeutic project? Freud's overarching aim was not the discovery of the truth but the relief of suffering.[13] But this was an aim that Freud approached from two different directions over the course of his career. In the first, Freud's method resembles an attempt to bring about something akin to catharsis. However, it is not only a discharge of energy that he seeks, but also, in the words of one philosopher, "a person's coming to experience his own desires and fears consciously and with appropriate emotional intensity."[14] This resembles the intellectual component of catharsis, the component that involves clarification, not just the purgation of disturbing emotions. Insofar as it occurs in dialogue with the psychoanalyst, it proceeds in manner akin to the philosophical cross-examination we see in some of Plato's dialogues:

> [The patient] is shown to have an inadequate conscious understanding of who he is, what has happened to him and how he feels about it. If a person is willing and able to undergo this "refutation," his own soul will lead the analyst and the analysand to the toxic split-off beliefs and emotions. (Lear, 45)

Freud's second path toward the relief of symptoms involved something that is called "transference." There are many understandings of what transference means, but it is "intra-psychic" transference that is at issue here (i.e., a shift within the patient's psyche, not between analysand and analyst). Freud thought that neuroses and other conditions of psychic malaise involve the distorted or unhappy association of some experience with a concept that does not belong to it. Intra-psychic transference involves shifting problematic associations to appropriate ones, and doing so at the right time. If problematic conceptual attachments can be shifted (transferred) toward ones that are appropriate, and if means appropriate to the patient's own underlying experiences can be found, then the suffering associated with the inappropriate conceptualizations may be relieved.

Consider the case of Little Hans in this context.[15] Hans's symptoms involve a fear of horses. But in telling his story, there comes a moment when Hans relates the fantasy of two giraffes: "In the night there was a big giraffe in the room and a crumpled one; and the big one called out because I took the crumpled one away from it. Then it stopped calling out; and then I sat down on top of the crumpled one" ("Analysis of a Phobia," X.37). The moment of the shift from horse to giraffe is the occasion when Hans can be offered a set of concepts through which he might relate to his own psychic productions more favorably. But in addition to concepts, Freud is able to offer Hans an opportunity for linking these concepts to the underlying psychic material that the concepts rationalize – that is, a fear of his father (see Lear, 111). If this were not the case, then Freud's procedure would amount to little more than the renaming of distorted associations. That would be an unlikely basis for therapy. Rather, the reinterpretation claims to be effective because it helps the patient find appropriate conceptualizations for the deeper upheavals within his psyche. It allows Hans to retell his story, ultimately in terms that deal appropriately with the archaic disruptions that were the source of his problems. The therapy is not a cure, and cannot be one, because the problems psychoanalysis takes up are rooted in the past and cannot be undone. But in relieving the repression through the work of appropriate redescribing, the patient may nonetheless find relief.

## Ideology and Interpretation

In *Ludwig Feuerbach and the End of Classical German Philosophy* (1888), Friedrich Engels said that art is both richer and more opaque than economic and political theory because it is not *purely* ideological. What goes by the name of "ideology" is the second opacity that we will consider here. Ideology is a term that had an established meaning before Marx and Engels adopted it. It was coined by the French philosopher Destutt de Tracy in his *Eléments d'idéologie* (*Elements of Ideology*, 1813–1814). In the Marxist context, "ideology" refers to a systematic distortion in the framework of ideas, or to accepted systems of beliefs that are false, especially as these are produced by the arrangements of power that control the productive forces in society. ("Ideology" does not mean anything like "doctrine" or "dogma" here.) The notion of "power" just mentioned is quite broad, but in the context of Marxist philosophy it always points to the ways in which the forces underlying social relations are masked.

Marxism is at bottom a philosophy of history, and as such depends crucially on the notion that value is made, just as human history is made. This is part of Marx's demystifying critique of the idealist assumptions about "spirit" that formed part of Hegel's view of history and consciousness. For Marx, "making" cannot be produced by an abstract spirit because it has its basis in human labor. Material making in the way Marx conceives it is a form of human self-production, but it does not tend to proceed as we might wish or believe. The most basic reason this is true in the modern world lies in the fact that under the conditions of capitalism a strange distortion occurs: as capital, the creative power of human labor becomes an "*alien power*."[16] At bottom this is the alienation of our creative, self-productive powers. While Marx may never explain why human beings allow this to happen, and to happen oftentimes with their apparent consent, he does explain how it is sustained – that is, by various systems of false belief, mystification, or "ideology."

These conditions require a practice of interpretation. As part of this practice, conventional Marxism asks us to reckon with the various factors that go between (mediate) the productive forces at work at the deep-structure level and what we see in the superstructure. The latter includes all the conventional materials of which literature is itself comprised (genres, styles, myths, etc.). This might, however, suggest that literature cannot play some active role in relationship to history and the forces of production. That is among the reasons why later Marxist thinkers sought to revise the simple base/superstructure model. French Marxist philosopher Louis Althusser argued that literature and art could not be reduced to ideology or to reflections of it. Rather, he placed literature in a critical relation to ideology. Literature may play a role in the critique of ideology while being itself subject to the forces of history. As Terry Eagleton said, "the task of literature is not to 'reflect' a fixed reality, but to demonstrate how character and action are historically produced, and so how they could have been, and still can be, different."[17]

Accordingly, this means that we have to revise the causal relationship between base and superstructure.[18] Since the base is as much something produced as the superstructure is, it is better to think of them as parts of the same structured totality. The relationship between them is not causal in the conventional way, but is rather that of a *structural causality*. In this relationship, history functions as an "absent cause," a term that Fredric Jameson adopts from Althusser and, before him, Spinoza. History is an absent cause since it is not anything independent of base and superstructure. There is nothing that stands outside history. We cannot see beyond it. History is the "ultimate ground as well as the untranscendable limit of our understanding in general and our textual interpretation in particular" (Jameson, 100). To this, Jameson adds the notion that narrative is not one form among many but is itself an epistemological category because it is the form of history. History and narrative are in the end two faces of the same thing.

## Writing, Difference

Suppose there is some fundamental opacity associated neither with history nor the unconscious, as Marx and Freud conceive them, but with texts and writing themselves. When dealing with texts there is invariably something that stands in the way of our access to the sorts of things that standard philosophical views of reason and morality would hope to encounter directly (e.g., truth, freedom, autonomy, the authority of the moral law). Whatever is "in the way" is often something we cannot definitively locate. Writing involves not just a system of internal, structural differences that produce meaning, but what Jacques Derrida called *différance*. *Différance* implies a deferral that is at once temporal, spatial, and metaphysical: it implies a critique of presence that also means: not (ever) here, not (ever) now. However much writing may be unwittingly in the thrall of the values that are associated with the living voice of a speaking subject, it is a system, a technology, in which presence and plenitude are always displaced.[19]

**"There is Nothing Outside the Text."**

This formulation, proposed by Jacques Derrida in commenting on Rousseau's *Confessions*, also means that "there is no outside-text"" (i.e., that even outside the text there is only writing) (*Of Grammatology*, 158).

> Beyond and behind what one believes can be circumscribed as Rousseau's text, there have never been anything but writing; there have never been anything but supplements, substitutive significations which could only come forth in a chain of differential references, the "real" supervening, and being added only while taking on meaning from a trace and from an invocation of the supplement. (158–159)

Metaphors and other figures of speech (tropes) provide one illustration of these issues. On the one hand, the notion of metaphor only makes sense if we contrast it to "literal meaning." Aristotle says that metaphor involves giving something a name that belongs to something else (*Poetics*, 1457b, 59). But the Aristotelian definition of metaphor is itself wrapped up in metaphors – "a philosophical discourse whose surface is worked by a metaphorics," as Derrida puts it.[20] There is no place outside the web of metaphors and other tropes. The idea of "metaphor" involves a theory of meaning in which some underlying thought (*dianoia*) is manifested in discourse; but thought in-itself always remains hidden, latent, and opaque. The same holds true where the idea of metaphor revolves around the notion that some kernel of sense – sense *experience*, rather than thought – always underpins metaphorical locutions.

But that kernel of experience seems never to reveal itself, or perhaps better put, never to reveal itself outside of a system of tropes. Taking Rousseau's *Essay on the Origin of Language* as a pivotal case, Derrida argued in *Of Grammatology* that writing effaces or conceals the "originary metaphor" (i.e., the fact that language is *originarily* metaphorical). "White Mythology" continues this argument in relation to Aristotle, who said that "it may be that some of the terms thus related have no special name of their own, but for all that they will be metaphorically described in just the same way. Thus to cast forth seed corn is called 'sowing'; but to cast forth its flame, as is said of the sun, has no special name" (*Poetics*, 1457b, 58). Derrida asks:

> Where has it ever been *seen* that there is the same relation between the sun and its rays as between sowing and seeds. … The figure [in Aristotle's explanation in the *Poetics*] is carried off into a long, implicit sentence, a secret narrative which nothing assures us will lead us back to the proper name. The metaphorization of metaphor, its bottomless overdeterminability, seems to be inscribed in the structure of metaphor, but as its negativity. ("White Mythology," 243; see text box).

**Nietzsche and Metaphor:**

"Metaphor is linked to the loss of the 'proper' understanding of the world, which is indecipherable and of which man can have only representations which are quite 'improper.'"[21]

This is the background informing some influential "deconstructive" interpretations of literature, including those put forward by J. Hillis Miller in his analysis of the notions of "respect" and the moral "law" in Kant's *Foundations of the Metaphysics of Morals*, and by Derrida in conjunction with Kafka's text "Before the Law." Their point of reference is what Kant says in *Foundations* about respect: "Respect" (*Achtung*), he says, is a particular "feeling" that we experience in relation to the moral law. Kant himself raises questions about this feeling. Is it a feeling like others? Does respect originate in fear, in which case our moral autonomy would clearly be compromised, since the moral law is supposed to be something we determine for ourselves out of our rational nature? We should not be in fear of it, or act out of fear of it, and if we do then perhaps we are not at all free but beholden to some other power. What, then, is the nature of the moral obligation we feel, and where does it come from? Kant puts it this way: "What I recognize directly as a law for myself I recognize with respect, which means merely the consciousness of the submission of my will to a law without the intervention of other influences on my mind."[22]

The decoupling of respect from inclinations is key for Kant. But there is a moment when Kant delves more deeply into the quality of this feeling of "respect" and it is in this discussion (in a footnote, it so happens) that deconstructive critics – Miller in particular – locate a clue as to the literary entanglements of Kant's project and, in turn, to its fundamental opacity. In "Reading Telling: Kant," Miller argued that Kant's discussion of "respect" introduces an unsolvable paradox. This is the paradox of a feeling (respect) that is not a feeling, or at least not a *subjective* feeling. Miller asks, "What, exactly, is the law? How can I confront it, or define it, or have access to it?" and responds by saying that

> Kant gives, and can give, only negative or indirect definitions of the moral law. The law is not, for example, any particular moral that can be formulated as a maxim: "Don't tell lies"; "Thou shalt not steal"; "thou shalt not commit adultery", etc. The law in question is the law as such. … [But] what then is the law as such? The reader would like to know. He would like to have access to it, to confront it face to face, to see it written down somewhere, so he can know whether or not he is obeying it. Well, Kant cannot tell you exactly where it is, or where it comes from. The law, as Jacques Derrida puts it, gives itself without giving itself.[23]

This line of questions echoes those Derrida raised in relation to Kafka's parable "Before the Law."[24] In Kafka's text, a man approaches the gateway to the law and requests permission to enter. The gatekeeper denies his request and tells the man that inside there are other gates with ever more powerful gatekeepers. The man grows old waiting to gain entry. Finally, as he approaches death, the gatekeeper tells him that the gate was for nobody else and that now, at his death, it is to be closed. This story is invoked as an example of the infinite, endless deferral of an encounter with the moral law; it is a presentation of what we have been calling its opacity. Likewise, the point is that Kant does not bring us face-to-face with the law *as such* but in its place offers hypothetical cases and narrative examples that serve in fact to distance it just where they are meant to make it perspicuous. It is the linkage of these two phenomena that creates the space in which the deconstructive wedge inserts itself. For Miller, it is specifically the narrative nature of "literary" examples that is essential *and* problematic for the kind of morality that Kant wishes to propose. With Kafka's story and Derrida's interpretation in mind, he suggests that "narrative enters as the relation of the search for a perhaps impossible proximity to the law" (*Ethics of Reading*, 25). He concludes that when narrative enters the discourse of ethics (as inevitably it does), we are faced with the "indefinite postponement of that ultimate direct confrontation of the law which narrative is nevertheless instituted to make happen in an example worthy of respect." The story takes place "in the space between the promise and the perpetually deferred fulfillment of the promise" (33).

The further implication is that since the seat of the law can never be located, there is no possible way of gaining any secure orientation in ethics. Like Kafka's character, we are somehow never able to know the true source of the moral law. Either it eludes us while we search for it, or we arrive too late. Ethics presents us with this insoluble paradox, which Kafka's story turns into a parable. Behind the parable lies a truth about texts themselves – that they never disclose the source of their authority, or their full meaning, but instead always defer or mask these things. From this we can surmise that the demand on anyone who searches for the moral law (or a final interpretation of it) is infinite and endless, and can never be met. We are endlessly responsible, responsible beyond what we can ever discern.

There is nonetheless the possibility that literature may open us to the possibility of ethical engagement with other human beings, even if we cannot know the moral law in-itself. The very fact that we are embodied beings means that others are always outside us. Our obligations are shaped by the fact that the others we encounter are never fully present to us, nor we to them. We remain, as it were, outsiders to one another and yet under some ethical obligation. This outsideness is itself a feature of the opacity that defines our relations with others; it goes beyond what the limits of our knowledge of or our sympathy for others may allow. How are obligation and ethical responsiveness shaped in this light?

One response can be approached via Merleau-Ponty. For him, it is the act of reading that allows for an encounter with the other and a transformation of the self. While reading Stendhal, for example, it is as if I become Stendhal in some provisional sense. That can happen only because we share a common language and because Stendhal "knows how to bring us to dwell within him."[25] The act of reading projects us beyond our own thoughts toward the other person's intention and meaning. How close can I get to Stendhal? There are limits, to be sure, not least among which is the embodied condition of every speaking or reading subject. And yet language is a means for the transcendence of those limits: "the power of transcending myself through reading is mine by virtue of my being a speaking subject capable of linguistic gesticulation, just as my perception is possible only through my body" (14). The implication is that reading, like speaking and listening, requires "the capacity to allow oneself to be pulled down and rebuilt by the other person" (20).

Another, not unrelated response can be framed in terms of a statement that Lévinas makes in "The Meaning of Meaning": "the law itself expresses my responsibility for the other to which I am bound in response … and which, by the face of the other, comes to me from I know not where."[26] The point is not that the "face of the other" is a veil for something we cannot fathom, or a mask for an opaque and elusive moral law that we cannot know. Rather, the point is that the revelation of the face makes a demand that exists before I can know my freedom to affirm or deny it. Subjectivity is fundamentally ethical, not epistemological: the very nature of our subjectivity rests upon our responsibility toward the other, and yet the limits of our responsibility cannot be known in advance. To fix its limits would be to deny it; by contrast, to place the encounter with the other at the heart of ethics may open us to forms of responsibility that depend upon the appearance of the other as much as on the opacity of other beings.

## Suggestions for Further Reading

Leo Bersani, *Baudelaire and Freud* (Berkeley: University of California Press, 1977).

Simon Critchley, *The Ethics of Deconstruction: Derrida and Lévinas* (Oxford: Blackwell, 1992).

*Very Little, Almost Nothing: Death, Philosophy, Literature* (London: Routledge, 1977).

Gilles Deleuze and Félix Guattari, *Kafka: Towards a Minor Literature*, trans. Dana Polan (Minneapolis: University of Minnesota Press, 1986).

Jonathan Lear, *Love and its Place in Nature: A Philosophical Interpretation of Freudian Psychoanalysis* (London: Faber and Faber, 1990).
Charles E. Scott, *The Question of Ethics: Nietzsche, Foucault, Heidegger* (Bloomington: Indiana University Press, 1990).
Slavoj Žižek, ed., *Mapping Ideology* (London: Verso, 1994).
*The Parallax View* (Cambridge, MA: MIT Press, 2006).

# Part III

## *Questions of Form*

## Chapter 9

# Ubiquitous Form

What do we indicate when we invoke the notion of "form"? And what do we mean when we make reference to the many different forms of discourse that span literature and philosophy (novel, essay, dialogue, treatise, aphorism, etc.)? How does form stand in relation to content? To what extent is form a matter of convention, whose roots lie in history and in the particular modes of expression that exist at any given time, within any particular community? While there is a long and deep tradition of thinking about many questions associated with form, definitions of the term are no more stable and fixed than are definitions of truth or value. But definitive answers are not the object here. Our aim is rather to see how the many senses of form crisscross literature and philosophy, and to outline the principal questions raised in conjunction with it. In the process, we also want to understand how form is involved with the questions of truth and value taken up in the Parts I and II of this *Introduction.* Indeed, one can't fully comprehend questions of truth or of value without also understanding form.

Yet form is surprisingly easy to miss. There is well-known line in Molière's comedy *The Bourgeois Gentleman* (*Le Bourgeois Gentilhomme*) that can serve as a reminder of this fact. Molière's protagonist, Monsieur Jourdain, comes to marvel at the fact that he has been speaking in prose for his entire life, thought without ever having realized this ("Par ma foi! il y a plus de quarante ans que je dis de la prose sans que j'en susse rien"[1]). The joke in the Molière play turns on the fact that M. Jourdain is naively enlightened – enlightened to something that should be obvious simply because he acquires a new name for the way he has always spoken. His naive sophistication notwithstanding, he does notice something true about his own speech: it has a *form.* He speaks in *prose.* The point can be extended broadly, and without the joke: form is ever-present, so ubiquitous in fact that we are apt to miss it unless we are obliged to notice it. Especially through language, form plays a vital role in the shaping of thought. It is at work everywhere in the domains of literature and philosophy. As symbol-using animals, human beings are constantly involved in the making of signifying forms; literature and philosophy are subsets of these.

We can't get away from form, and yet there are questions about when, why, and how it is made prominent. Form can sometimes seem invisible, and sometimes aspires to be so, but this may be all the more reason to attend to it. We need to think about form across a spectrum that ranges from the transparent at one end to the opaque at the other. Form is something we can choose to look "through," or something we can choose to look "at."[2] We can look *at* the form of a novel or a poem or a stretch of philosophical writing just as we can choose to be absorbed in it – looking, as it were, through the form.[3] Likewise, we can look at the form of philosophical writing, or we can look through it to arguments and ideas. But we should resist the temptation to think that form is unique to literature and absent from philosophy. Descartes wrote *Meditations on First Philosophy* as a quasi-autobiographical text. Wittgenstein's *Philosophical Investigations* involves both interior dialogue and fragmentary construction. St. Augustine and Rousseau both wrote confessions. Every work, including every philosophical work, whether treatise, essay, or dialogue, has a form. The fact that Plato wrote dialogues, and not essays or treatises, whereas Montaigne and Emerson wrote essays, bears noticing because the dialogue shapes what Plato means just as the essay shapes the thought of Emerson and Montaigne.

Walter Benjamin took up the question of transparency and opacity in form in a highly concentrated essay at the beginning of his book on German baroque tragic drama, *Ursprung des Deutschens Trauerspiels* (*The Origin of German Tragic Drama*). On one side of a continuity he placed a "mathematical ideal," in which genuine knowledge and truth would be independent of any form of mediation (including sign-systems, writing, text, and language itself); on the other side he placed various forms of writing in which form is prominent – literature above all, but not exclusively so. He emphasized the fact that no matter how much it might try, philosophy could never hope to achieve the mathematical idea of a formless expression. What Benjamin calls "representation," and what we might call form in general, is essential to philosophy insofar as it is a method for acquiring knowledge and not the self-revelation of truth. Truth itself would in principle be self-representing, "imminent in its form."[4] Instead, Benjamin saw philosophical writing as having a mosaic-like structure. Its prose style, he suggested, remains under an obligation to stop and restart with virtually every sentence, causing the reader continuously to pause and reflect rather than to get swept along in a flow of language (29). In *Culture and Value*, Wittgenstein says that "philosophy ought really be written only as a *poetic composition*."[5]

**Forms and Form**

Every work of literature or philosophy has a particular form, as determined in some measure by the arrangement of its words and parts. But there are also the larger verbal forms mentioned above (novel, drama, dialogue, essay, etc.), sometimes called genres. These are built of the elements of language and depend on the expectations of the speakers of that language. A language is comprised of utterances as a genre is comprised of works. These relationships are dynamic and reciprocal: each utterance that is spoken and each work that is produced also helps to shape language and genre. We can't speak an utterance without there first being a language, and we can't comprehend a work without having some expectation about what kind of work it will be. We always begin our understanding of a work as being of a certain kind; we read and understand with generic predispositions in mind. In the field of hermeneutics (the philosophy of interpretation) this relationship is called the "horizon of expectations."

Surprisingly, perhaps, our predispositions remain largely in force even where a given work confounds our expectations by breaking with convention. We sometimes need to read against the grain, but there always is some given grain to read against. There is always what Heidegger called the "background" of our practices; so too there is always some preexisting structure of understanding by virtue of which we can say or do anything meaningful at all. The notion that we begin from a "blank page," bereft of any and all expectations, is a myth. Many of our expectations, moreover, are carried by form.

Questions of form in literature and philosophy have ancient roots and many modern interpretations. They involve some of the most fundamental links and differences between the two fields, ranging from basic questions about language and meaning to changing views about the relationship between nature and convention. Because questions of form span such a wide spectrum, we will begin by outlining some very basic issues regarding form and content in language. Then we will take up a set of further questions about the role of form in literary and philosophical discourse. Throughout all this, it will be important to bear in mind that form is not one thing but many, and that while we can track a number of the most important perspectives about it, form has itself been interpreted in many different ways over time. These have all had a bearing on the relationships between literature and philosophy.

## Form and Content: Deep-Structure Theories

Since at least Aristotle, it has been conventional to think about form in contrast to content. "Form" here translates Aristotle's term *morphē*. Especially for Aristotle and for the lines of interpretation that have their roots in his ideas, it has been thought that content precedes form, and that form involves some kind of work on some preexisting content. The term "hylomorphism" (see text box) describes the belief that *content* – especially as matter – is independent of form, and that form is something added to matter. This belief has its roots in Aristotle's ideas about change in general. Aristotle believed that in the course of any kind of change, there is something that persists and something that is gained or lost: matter persists, while form is gained or lost. As bronze is heated it loses its solid form and takes on the form of a liquid; the matter (bronze) nonetheless persists. Much later, Descartes would apply similar ideas to the question of personal identity, although concluding that what persists is consciousness, not the material substance of the body. Since Aristotle was interested in accounting for all manner of phenomena, he regarded matter and form both as features of the world, independent of mind. This also helps explain why Aristotle's ideas about tragedy in *Poetics* are largely about the best ways to give dramatic form to tragic plots; *Poetics* also describes which plots lend themselves best to tragic form, but the story of a hero's downfall is independent of any dramatic imitation of it. Plato also had much to say about the question of form (and about forms), as previously noted, but Plato's forms are non-temporal and non-spatial. Even their language is different. Plato's "form" translates *eidos* rather than *morphē*. The ideal Platonic forms do not ever change; they are eternal, and so do not come into being or pass away.

## Hylomorphism

The term "hylomorphism" derives from the Greek *hylo* (matter) and *morphē* (form). On Aristotle's account, there is a continuity of matter throughout changes in its form.

> When a lump of bronze comes to be enformed with the shape of Hermes, a statue of Hermes comes into existence. When this same bronze is later melted and recast as a statue of Domitian, then the Hermes statue goes out of existence and a statue of Domitian comes into existence. ... [T]he bronze which first acquires and then loses one shape (the Hermes shape) and then acquires a new shape (the Domitian shape) is itself only contingently enformed by either shape. We speak of the lump or quantity of bronze as continuing through the entire process; and this seems plausible, since the bronze itself has no one shape essentially. Perhaps it is essentially bronze or essentially metal, but it is not essentially either Hermes- or Domitian-shaped.[6]

Thanks to both Aristotle and Plato (although in contrasting ways), the concept of form has often been linked to the notion that all language expresses a "kernel" of meaning. This is sometimes described as a kind of pre-linguistic "sense," a notional content that is independent of language, although given shape by it. Typically, this kernel of sense is thought of as lying "below" language, at some deep-structure level. Consider the relationship between *Sinn* (sign) and *Bedeutung* (meaning) in the philosophy of Edmund Husserl.[7] In Husserl's model, these relationships are explained in terms of strata or layers. Language is a representation (i.e., a copy or portrait) of some "sense" that is not itself linguistic. Sense is described as an "infrastructure" that is "guided secretly" (171) by the superstructural possibility of meaning. This is a model in which pre-linguistic content (sense) is imprinted in an expressive thought (*noema*); "thought" here is without form, and offers itself "as a blank page or virgin tablet" (164).

As we will see at several points in this section, however, this is very much the relationship that has been called into question by a number of contemporary thinkers working across literature and philosophy. In one respect, it does not matter for these arguments whether the kernel of sense, or the underlying content of utterances is linguistic, historical, or of any other kind. The important questions are the ones we have already begun to identify: Is there any content that is truly independent of form? Is the relationship between form and content that between some "underlying" stratum and a "representation" of it? Is there a deep structure of experience which can then be rendered literarily or philosophically? Most contemporary work in the areas between literature and philosophy revolve around (1) a critique of the deep/surface structure model and (2) attempts to find alternatives to it.

To take one example, Jacques Derrida made Husserl's model of sense and meaning a centerpiece of his critique of the phenomenology of language. Derrida did not want to suggest collapsing these layers as a solution; to question this model meant

> neither to reconstruct the experience (of sense) as a *language*, above all if one takes this to be a *discourse*, a verbal fabric, nor to produce a critique of language on the basis of the ineffable riches of sense. It is simply to ask questions about *another relationship* between what are called, problematically, *sense* and *meaning*. (172; emphases in original)

What might this be? Derrida described it as "elliptical," from which we can infer that their relationship is one of interdependence and of co-construction; it means that the one can and does influence the other, and that neither one has priority over the other.

### Form and the Privilege of Fact?

Are statements of fact different from other types of statements when it comes to the question of form? Is it possible that there is an underlying and independent kernel of sense in a statement like "the sum of the angles in this triangle equals 180 degrees" but not in the expression "my mistress' eyes are nothing like the sun"?[8] Derrida suggests that we tend to privilege statements of fact and that we are apt to believe that all statements can be understood according to some of the basic principles underlying them. The most basic reason, he argues, is that statements of fact are predications grounded in being-present – that is, in the present indicative form of the verb "to be" (i.e., statements of the type "it is thus"). Correspondingly, we are inclined to believe that we can always understand expressions of affect or value as relying on this same underlying form:

> It is because this silent stratum [doxic kernel] always bears within it – or always has the power of restoring – a relation to form, that it can always convert its affective or axiological experience, its relation to what is not being-present, into an experience in the form of being-present ... and that offers itself without reserve to the logical discourse watched over by predicative form, that is, by the present indicative of the verb to be. (Derrida, 170)

Form plays a crucial role in this model because it is complicit with thinking about meaning as predication about things as they *are*.

Others, including Kant, thought very differently about this. In *Critique of Judgment*, for example, Kant argued that claims about beauty have the form of assertions about objects ("x is beautiful") but are in fact assertions about a type of pleasure felt in response to them. The challenge he took up was to determine how such claims can also have universal validity.

Similar questions about deep and surface structures have become important not just in reflections on language and meaning, but also for questions raised by philosophers of history and historiographers. Consider the work of philosopher Arthur Danto in *The Analytical Philosophy of History* and of Hayden White in *The Content of the Form*. Danto and White both reached the conclusion that form plays a determinative role, not an accidental one, with respect to content in the writing of history; "content" scarcely exists without form. They both argued against the claims of an earlier, "scientific" historiography that saw narrative form as an unnecessary distortion of the underlying historical "facts." Danto and White concentrated principally on narrative form, but their arguments are broadly generalizable. One of the implications of their work was that form is at work creating content even where it might appear to be inactive or invisible.

To invoke one of White's examples, the difference between a historical annal, in which dates and events are simply recorded sequentially, and a full-blown historical narrative with an authorial voice and point of view does not lie in the fact that the annal has no form while narrative has a robust and discernible shape; rather, it lies in recognizing that the form of each contributes to our understanding of history. An older distinction that separates "history" into actions or deeds on the one hand and their recorded form on the other (history as *res gestae* and history as *historia rerum gestarum*) no longer stands. Certainly in its narrative form, history is a kind of discourse that can be placed under the broad umbrella of "literature"; but the more important point is that its literary *form* is not isolated from its *content*. Rather, the content is given a determinative shape by it. As White showed in *Metahistory*, this is especially true of the overarching plot structures according to which histories are shaped (e.g., as tragedies with disastrous outcomes, as satires, as comedies, or as romances, with endings that are by and large happy ones). The question that neither White nor Danto answered directly, and which we will turn to later, is whether there is a deep structure at work in history as a function of human experience itself – perhaps not a content, but a *structure* that drives the form. The answer has an important bearing on how we regard the interpretation of literary forms, and in turn marks one of the areas where literature and philosophy have often diverged. We will address it in the final section of this chapter. For now, we turn to the role of form in poetry, and from there to questions about the relationship between poetry and "ordinary" language, and to the relationship between ordinary language and philosophy.

## Form and *Poiēsis*: The Example of Poetry

Poetry epitomizes the work of form in language; it is language in which the power of form is itself on display. This is a version of what Heidegger meant when he wrote about the way all art roots in the activity of *poiēsis* (making). "When a work is created, brought forth from out of this or that work-material – stone, wood, metal, color, language, tone – we also say that it is made, set forth out of it. … The work as work, in its presencing is a setting forth, a making."[9] Works of art are not mere things; so too, poetic utterances are not just assertions. Any utterance gives a specific shape to the claim it makes, and in poetry this specific shape (which falls among the many things that "form" designates) creates a bridge to value. Form creates this bridge to value in poetry because poetry shapes and directs our attention to the power of language in the work of making. This may involve ordering (and reordering) the way we put words to the world, but in the process it involves the revaluing of the world. As Simon Critchley said of Wallace Stevens, "Poetry reorders the order we find in things. It gives us back things exactly as they are, but beyond us. … The imaginative reordering of the world through the sound of words both touches a common reality and gives us that reality back under a new aspect, anew, transfigured."[10]

**Work and World**

Heidegger asks: "What does the work set forth?" By way of an answer, Heidegger invoked the term "world": "To work-being belongs the setting up of a world."[11]

Poetry is a matter of *significant* form, even in the context of what would seem to be simple statements of fact. Thus, rather than think of form as element of language that can be added to or subtracted from the truth-content of an utterance, we do better to think of form as a route toward the kind of value we would associate with the importance of the truth. This can best be illustrated in relation to some specific examples. Consider what would seem to be a simple statement of fact in a poem by Wallace Stevens, "Examination of a Hero in Time of War." Stevens writes: "There is no image of the hero."[12] This statement goes against a number of common assumptions, since we do in fact have all kinds of images of heroes – in paintings, statues, literary texts, coins, medals, folktales, myths, and so forth. Whatever the line means must somehow be contrary to these facts, or be *otherwise* than the facts as we ordinarily take them to be. What it means, and why it matters, depend upon the specifics of the utterance itself, including its formal qualities and the contextual relationships established within the poem:

> It is not an image. It is a feeling.
> There is no image of the hero.
> There is a feeling as definition.
> How could there be an image, and outline,
> A design, a marble soiled by pigeons?
> The hero is a feeling, a man seen
> As if the eye was an emotion,
> As if in seeing we saw our feeling. (278)

The plainness of Stevens's language, the directness of this phrasing, and the order of lines in the poem all produce a surprising clarity about something that might seem contradictory, if not untrue. By virtue of its form the poem makes sense out of utterances that might not seem to be meaningful. Stevens's lines suggest that when it comes to heroes, the image is not in fact an image, but rather a feeling. And if the image of the hero is a feeling, then the eye acts in an emotive capacity: emotion becomes visible in the image of the hero. What the poem gives us in these lines, through their specific arrangement and articulation, is the experience of a truth that builds with gradual insistence and increasing clarity toward a conclusion that might otherwise seem contrary to fact.

**Is it Beautiful?**

Questions of beauty have plagued philosophy for centuries. Properly speaking they fall under the branches of philosophy known as aesthetics and the philosophy of art. One important strand of thinking, which has its roots in Kant, associates questions of beauty with questions of form. Kant did not think that objects are beautiful because of some formal properties they have. Wildflowers in nature have a particular form that may be considered pleasing. So too, a painting, a poem, or a musical composition. But these pleasures derive from the mere play of their elements. Kant has something else in mind – something "higher" – when he speaks of form in relation to beauty. Here, the locus of form lies in the subject. It is an organization of the faculties involved in making judgments about beauty. That organization is peculiar insofar as it is prompted by our experience of things for which we have no available concepts, or for which our concepts leave something unaccounted. The organization of our faculties achieved in these circumstances is what Kant calls the "free play" of the faculties.[13]

Heidegger remarked that poetry involves thinking, but "without science, without philosophy" (*OWA*, 61). "Thought" has long been thought of as an important component of literature. Aristotle spoke about *dianoia* (discursive thinking) as an element of tragedy (although for Aristotle, it could also be considered independent of the form of tragedy).[14] Helen Vendler likewise spoke about "poets thinking."[15] It might be tempting to imagine that when poetry thinks "without science" it thinks either unclearly or by mere intuition. But it would be better to say that when poetry thinks, it does so by virtue of form. A poem places truth in the debt of the language that shapes it and lends it value. It does not aim to give us knowledge of any particular thing; rather, it shows how language underpins the value of any "thing." This is the end to which Heidegger interpreted a pregnant line from a poem by Stefan George ("The Word," 1919): "Where word breaks off no thing may be."[16]

Poetry offers what may well be the clearest set of examples in which the various elements of linguistic form play a role in giving shape to truth and in creating a bridge to value. As the paragon of formed language, as *significant form*, poetry also shows how value and truth are linked by showing the value of truth. It was Heidegger who most forcefully argued that the "making" we associate with poetry, as with all art, involves a kind of "disclosing." As mentioned in Part I, Heidegger used the Greek term *alētheia* for this. Heidegger argued that the deepest, and oldest, function of poetry was to reveal the truth by bringing it out from concealment into the open. By virtue of its form, poetry is a disclosure of truth, not a representation of underlying facts. In the process, poetry establishes value in a way that cannot be accounted for if we think of language simply as a way of representing facts.

Consider the following lines from Shakespeare's *Richard II*:

> This royal throne of kings, this scepter'd isle,
> This earth of majesty, this seat of Mars,
> This other Eden, demi-paradise,
> This fortress built by Nature for herself
> Against infection and the hand of war,
> This happy breed of men, this little world,
> This precious stone set in the silver sea,
> Which serves it in the office of a wall,
> Or as a moat defensive to a house,
> Against the envy of less happier lands,
> This blessed plot, this earth, this realm, this England.[17]

The difference between this passage and a geographical description has everything to do with its form, from the formal repetitions ("This royal throne," "This earth of majesty," etc.) to its metaphors ("precious stone set in the silver sea"). Taken together with the fact that they are spoken at a particular moment and by a particular character (the dying Gaunt) these elements of form lend a particular salience to what is said. Moreover, they invite an engagement with the truth that is not instrumental (i.e., that cannot be enlisted to accomplish other ends but that is intimately connected with our capacity as human beings to ascribe value to truths beyond their status as facts). It shows us a face of truth that involves something other than the accuracy of propositions or "correctness in representation." What we have been calling the value of truth, as shown by form, is what Heidegger describes as beauty.[18]

What has been said thus far may help to dispel any idea that a poem (or a novel or a play, for that matter) is susceptible to paraphrase without considerable loss. What is lost in paraphrase is form, and with it the value of poetry. To consider another example, the themes that critics most commonly identify in Emily Dickinson's poetry are easy enough to paraphrase: death is a certainty;

the adoration spawned by love is likely to bring grief; the promised truths of religion are liable to disappoint us, even though comfort may be found in more secular forms. But as literary critic Helen Vendler remarked, these are scarcely the adequate renderings of the temper of Dickinson's thinking. One might even summarize the emotional crises in her poetry as instances in which a soul of great sensitivity strives to find stability in religion or love but is brought to grief.[19] And yet what Vendler calls Dickinson's *style* of thinking means that these capsule summaries are bound to be insufficient. Consider these lines:

> The Outer – from the Inner
> Derives its magnitude –
> 'Tis Duke, or Dwarf, according
> As is the central mood –
> ...
> The inner – paints the Outer
> The Brush without the Hand –
> Its Picture published – precise –
> As is the inner Brand.[20]

We can think of a paraphrase as an attempt to render the meaning of a given text in some more condensed or literal way, but the passage quoted above is already remarkably condensed. Indeed, condensation is one of its characteristic features. If we think of a paraphrase as the "prose sense" of a poem, then it is hard to imagine how, here, it might not also be a distortion of the poem's sense. The lines quoted speak clearly, and with a compact intensity, about the revelation of the "inner" (of inward character) by the outer (e.g., by the body, by gestures, by the face, by habit), as if a brushless hand were to paint a perfect resemblance between the two. In expanding further on these lines in an effort to paraphrase them, we would sacrifice their precision, economy, and exactness. In so doing we would perforce lose everything about form that contributes to the sense of the poem. In 1817, literary critic William Hazlitt wrote, "Shakespeare was as good a philosopher as he was a poet," and he wrote with "the spirit of a poet and the acuteness of a philosopher."[21] This may well be true, but Shakespeare's "philosophy" exists only through the form of his plays. The mistake would be to think that we can strip away the dramatic form and still leave Shakespeare's philosophy intact.

In concluding this section, we ought to remember that what has been said about poetry holds true for literature in general. As one recent philosopher, Jacques Rancière, said, "If the function [of literature] is not to represent ideas, situations, objects, or characters according to the norms of resemblance, it is because it already presents, on its very body, the physiognomy of what it says."[22] Indeed, this was key to Flaubert's wish to make a "book about nothing" (i.e., a book in which the work of representation or the relationship of "aboutness" to the world would recede to the point where it would all but vanish). For Flaubert, style was crucial to this project. Here is how he framed the issue in a famous letter to Louise Colet:

> What seems beautiful to me, what I should like to write, is a book about nothing, a book depending on nothing external, which would be held together by the eternal strength of its style, just as the earth, suspended in the void, depends on nothing external for its support; a book which would have almost no subject, or in which the subject would be almost invisible, if such a thing is possible. The finest works are those that contain the least matter; the closer expression comes to thought, the closer language comes to coinciding and merging with it, the finer the result.[23]

And yet there seems always to be *something* that a work is *about*, even if it strives toward an ideal of complete self-containment. This becomes apparent in the works of Samuel Beckett. Beckett presses action and meaning toward the limit of nothingness, toward stasis, and to the edge of nonsense. But even in works like *Endgame* and *Waiting for Godot*, it turns out that something is said, something done, something meant. Waiting is a form of action. So too with meaning, which we can't seem to stop making. Hamm asks Clov in *Endgame*, "Did you ever think about one thing?" Clov responds, "Never," meaning of course that he has always thought of many things, and certainly not ever of no-thing.[24] We will see next how this particular idea was central to the work of philosopher Stanley Cavell.

## Poetry vs. Ordinary Language

Some of what has just been said might suggest that there is a fundamental difference between poetic language and "ordinary" speech. There are of course numerous ways in which the two might be characterized as different. But, since at least Wordsworth's *Lyrical Ballads*, the opposition between "ordinary language" and "poetry" has been tenuous at best. It is of course true that form is given a prominence in poetic language, and that we can think of poetic language as significant form. (We'll later turn to instances of philosophy that are no less significant in formal terms.) What we should *not* assume is that the description "ordinary" with respect to language indicates an absence of form; or that ordinary language is unmarked, neutral speech (like M. Jourdain's "prose"); or is not the potential source of significant philosophical insights. The work of so-called ordinary language philosophy, of certain strands of pragmatism, and of some followers of Wittgenstein (Cavell most notably), have shown that none of this is true.

The term "ordinary language philosophy" was developed to describe some of the work of modern British philosophers such as Gilbert Ryle, H. L. A. Hart, and P. F. Strawson; sometimes it was also associated with Wittgenstein's *Philosophical Investigations*, J. L. Austin's work on speech acts, and Stanley Cavell's books *Must We Mean What We Say?* and *The Claim of Reason*. Strictly speaking, ordinary language philosophy names only a subset of their work, and yet they do all share some important features. Aside from the fact that they all take language itself as the *materia prima* of philosophy, their impulses were all corrective and therapeutic: corrective of the path that academic philosophy had come to favor by framing its questions in highly technical terms oriented toward metaphysics and disconnected from the (ordinary) world at hand, and therapeutic to the extent that those technical approaches had generated an artificial series of questions that needed to be overcome or dissipated rather than answered. The hope was that, by carefully inspecting the utterances of ordinary speech, philosophy could respond to the most important questions about truth and value while allowing the artificial questions to dissolve. Wittgenstein said that he would treat a philosophical question as he would treat an illness.

As noted previously, most of these "artificial" questions originated in some involvement with questions of metaphysics. Wittgenstein famously said that he was trying to bring words "back from their metaphysical to their everyday use."[25] If metaphysics was concerned with the "essential" nature of things, either with their ideal forms (Plato) or their formed substance (Aristotle), then ordinary language philosophy was clearly anti-essentialist. And whereas metaphysics thus tended to approach questions of truth and value on an abstract plane, ordinary language was adherent to particulars.

## Beyond Wittgenstein: Cavell

It was Stanley Cavell who brought an awareness of what ordinary language philosophy and Wittgenstein's later writings could contribute to and learn from the methods of reading and interpretation associated with literary study.[26] Richard Eldridge and Bernie Rhie remarked that

> the art of attentive, careful reading lies at the very heart of Cavell's conception of philosophical method. … The philosopher's activity therefore resembles the compositional activity of the modernist writer, seeking to make new sense through situated engagements with, and

> departures from, precursors. Hence it is natural that Cavell would devote so much time and energy to the study of literary texts, where efforts to find and make sense are foregrounded over proofs and fixed results.[27]

While there are significant differences in both method and consequence between Cavell's work and the practice of ordinary language philosophy, that work was nonetheless a starting point for much of what Cavell went on to develop, ultimately offering him a point to press against in his own work on questions of skepticism, knowledge, and acknowledgment. Cavell outlined some of the basic ideas that informed his way of reading literature philosophically in *Must We Mean What We Say?* as involving a careful inspection of particular claims as they were spoken in ordinary language. These were typically truth-claims – propositions stating that something is thus and so. Answers to larger philosophical questions (e.g., questions about truth itself) were, in this process, redirected to what "we" ordinarily say. And yet the "we" in ordinary language philosophy typically went unquestioned. How was this "we" actually constituted? How far did it reach? Was it fixed, and if so how? Indeed, Eldridge and Rhie aver that appeals to ordinary language might well seem to be nothing more than exercises in self-congratulation, embodying a "'commons-room' authoritarianism that is both class-based and inattentive to the varieties of demotic speech" ("Introduction," 3). Regardless of whether or not this was ever true of ordinary language philosophy, it was never true of Cavell, much of whose enterprise was designed to keep questioning the grounds of the "we" to which judgments appeal and, beyond that, to keep pressing the question of any individual's relationship to that "we." In philosophically significant appeals to ordinary language, we can arrive not merely at a confirmation of what we say, but a sense of better attunement, of "felt rightness – in the ear both of the one entering the claim and the ear of anyone who follows its rightness" (4). When this happens, our relationship to the "we" may be transformed, as our selves may be: The process may yield "new or transformed subjects, who have entered into this new we from the resources of their own subjectivities" (4).

Transposed to literature this meant, first and foremost, attending to the words spoken by characters as fully *meant*, rather than allowing the figural or metaphorical sense of their words to relieve that obligation. When Cavell took up *King Lear*, he was loath to follow the lead of prior literary critics in tracing particular images throughout the play. There are, to be sure, important figural patterns in *King Lear*. More important, there is a pattern of figures that has to do with seeing, the eyes, light, and blindness. But attending to this figural pattern can distract us from the fact that the characters speak and mean what they say, and sometimes quite literally. Thinking about figures of speech can make it impossible to ask questions about how and why the characters mean what they say, and how they take responsibility for what they say or avoid that responsibility. The effect of concentrating on figures is like the pursuit of metaphysics, which can be flawed by looking "too high" for the answers to basic philosophical questions.[28] Cavell's point is that characters are bound more closely to their words than critics have tended to suppose. Literary language in no way relieves the characters from meaning. On the contrary, it binds characters to what they say. And as with words, so too with human relationships. To see another person or to ignore them; to be seen by another or to avoid being seen: these are figural notions that point directly to human relationships. What critics had come to call the "sight pattern" in *King Lear* is in fact a matter of the acknowledgment or avoidance of others; hence the title of Cavell's essay, "The Avoidance of Love."

Cavell's engagement with literature exemplifies the ways in which many of the central, inherited problems of philosophy required a shift of their register and zone of engagement if their importance was to be recognized. This was especially true of the way Cavell dealt with the problem of skepticism. For Cavell, skepticism is not at bottom an epistemological problem, although it typically presents itself that way. It is, rather, a condition of our relationship to others and to the world in the *guise* of a question about knowledge. The "answer" to skepticism lies in acknowledgment rather than in knowledge. Acknowledgment – our response to others both as human beings and as outsiders to ourselves – lacks the kind of closure that epistemology would hope to achieve because acknowledgment must be acted or enacted in every instance in which it is required. In tracing the route from questions of language and meaning to questions of acknowledgment, Cavell is suggesting a homology: both in language and in acknowledgment, it is incumbent upon us to mean what we say as fully and responsibly as possible. One source of this homology lies in the fact that language is the primary space in which our relationship with others is realized.

We have already pointed out some features of Cavell's concept of acknowledgment, but there are two additional points to be made. First, that its link to skepticism is underpinned by the form of tragedy. The point is not that tragedy is the working out of skepticism but rather that skepticism is the playing out of a tragedy, one that is enacted in our ordinary lives as much as it is on the stage.[29] This leads to the second point, which Cavell addressed in his engagement with romanticism's attempt to reclaim the ordinary in language and experience. It has to do with our discomfort with the ordinary, or perhaps better said, with the difficulty of arriving at a wholly natural and settled relationship to it. "An irreducible region of our unhappiness is natural to us but at the same time unnatural," he wrote; "skepticism is as live in us as, let me say, the child" (9).

These insights derive largely from Cavell's engagement with the writings of Emerson, Thoreau, Coleridge, Wordsworth, and Beckett. While his project was at one level to (re)claim their work as philosophical, in spite of its formal appearance to be otherwise, at another level his goal was to redirect our attention toward that which is so often overlooked (the ordinary, the everyday). The outcome is not, as his remark about unhappiness suggests, the reestablishment of a naïve or innocent relationship to the ordinary world, but rather to capture how provisional and strange that relationship may be. Thoreau calls the condition of the everyday one of "quiet desperation." Emerson described it with the phrase "silent melancholy." Coleridge and Wordsworth use terms like "despondency" and "dejection." Cavell accounts for all these, along with what Heidegger called "bedimmed averageness" and Wittgenstein "bewitchment." The strangeness of Beckett's writing roots in his perception of the "weirdness, or surrealism" of what we ordinarily take as usual and real.[30] Cavell's own account turns to the fragility of our relationship to home: "The everyday is ordinary because, after all, it is our habit, or habitat; but since that very inhabitation is from time to time perceptible to us – we who have constructed it – as extraordinary, we conceive that some place elsewhere, or this place otherwise constructed, must be what is ordinary to us, must be what romantics … call 'home'" (9).

Cavell has for this and similar reasons often been called a "humanist," which is to say a thinker who may well press against the limits of our language, and who looks to literature to probe questions about our generosity, love, callousness, and even our inhumanness toward others, but whose thinking assumes that we can only adopt a human-centric stance as the basis for our relations with all other beings in the world. As a thinker whose work revolves so deeply around language and literature, it is not surprising that he would work within these bounds. Two of Wittgenstein's remarks speak in some measure to this issue; one from *Philosophical Investigations*: "If a lion could talk we could not understand him" (223); and another from *Tractatus Logico-Philosophicus*: "The limits of my language mean the limits of my world."[31]

## Suggested Further Reading

Giorgio Agamben, *The Idea of Prose*, trans. Michael Sullivan and Sam Whitsitt (Albany: SUNY Press, 1995).

*The Man Without Content*, trans. Georgia Albert (Stanford, CA: Stanford University Press, 1999).

Arthur Danto, *Analytical Philosophy of History* (Cambridge: Cambridge University Press, 1964).

John Gibson and Wolfgang Huemer, eds., *The Literary Wittgenstein* (New York: Routledge, 2004).

Wlad Godzich and Geoffrey Kittay, *The Emergence of Prose: An Essay in Prosaics* (Minneapolis: University of Minnesota Press, 1987).

Jean-Luc Nancy, *The Sense of the World*, trans. Jeffrey Librett (Minneapolis: University of Minnesota Press, 1997).

Marjorie Perloff, *Wittgenstein's Ladder: Poetic Language and the Strangeness of the Ordinary* (Chicago: University of Chicago Press, 1996).

Elaine Scarry, *On Beauty and Being Just* (Princeton, NJ: Princeton University Press, 1999).

Hayden White, *The Content of the Form: Narrative Discourse and Historical Representation* (Baltimore, MD: Johns Hopkins University Press, 1987).

*Metahistory: The Historical Imagination in Nineteenth Century Europe* (Baltimore, MD: Johns Hopkins University Press, 1973).

## Chapter 10

# Linguistic Turns

"*Truth* consisteth in the right ordering of names in our affirmations."

Hobbes, *Leviathan*[1]

The area of ordinary language philosophy discussed in Chapter 9 is one of a number of instances where philosophy in the twentieth century made a turn toward language. This "linguistic turn" implied a turn *away* from a set of questions that had been dominant in philosophy for the previous few centuries. Beginning with Descartes, those questions had come to center around the relationship between the mind and the world. Questions of truth and value were organized around epistemology, which saw itself as "first philosophy." The linguistic turn displaced those concerns with an interest in the relationship between language and the world. This did not come about for any accidental reason, but rather because it was hoped that the philosophy of language could answer questions that epistemology could not resolve. The linguistic turn did not leave everything else in place. Language involves questions of reference and meaning, and a satisfactory understanding of such things can't be produced simply by replacing the notion of mental representations with the notion of linguistic representations.

I will have more to say about this shifting terrain over the course of what follows, but first we should indicate the role that literature had to play in the evolution of these views. First, literature is a form of discourse where meaning is crucial and yet is hardly dependent on a belief that the function of language is to represent the world. It is not at all clear that all literary language "represents" or "refers" at all. Second, literature is a domain where various kinds of "non-literal" meanings (including metaphor and other examples of figurative speech) are fundamental. Third, literature is a domain in which the "intentions" of speakers cannot be assessed in the ways in which we might assess the intentions of speakers in other contexts. The intentions of the narrator in a novel by Tolstoy, of a character in a play by Schiller, or of the speaking "I" in a poem by John Ashbery are not fathomable according to a single scheme of what "intention" may mean, and may not align with our understanding of intentions in ordinary speech at all. The evolution of the philosophy of language did not begin from literature, but its development was nourished by an awareness of the different ways in which literature uses language and makes meaning.

In this chapter, I begin with some of the basic background of the linguistic turn in philosophy, starting from the philosophical interest in "propositions," and moving from there to Wittgenstein's *Tractatus Logico-Philosophicus*, written largely in the spirit of logical positivism. By the time Wittgenstein was writing the later *Blue and Brown Notebooks* and *Philosophical Investigations*, the relationship between language and world was no longer center stage. Rather, Wittgenstein moved to the domain where the concepts of "language games," "family resemblances," and "forms of life" are far more important than linguistic representations. Next, I turn to J. L. Austin's development of the theory of "speech acts," its implications for literature, and its expansion to a much broader range of performance. Austin is an especially good example of a philosopher who recognized that language was doing much more than "representing" the world; he saw it as playing an active role within it – literally allowing us to do things with words.

## Propositions

The first element in the linguistic turn came with the shift of the ground on which the basic problems of philosophy were engaged: from representations in the mind to linguistic representations (i.e., the propositions of language). The term "proposition" here means a statement that such and such is the case. The opening passages of Wittgenstein's *Tractatus* provide a basic orientation.

1 The world is everything that is the case.
  1.1 The world is the totality of facts, not of things.
    1.11 The world is determined by the facts, and by these being *all* the facts.
    1.12 For the totality of facts determines both what is the case, and also all that is not the case.
    1.13 The facts in logical space are the world.[2]

The alignment between propositions and statements of fact is quite close. The statement "There are storm clouds on the horizon" aligns well with the proposition "It is the case that there are storm clouds on the horizon." This model works well for determining the truth-value of utterances of this empirical sort. "There are storm clouds on the horizon" is true if it is in fact the case that there are storm clouds on the horizon. In the philosophy of logical positivism, such matters would have to be verified empirically. By contrast, analytical propositions, such as those of mathematics, could be deduced from their presuppositions, and could be verified a priori. This model can be adjusted to cover utterances that are neither analytical nor empirically verifiable, such as the ones that apply in fiction, which do not refer to things or states of affairs in the (real) world, but do make sense in relation to entities or states of affairs in fictional worlds. "Emma Bovary is unhappily married to Charles" is true in the fictional world of *Madame Bovary*.

Whether the context is fictional or not, the fundamental effort behind the work of "representation" and "reference" remains constant: to match a scheme or frame of some kind to some particular content. In fact, the ambition was a broader one: to find some *invariant* scheme that could be matched to whatever content might be at issue. This first moment in the linguistic turn in philosophy was thus a transposition of what Kant had attempted to accomplish by identifying basic and invariant categories of the mind that could be matched to any particular experiential content. The ideal was to find a scheme of representations that would make clear its tie to whatever content we might wish to represent.[3]

The notion of "picturing" runs throughout the *Tractatus* as the model for what the basic scheme of representation involves. Wittgenstein wrote that "We make pictures to ourselves of the facts. … The representing relation consists of the coordination of the elements of the picture and the things" (2.1, 2.1514; all references to this work are by section numbers). This is not the work of mental picturing, as it was for Descartes and the empiricists, but of linguistic representation. "Picture" here means "logical picture." In turn, "representation" indicates the structure that the picture shares with what it represents: "The picture has the logical form of representation in common with what it pictures" (2.2). Two additional features are crucial to the construction of this platform. One is that any proposition has one and only one complete analysis (3.25); the second is that every proposition is articulate; it expresses what it does "in a definite and clearly identifiable way" (3.251). The picture may agree with reality or not; it is right or wrong, true or false (2.21). But pictures are value-neutral. Indeed, the value-neutrality of the picture is an inescapable feature of the way in which Wittgenstein understood propositions: "All propositions are of equal value" (6.4); "In the world everything is as it is and happens as it does happen. *In* it there is no value" (6.41; emphasis in original). Accordingly, there are things, such as the will, of which we cannot speak; the will may be of interest to psychology, but not to philosophy (6.423).

Already in the *Tractatus*, Wittgenstein saw his work as delineating meaningful from senseless questions, rather than trying to answer all the inherited questions of philosophy. We can discern the difference between the two by paying attention to the logic of language: "Most propositions and questions, that have been written about philosophical matters, are not false, but senseless. We cannot, therefore, answer questions of this kind at all, but only state their senselessness. Most questions and propositions of the philosophers result from the fact that we do not understand the logic of our language" (4.003). This is very close to what Wittgenstein says in *Philosophical Investigations* – that philosophical problems occur "when language goes on holiday" (19e). *Philosophical Investigations* remains nonetheless committed to the idea that the answers to philosophical questions depend upon the grammar of propositions. "*Essence* is expressed by grammar. … Grammar tells what kind of object anything is" (371, 373, 116e; emphasis in original).

Among the many reasons why the project of *Tractatus* and others like it were bound to fail, one has to do with our experience of certain kinds of theoretical claims over the course of history. "Theories" in this sense are the ways in which phenomena are explained; they often evolve by invoking (new) theoretical entities and abandoning old ones. Just as epistemology has a history (e.g., of the kind outlined by Mary Poovey in *A History of the Modern Fact* and Arnold Davidson in *The Emergence of Sexuality: Historical Epistemology and the Formation of Concepts*) so do theories and theoretical entities in science. The "atoms" in Lucretius's *On the Nature of Things* are not the same as the atoms in modern physics. In the seventeenth century, the theory of phlogiston was invented as a way to explain how things burn; in the eighteenth century, Lavoisier proposed instead that there was a substance of heat called "caloric." Neither of these accounts has any place in what we understand to be the correct explanation of combustion. But with the ongoing correction of scientific understanding there comes a worry. Hilary Putnam presented the worry this way: "What if this keeps happening? What if the theoretical entities postulated by one generation (molecules, genes, etc., as well as electrons) invariably 'don't exist' from the standpoint of later science?" The worry, as he frames it, is that if no term used in the science of fifty years ago (or whatever time) ever "referred," so it is bound to turn out that no term used now "refers" either.[4] One answer is to give up the notion of "reference," which is close kin to the term "representation," and to turn instead to notions that make no claim to be grounded in anything but the ways we speak. This is consistent with Thomas Kuhn's thesis of paradigm shift within the history of science.[5]

**Practice**

"Practice is a set of relays from one theoretical point to another, and theory is a relay from one practice to another. No theory can develop without eventually encountering a wall, and practice is necessary for piercing this wall. … A theory is exactly like a box of tools. It has nothing to do with the signifier. It must be useful. It must function."[6]

Rorty proposes that the solution is to accept the fact that we are constantly producing new descriptions of the world; our effort can only be to (re)describe things in a way that works, not to aspire to find a theory of reference or representation. Wittgenstein's much earlier approach to the problem of representation involved a shift toward the notions of "grammar" and "language games" discussed previously.

These meta-worries may seem troublesome from within disciplines that take the theoretical framework of natural science (rather than the history of the sciences) as normative. They are far less troublesome from within the horizon of literature. That is one reason why literature was regarded as an ally among those thinkers (such as Rorty) who favored abandoning the idea of representations, but also why it was taken as a threat by those who were concerned about the evisceration of the very notion of "truth." Certainly in literature one does not face a set of circumstances in which the work of a later generation "disproves" that of an earlier one. The poetry of Dryden did not render Milton's false or less meaningful, just as Milton did not have such an effect on Shakespeare. These dynamics are better understood in relation to power and to what Harold Bloom called the "anxiety of influence" rather than in relation to enduring conceptions of what is "true" or of what constitutes an accurate representation of anything that is independent of the works themselves. This is one of the many reasons why literary theory has seldom resembled theory in the natural sciences. Attempts to define and defend poetry, from Aristotle to Sidney to the romantics and beyond, have sometimes attempted to say what the "essence" of poetry is; but the awareness that the definition of poetry keeps changing does not threaten to undermine literary theory in the way that the troubling meta-induction about the validity of "theory" in science was regarded as a threat to truth.

Changes between *Tractatus* and *Philosophical Investigations* in what Wittgenstein means by "grammar" helped alleviate the worries that accompany the problems of reference and representation. Perhaps most important is that "grammar" no longer indicates a basic, invariant scheme that accommodates content. Grammar does not try to accomplish what transcendental philosophy could not do (i.e., clarify the constraints that rationality *itself* exerts, and explain why our ideal theories must correspond to reality). Rather, it refers to the web of relations among the things that are spoken within a community of language users. A grammar is the set of rules that language users establish for themselves. The distinction is not between true and false statements but rather between sense and nonsense. To take one of Wittgenstein's examples, we can understand "Bring me milk" and "Bring me sugar," but to say "Milk me sugar" is nonsense (*Philosophical Investigations*, sec. 498, 138e). Here, grammar no longer plays the role of providing the context-independent set of possibilities that underlie truth-claims; it is entirely decoupled from grounding in a "deep structure." With this, there is also a decoupling of the apparent connection between "meaning" and "thinking"; in *Philosophical Investigations*, meaning is no longer a mental activity. Similarly, *Philosophical Investigations* moves decisively away from the idea that language pictures anything, mentally or otherwise. In fact, it is the "picture theory" of language that Wittgenstein famously said "held us captive": "A picture held us captive. And we could not get outside it, because it lay in our language and language seemed to repeat it to us inexorably" (sec. 115, 48e).

Several consequences follow from Wittgenstein's turn away from the picture theory of language. One is that we don't need to make special adaptations of a theory of meaning to cover the "special case" of literature. This is because verification is not at issue in distinguishing between sense and nonsense. Indeed, the entire distinction between "synthetic" (verifiable) and "analytical" truths that was important for logical positivism is no longer of concern. Returning to points made previously, this does not mean *either* that there is no difference between literature and other forms of language *or* that all uses of language are metaphorical. It does, however, mean that we go astray in trying to map the literary meaning of words onto some other, literal meaning, especially if we take the "basic scheme" underlying literal meaning as a representation of the way things "truly are." But it also suggests why it is legitimate to look at literary utterances with some of the same expectations that we bring to ordinary language. Those include the difference between sense and nonsense and between what can and cannot be said, as well as expectations about the criteria implicit in the claims we make.

At various points in *Philosophical Investigations*, Wittgenstein or one of the questioning voices asks about "how we know" something. In these instances, there is typically a consideration of whether are not there are criteria for knowing, and especially criteria of the kind that might either be independent of the circumstances in question or independent of those raising the question. How do I know that in the series of numbers 2, 4, 6, 8, 10, the next is 12? How do

I know that one triangle resembles another in a way that neither resembles a circle? How do I know what a sign means (e.g., an arrow pointing in a particular direction)? Wittgenstein's reader may feel some frustration in all these instances, because he refuses to say what the criteria for knowing are. Better said, perhaps, he allows the reader to experience the desire for criteria, not unlike an itch that wants to be scratched. Wittgenstein's purpose in doing this was twofold. One was to demonstrate that the "itch" for criteria was artificial and contingent; this is the "standard" reading of Wittgenstein, and it is not unfaithful to his purpose. After all, he said that his aim was to show the fly the way out of the fly-bottle (sec. 309, 103e). The second set of purposes was one that Cavell drew out in his engagement with Wittgenstein in *The Claim of Reason*. Cavell's argument there is that searching for independent criteria is a strategy of avoidance. That avoidance is broad-based, and central to it is the avoidance of the responsibility that befalls us as participants in any given language game – that is, in any given set of practices (linguistic and otherwise) that we sustain by mostly tacit agreements.

The appeal to criteria is one way the philosopher attempts to answer questions, respond to doubts, and avert skepticism. Criteria tell us the terms by which we know something. They are integral to matters of judgment, but they are not the same as standards.

> Both criteria and standards are means by which or terms in which a given group judges or selects or assesses value or membership in some special status; but criteria, we might say, determine whether an object is a relevant candidate at all, whereas standards discriminate the degree to which a candidate satisfies those criteria.[7]

Cavell offers the following example: a diving judge who enters a score of 5 out of 10 next to "Water Entry" is not saying that there is a 50 percent chance that the diver satisfied this criterion, but rather is judging how well it was satisfied. Judgments about "standards" can only apply once a more basic criterion is met (e.g., that this is a water entry). In Wittgenstein's exploration of questions about criteria there is never a moment in which an appeal is made to standards. Everything depends upon criteria, and yet criteria do not lie outside the language games that depend upon them.

> It is [for Wittgenstein] always *we* who "establish" the criteria under investigation. The criteria Wittgenstein appeals to … are always "ours," the "group" which forms his "authority" is always, apparently, the human group as such, the human being generally. When I voice them, I do so, or take myself to do so, as a member of that group, a representative human" (*Claim*, 18; emphasis in original).

As Cavell goes on to say in continuing this line of thought, claims to criteria are claims to community, "and the claim to community is always a search for the basis on which it can or has been established. … The wish and search for community are the wish and search for reason" (20).

## Performatives, Performances

The second set of pathways marked by the linguistic turn in philosophy is anchored in the work of J. L. Austin on "speech acts." This work intersects with that of Wittgenstein and Cavell at various junctures. For instance, Cavell's notion of a "claim," and his account of the process of establishing criteria involve something considerably more active than what is usually understood in the notion of a philosophical "claim" – something which at times verges on a performative action.

Austin's interest in "performative utterances" and "speech acts" originates in a very basic intuition: that many types of language are not propositional at all. In concentrating almost wholly on propositions, philosophy had been missing a large swath of language. Some of its fundamental assumptions were at best incomplete, and at worst entirely wrong. The opening pages of *How to Do Things with Words* are as instructive as anything one might possibly read on the subject: "It was for too long the assumption of philosophers that the business of a 'statement' can only be to 'describe' some state of affairs, or to 'state some fact,' which it must do either truly or falsely."[8] There are many utterances that neither describe nor report, hence are not true or false. In some instances, "the uttering of a sentence is, or is a part of, the doing of an action, which again would not *normally* be described as, or as 'just,' saying something" (5; emphasis in original). Some of Austin's examples were perfectly ordinary and have since become notorious: "'I do' (take this woman to be my lawful wedded wife)," said in the context of a marriage ceremony; "I name this ship the *Queen Elizabeth*" spoken while smashing a bottle against the bow; "I give and bequeath my watch to my brother" (5).

Austin goes on to describe the conventions and contexts that need to be in place in order for these utterances to be effective (felicitous). There are many opportunities for misfires and infelicities, where "infelicities" are situations in which the conditions for the performance are not fulfilled. I can walk up to a ship up on the stocks (Austin's example), smash a bottle against its bow, and say "I name this ship the *Mr. Stalin*" (23), but if I am not the one appointed to do the naming, this will be ineffective, or worse. The contrast Austin draws is with "constative utterances," which can be judged true or false according to some set of criteria or norms ("constative" is Austin's word for "descriptive"). Once we accept the idea that things *can* be done with words, however, we have to reckon with the fact that language seems to behave uniquely in literary contexts. If two characters in a play exchange marriage vows, we understand that they are not married once they walk off the stage (indeed, that they are not "really" married onstage either). We either have to say that "special conditions" apply, or that the conditions for a felicitous (effective) speech act do not apply. The situation with performative utterances in literary contexts parallels the situation with reference in literary contexts, and with the question of metaphorical versus literal meaning, or meaning in "serious" versus "non-serious" contexts. If I say, "Her face froze over," we understand that the meaning is metaphorical. Likewise, we understand that statements about Lilliput refer, but do so only in the context of Swift's fictional world. A considerable amount of work has been devoted to specifying the particular conditions that must (or must not) apply in such instances, and likewise to specifying the particular nature of the intentions that must accompany such locutions. Austin further parses the difference between "locutionary acts," "illocutionary acts," and "perlocutionary acts." These fed the development of a "speech act theory" of literary discourse and fueled many debates about the differences between literary and non-literary meaning. Not surprisingly, none of these debates was ever "resolved," not least because the questions they raised were not resolvable.

For Austin, literary meaning is regarded as dependent upon (sometimes said to be "parasitic upon") non-literary meaning. In debates with John Searle over Austin's theory, however, Derrida pointed out that the very idea of "non-literary" meaning, or of words used "seriously," depends upon a correspondence between a psychic structure (a speaker's intention) and what is said. Henry Staten elegantly summarized the key assumptions underlying "literal meaning" and "serious speech" as follows: "The telos of serious, literal speech is the ideal of perfect correspondence between mental act and linguistic formula, in which logos as speech act gives the true form of logos as psychic act."[9] But it is not at all clear how this correspondence might be established. Derrida remarked that "No criterion that is simply *inherent* in the manifest utterance is capable of distinguishing an utterance when it is serious from the same utterance when it is not."[10] The notions of "seriousness" and "literal meaning" depend upon a mental form that is inscrutable and to which the ideal of a perfect correspondence is impossible to achieve, if not unimaginable.

None of the local issues that arose in the many debates surrounding these questions was as important as their overarching consequences. These point in two directions. The first has to do with what may seem to be the surprising fact that speech acts carry with them a set of commitments: they have a moral force which from which it may not be possible to break free. Austin cites the line from *Hippolytus* at the very beginning of *How to Do Things with Words*: "my tongue swore to, but my heart (or mind, or other backstage artiste) did not" (9–10). His claim is that there are no alibis in the case of promising or vowing: "Accuracy and morality alike are on the side of the plain saying: *our word is our bond*" (10; emphasis in original). As with promising, so too with other speech acts. It is appropriate that the person uttering the promise should have a certain intention (e.g., to keep his word); otherwise, we would speak of a "false promise," or of a promise made in bad faith. But we are (morally) bound by our words nonetheless. Indeed, there are consequences that follow from what we say that are not dictated by our intentions at all, and from which we cannot simply exempt ourselves by some private mental gesture.

The second set of consequences revolves more broadly around the insight that the role of language is not just to mirror the world, but to shape it. Alongside this insight stands another one: that we constitute ourselves through language and thorough other discursive practices for which language is emblematic. Both these insights have contributed to a broad-gauge reassessment of the boundaries between nature and convention and to an expansion of the notions of "performance" and "performativity" beyond language in the narrow sense. "Self-constitution" is something that Cavell argued is implicit in the Cartesian *cogito* even though it has gone largely suppressed. The *cogito* is in one sense a performative act. It demands an alignment between saying and being, not just between thinking and being. This is true more broadly for questions of personal identity and communication because the "agreements" that underlie our various language games are held in place not in spite of us but because (and as) we enact them.

## Self-Assertion, Self-Reliance, and the Cogito

Descartes states the *cogito* several times: in *Discourse on the Method*, in *Principles of Philosophy*, and in *Meditations*. There, he writes: "After considering everything very thoroughly, I must finally conclude that this proposition, *I am, I exist*, is necessarily true whenever it is put forward [i.e. spoken] by me or conceived in my mind" (17).

Emerson echoes this in his essay "Self-Reliance": "Man is timid and apologetic, he is no longer upright; he dares not say 'I think,' 'I am,' but quotes some saint or sage."[11] Stanley Cavell in turn reads Emerson as drawing us toward the need for acknowledgment rather than a reliance on truths established generally: "One can describe Emerson's progress as his having posed Descartes's question for himself and provided a fresh line of answer, one you might call a grammatical answer: I am a being who to exist must say I exist, or must acknowledge my existence – claim it, stake it, enact it."[12] Yet Emerson is more complex still, for in "Nature," he also claims to be the ultimate omniscient observer, a "transparent eyeball": "I am nothing; I see all" (*Essays and Lectures*, 10).

To speak of the self or of personal identity in terms of "performance" is not to suggest that it can be any way we might wish. But the alternative is not to commit ourselves to the notion of an ideal identity, fixed and unchanging, common to all human beings, that persists over time. Take the case of gender identity as an example. There is gender and there is sex. We can think of the one (gender) as conventional and the other (sex) natural, as long as we are careful not to think of the conventional as the necessary expression of a natural essence. This is the point Judith Butler made in *Gender Trouble*: "Because there is neither an 'essence' that gender expresses or externalizes nor an objective ideal to which gender aspires, and because gender is not a fact, the various acts of gender create the idea of gender, and without those acts, there would be no gender at all."[13] The various "acts" referred to here include the elements that comprise the performance of gender identity. The difference between expression and performance is crucial:

> gender is an identity tenuously constituted in time, instituted in an exterior space through a *stylized repetition of acts*. … If gender attributes, however, are not expressive but performative, then these attributes effectively constitute the identity they are said to express or reveal. The distinction between expression and performativeness is crucial. If gender attributes and acts, the various ways in which a body shows or produces its cultural signification, are performative, then there is no preexisting identity by which an act or attribute might be measured … and the postulation of a true gender identity would be revealed as a regulatory fiction. That gender reality is created through sustained social performances means that the very notion of an essential sex and a true or abiding masculinity or femininity are also constituted as part of the strategy that conceals gender's performative character. (140–141; emphasis in original)

This position is consistent with the broadly Foucaultian background that Ian Hacking brings to his work on "historical ontology," and which is in turn indebted to the Nietzschean view that the self is not something essential and abiding, but is in fact *fashioned*. Alexander Nehamas was one of the first to draw attention to this dimension of Nietzsche's thought, by way of a set of contrasts with ideas commonly attributed to Freud: "the vulgar Freudian idea that the core of one's self is always there, formed to a great extent early on in life, and waiting for some sort of liberation is incompatible both with Nietzsche's view that the self is a fiction and with his general denial of the idea of a reality that underlies appearance."[14]

Among the elements that help hold the idea of a "core" identity or underlying essence in place are some of the strongest associations binding language and metaphysics together. One of Nietzsche's modern interpreters, Michel Haar, signals the extent to which certain long-held views about language work in concert with metaphysical beliefs about subjectivity and personal identity:

> [A]ll psychological categories (the ego, the individual, the person) derive from the illusion of substantial identity. But this illusion goes back basically to a superstition that deceived not only common sense but also philosophers – namely, the belief in language and, more precisely, in the truth of grammatical categories. It was grammar (the structure of subject and predicate) that inspired Descartes' certainty that "I" is the subject of "think," whereas it is rather that thoughts come to "me."[15]

The privileging of "literal" over "metaphorical" usage, or of "serious" over "non-serious" utterances that we find in Austin and Searle amounts to a protection of identity as self-sameness against the perceived threat that identity would be permanently undermined by the view that language is at bottom performative, decoupled from an underlying substance or mental/psychic essence.

With this we can return to Wittgenstein's critique of the "inner act of meaning" in *Philosophical Investigations*. To say that there is no underlying, internal mental content that language expresses points to the fact that propositions about identity are not so much wrong as useless. "We seem to have an infallible paradigm of identity in the identity of a thing with itself. … Then how are two things the same when they are what *one* thing is? And how am I to apply what the *one* thing shews me to the case of two things?" (sec. 215, 84e; emphasis in original). "'A thing is identical with itself.' There is no finer example of a useless proposition" (sec. 216, 84e). Wittgenstein's point is to illustrate how deeply we are attached to such "useless" propositions. His aim was to find a different way of putting these problems, and by so doing to help us get free from the artificial puzzles they create. This is consistent with the idea that philosophy causes the problems for which it proposes itself as the cure. What we have instead of "inner meaning" and "mental content" are language games and forms of life, both of which are practices that involve rule-following behavior. We must allow for the rules to determine some things, or they would not be rules at all; similarly, forms must establish boundaries of some sort. Games, including language games, have bounds. But these need not be determinative. We determine them as much as we are determined by them. Staten comments that "we learn to follow it, obey it, or manipulate it, and yet the rule itself is structurally or essentially indeterminate" (134). Language games and forms of life are always under construction. The conclusion to be reached from a Wittgensteinian vantage point is that neither forms of life nor language games have a self-identical and unitary form, and neither do we.

## Suggestions for Further Reading

Charles Altieri, *Act and Quality* (Amherst: University of Massachusetts Press, 1981).

Isaiah Berlin, *Concepts and Categories* (Princeton, NJ: Princeton University Press, 1999).

Arnold Davidson, *The Emergence of Sexuality: Historical Epistemology and the Formation of Concepts* (Cambridge, MA: Harvard University Press, 2004).

Martin Heidegger, *On the Essence of Language*, trans. Wanda Torres Gregory and Yvonne Unna (Albany: SUNY Press, 2004).

*On the Way to Language*, trans. Peter D. Hertz (New York: Harper and Row, 1971).

Peter Lassman, *Pluralism* (Cambridge: Polity Press, 2011).

J. Hillis Miller, *Speech Acts in Literature* (Stanford, CA: Stanford University Press, 2001).

Mary Poovey, *A History of the Modern Fact* (Chicago: University of Chicago Press, 1998).

Mary Louise Pratt, *Toward a Speech Act Theory of Literary Discourse* (Bloomington: Indiana University Press, 1977).

Richard Rorty, ed., *The Linguistic Turn* (Chicago: University of Chicago Press, 1992).

John Searle, *Speech Acts* (Cambridge: Cambridge University Press, 1969).

Chapter 11

# Form, Narrative, Novel

In this chapter, I turn to the place of narrative in the relations between "deep" and "surface" structures. Our working hypothesis will be a strong one: that narrative is not just a form that is laid over neutral content, but is itself both an epistemological category and an ethical/moral one. It orders knowledge and value according to the elements of time and action that are basic to experience itself. Proponents of the strong view of narrative would say that narrative is basic to questions of truth and value because cognition and morality are themselves narratively structured. On this view, the Kantian categories of space and time are not sufficient to capture what is fundamental about experience because they leave narrative out.

There would be little reason to think of narrative as integral to questions of truth and value if one were to believe, as a philosopher like Kant did, that pure reason determines what we know and that morality is a matter of obedience and respect toward a categorical imperative. Indeed, Kant found narrative a useful but insufficient way to fathom the idea of human progress toward the good. Kant took up the question in the essays "An Old Question Raised Again: Is the Human Race Constantly Progressing?" and "Idea for a Universal History," and his review of Herder's *Ideas for a Philosophy of History of Mankind*. In these writings, Kant drew on the story-like form of history in order to explain how we could discern the shape of human history as a whole without in fact being able to see the end of it. His reasoning was formal rather than grounded in evidence drawn from particular moments in society or other empirical sources. Kant wished to assert that human history has a purpose and a goal (teleology) that lead toward the good. Though we cannot know with absolute certainty where we stand with respect to progress, we can nonetheless posit it as a complete narrative, and we can place ourselves in relation to it as we might in relation to some "as if" story. We are "inside" the story of progress, although we also need to stand "outside" in order to grasp it as a whole. To do that, however, we need to adopt the stance of spectators of history ("sympathetic spectators," to be precise); in Kant's view, this in turn ensures that we will have the right role in the course of progress. We will see later in this chapter that the difficulty of aligning two such positions is the basis for a fundamental irony when it comes to narrative form.

Kant recognized that temporality was central to knowledge, representation, and experience. We can think of an experience as a moment within time, but these moments have a continuity over time. Kant did not think about narrative as the way to give form to experience by binding these moments together. Thinking about narrative is nonetheless crucial if one wishes to capture such things as the emerging nature of truth in experience, the development and transformation of moral consciousness, or what it means to consider life as a whole. J. David Velleman explains that whereas the principle of intelligibility in natural phenomena is called a "law," the principle of intelligibility in a narrative is called the "plot." It stands in very close relation to the principle of intelligibility that can be invoked for human action, which has been called a "rationale."[1] Narratives render events intelligible by linking beginnings to ends. In an essay entitled "History and Fiction as Modes of Comprehension," Louis Mink described this aspect of narrative as a kind of "grasping together," "a characteristic kind of understanding which consists in thinking together in a single act … the complicated relationships of parts which can be experienced only *seriatim*."[2] Though Mink was writing about history, what he says applies to fiction just as well: when history is presented as a coherent narrative "actions and events, although represented as occurring in the *order of time*, can be surveyed as it were in a single glance as bound together in an *order of significance*" (*Historical Understanding*, 56; my emphasis). Mink's conception of narrative implies a kind of grasping together.[3] As a "principle of intelligibility," this grasping together is not an act of synthesis as it was in Kant's theory of cognition. Rather, it is a principle of intelligibility that allows us to make sense of events and of ourselves.

It was Hegel who went beyond Kant's ideas most emphatically in this regard, and it was he who played a decisive role in replacing the Kantian view of truth and morality with something more responsive to the evolving nature of human consciousness and thus more akin to narrative. "Consciousness" for Hegel includes the experience of repeatedly discovering that the world is different from the way we thought it to be. There is an element of repetition involved in this process, but there is also transformation. Hegel's *Phenomenology of Spirit* is built on the awareness that there is a basic incongruity between things as they are "for consciousness" and things as they are "in themselves." However, Hegel proposed that there was not a simple gap between them that needs to be spanned, but rather a developing relationship of insight and disillusionment, of fulfillment and desire, of connection, refusal, and continuity, all of which together have a story-like form. "Truth" is something that can't adequately be captured in the static form of the "in-itself," as it was for Kant, because it has a temporal dimension; a truth is first grasped, then recognized as inadequate, and then replaced by a new and richer one. This process involves the activity of "overcoming" (*Aufhebung* or "sublation") where recognition of the inadequacy of one stance or "moment" enables the advancement to a higher one. Hegel explains the process by means of an organic metaphor that itself suggests a story: "The bud disappears in the bursting forth of the blossom, and one might say that the former is refuted by the latter; similarly, when the fruit appears, the blossom is shown up in turn as a false manifestation of the plant, and the fruit emerges as the truth of it itself."[4]

One could well protest that the terms "true" and "false" are strained in the work they are asked to do here. We might do better to think in terms of the relationship between parts and wholes: each "moment" is true, but in a partial way. In terms of the example given, this would imply that only something like the story of the plant as a whole could encompass what is fully true about it, including the relationship of each of its manifestations to one another. Hegel himself addressed this issue by proposing a radical notion of the whole ("the True is the whole"[5]). In the words of one recent commentator, it is "the whole of the coherent, completed system, projected back retrospectively from the end of absolute knowledge onto the path of phenomenal consciousness, the path of doubt and despair in which one truth replaces another in seemingly unending contingency."[6] Kant had posited time as a basic category of the mind. Heidegger established temporality as basic to *Dasein* (being in the world). But Hegel had already established a narratology that goes beyond lived time.

And yet the Hegelian idea of the totality also introduces something more than a narratology requires. It does more than say that consciousness, whether in the work of knowing (truth) or in the work of valuing (morality), or in its collective historical manifestations, has a story-like form, where time and action give shape to events. Rather, it says that the highest form of consciousness (Spirit as "Absolute Knowing") is an integrated whole configured in such a way that the end is implicit in the beginning, the beginning in the end, and that every part along the way likewise is not just a "piece" of a larger whole, but is itself a moment that only makes sense because the whole is also within it. We could not be farther from the fragment or from fragmentary forms like the essay, the aphorism, or the proverb. When we read an aphorism, we have no expectation that it is an integral part of a system of aphorisms or that it contains the germ of all wisdom. Similarly with a proverb. On the contrary, we know that these will have to be understood – and understood oftentimes quite differently – in relation to particular circumstances that will themselves always be changing (see text box).

**Hegelian Aphorisms**

It might seem surprising to find aphorisms in Hegel's writings. After all, he insisted that one could not say anything about philosophy in a single statement. And if he believed that truth is a whole that unfolds in a dialectical fashion, then why would he avail himself of a form that attempts to capture truth in an especially succinct and concise way? And yet, Hegel does make ample use of aphorisms. Some examples: "The Owl of Minerva spreads its wings only at dusk"; "It is as absurd to fancy that a philosophy can transcend its contemporary world as it is to fancy that an individual can overleap his own age, jump over Rhodes"; "What is rational is actual and what is actual is rational"[7]; "The True is thus the Bacchanalian revel in which no member is not drunk" (*Phenomenology*, sec. 47).

Why does Hegel do this? Two reasons have been suggested. One is that he wanted philosophy to operate in a language that was close to that of the times in which it was written, and not depend on a special, technical idiom. The second is that many of these aphorisms, while true, are comprised of elements that seem to contradict one another. Their role is to impel us to see that philosophy cannot in fact be contained in single statements but requires the unfolding of the dialectic.[8]

Despite its ambitions and its problems, the Hegelian totality as construed in *Phenomenology* makes it clear that there is one overarching "subject" of narrative, and that is human consciousness writ large. In this narrative, the work of knowing and the work of valuing are both *by* and *about* that subject. Kant said that we can know only what can conform to the categories of consciousness, that we can know only what we make. This is the sense of the phrase "the productivity of spirit," which we will discuss later in relation to the novel. To speak about the "productivity of the spirit" is to acknowledge that forms are not given, but that we are the creators of form. While *Phenomenology* is wholly consistent with this notion, Hegel proposes a system that is ultimately more encompassing than what narrative either offers or requires in this regard. Its limitations are directly related to its ambitions. Because Absolute Knowing is *absolute*, there is no clear first point of entry into it; Hegel imagines a beginning for consciousness in sense-certainty, but that is at some level a fiction. And because Spirit is a totality, transformations are always transformations within it, as in the example of the plant.

Consider the very different approach proposed for the case of narrative in moral philosophy by MacIntyre. When MacIntyre spoke of "the narrative unity of a life," he put a narrative spin on an expression of Wilhelm Dilthey's (*Zusammenhang des Lebens*, the connectedness of a life). An individual life is situated within a larger social context, and so too the meaning and unity of that life. MacIntyre likewise argued that moral practice and moral philosophy are both inextricable from social contexts. Even more important, he proposed that every moral philosophy presupposes a sociology. "Presupposes" is the active term here. MacIntyre did not say that moral philosophy is influenced by society, or that social behavior can be directed by moral philosophy. He said that a moral philosophy is unthinkable outside of some particular set of social contexts, roles, and circumstances. To illustrate how and why this happens, MacIntyre had recourse to the notions of narrative and of "character." As noted in Part I, a character is an agent who embodies the most significant moral views of a society in his or her action and attitudes.

In the particular area of MacIntyre's interest within moral philosophy – the virtues – his framework was both narrative and historical. His aim was to understand two intertwined questions: (1) what had become of the virtues since Aristotle, both in thought and in practice, and (2) what had become of society since the heroic age, where epic poetry was a primary vehicle for representing and transmitting the virtues. In the epic world, heroes served as exemplars of the virtues. The virtues had to be presented narratively because virtue implies action, not just the possession of a character trait. Because MacIntyre argued that virtue, character, and action were intimately connected (as they were for Aristotle), he also argued that that moral philosophy and narrative were inseparable.

Others, including Paul Ricoeur, have offered similarly narrative views of character, although without quite the level of emphasis on social context that MacIntyre introduced. For Ricoeur, character is a feature of personal identity; it is both "descriptive and emblematic."[9] At one level it describes a set of traits that remain associated with one's qualitative identity rather than with one's mere self-sameness or *numerical* identity. But because character describes the continuity or permanence of those traits over time, and because it describes the individual as an agent, it requires that we understand it in narrative terms. Aristotle, for instance, spoke of justice as "that kind of state of character [*hexis*] which makes people disposed to do [*praktikoi*] what is just and makes them act justly and wish for what is just."[10] We can think of character in relation to personal identity as designating the "who" of action. The question "Who am I, actually?" needs to be answered narratively because we need to "fill in" what Ricoeur called the "gap of sense" between the discrete moments of our identity that would otherwise be left empty across time. Some dimension of character may be thought of as "given," which is why it is sometimes said, following Heraclitus, that "character is fate." But, as Ricoeur argues, only a being that is free to act can have a fate:

> Only a freedom is or has a fate. This simple remark restores to the determinations put forward by characterology the equivocalness that makes it partake simultaneously of two orders, that of objectivity and that of existence. A portrait painted from the outside? But also a manner of being that is one's own. (*Oneself as Another*, 119).

Character also involves action and consent, including consent to what we do and who we are.

We can thus think of narrative in relation to character not just as "framing" personal identity but as offering solutions to some of the basic questions posed by human life. These include questions of the kind that Aristotle addressed across *Poetics* and *Nicomachean Ethics*: can we give sense to the unity of life and to the nature of morality by linking actions through beginnings, middles, and ends? As noted in Part I, Aristotle regarded tragedy not as the imitation of *an action* but as the imitation of *men in action* (see text box). The structure of plot (*mythos*), which is narrative in form even when it is dramatic in presentation, is basic to character insofar as stories are "about" persons who act. But it is more than that insofar as it structures and shapes a response to the question about *how* to act and determines the *meaning* of action beyond what is true or false about it.

**Mimesis and Completeness**

Aristotle says of the imitation of action in tragedy that it must be whole and complete. Plots are to have beginnings, middles, and ends. This can be taken to parodic extremes. Consider the hyper completeness suggested by Italo Calvino's "Meiosis," which proposes to begin from the "absolute" beginning:

> Narrating things as they are means narrating them from the beginning, and even if I start the story at a point where the characters are multicellular organisms, for example the story of my relationship with Priscilla, I have first to define clearly what I mean when I say me and what I mean when I say Priscilla, then I can go on to establish what this relationship was. … Narrating the story of me and Priscilla means first of all defining the relations established between my proteins and Priscilla's proteins, commanded, both mine and hers, by chains of nucleic acids.[11]

The idea that narrative helps answer basic questions about human existence and/in the world is already evident from the work of myth. Persons are not just entities knit together of a body and a mind. They have lives, and that means they are narrative creatures. Richard Eldridge frames the matter this way:

> Persons are not, it seems, "just" real material entities. … They lead lives out of ongoing narratives, make choices out of them. These narratives

> and the lives and choices that they shape are in turn structured by assumptions about narrative unity, coherence, and closure that are tested in narrative writing in general, and in particular in fiction, where the influence of contingencies can yield to the imperative to achieve coherence. ... Literary narratives come from our expressive acts and their narrative backgrounds; the narrative backgrounds of our acts are structured by assumptions that literary narratives help make manifest. It seems that literary narratives and personhood are, one might say, internal to one another.[12]

The novel exemplifies the challenges we face in needing to make whole and meaningful forms where these are not available in advance or guaranteed. It helps "solve" the problem of binding beginnings and endings together under conditions where we have no direct access to any "ultimate" sources of truth or value, much less to the totality of experience, but have to establish those for ourselves. In the modern world, that task falls largely to the novel, although with the caveat that the novel is not a form in which meaning is ready-made. These are matters of form, not theme. To give an example, Fernando Pessoa thematizes the predicament of the problematic individual at the very beginning of *A Book of Disquiet*: "these random impressions, and with no desire to be other than random, I indifferently narrate my factless autobiography, my lifeless history. These are my Confessions, and if in them I say nothing, it's because I have nothing to say."[13] If this were a novel, its task would be to find some way to bind these "random impressions" together. But this is rather a book of fragments – *not* a novel, in part because it does not have a narrative form. But even within narrative works, we need to be careful to distinguish between what it means to grapple with "existential" questions at the thematic level, and what it means to address those formally. Many of D. H. Lawrence's characters address questions about the meaning of love and death quite explicitly. In some instances, these moral difficulties are posed internally, as questions requiring self-interpretation by the characters themselves.

Beyond such moments of moral doubt is the problem of form in the novel itself: of how to lend experience meaning and unity without turning it into what Jay Bernstein aptly described as "a merely pedagogic or illustrative function."[14]

## Novels and Narrative Form

In *The Theory of the Novel*, Lukács famously said that the novel was what had become of epic literature, characteristic of "whole" societies, in an age that had been "abandoned by god."[15] In this (modern) age, truth comes under the pressure of skepticism and the demand for empirical proof; virtue and value become susceptible to the contingencies of time and place; and the hope for resolving any of these questions can at best aspire to a standpoint of omniscience that is itself a device of fiction. It must ultimately be ironic. (I will return to this question in the conclusion of this chapter.) Regardless of whether novels self-consciously acknowledge these things and display that awareness or not, the fact remains that novels are at liberty to respond either with optimism at the human freedom that these conditions imply, or with despair at the prospect of never getting things right. Whether optimistic or pessimistic, the novel transposes these problems into questions of narrative form.

*The Theory of the Novel* speaks of the epic as a form of narrative that corresponds to what Lukács nostalgically viewed as the "wholeness" of the ancient world; the novel, by contrast, is a form of narrative that corresponds to the world in which we are ourselves responsible for the production of forms by virtue of the "productivity of the spirit." This phrase means that we, and not God, are the source of forms, including the forms of consciousness (space and time), the faculties that Kant called reason (truth) and the understanding (freedom), and that we are in addition responsible for binding moments of experience together. Unlike the parable or allegory, the meaning of events in the novel cannot be derived from unchanging models or paradigms. Nor can we step outside time, even provisionally, to see things as a whole, as Kant's essays on history suggested. The novel deals with time in a way that is much closer to Heidegger's account of temporality in *Being and Time*, where the task of establishing meaning for Being can only be accomplished within the horizon of time. This includes our relationship to the world (including the "everyday"), to our own ultimate end (death), and to the potential for Being as a whole, which we cannot readily see.[16] Time in the novel is governed by the connections among series of events in search of a meaning as a way to address the problem of the wholeness and meaning of a life.

To reinforce the points we have been making, here is Lukács writing in *The Theory of the Novel* about the challenge of producing whole forms in the "disenchanted" world:

> The composition of the novel is the paradoxical fusion of heterogeneous and discrete components into an organic whole. … The relationships which create cohesion between the abstract components are abstractly pure and formal, and the ultimate unifying ground there has to be the ethic of creative subjectivity. (*TN*, 84)

What Lukács calls the "ethic of creative subjectivity" is his way of articulating a number of common beliefs about the power of individuals in the modern world to carry out the projects of synthesis, invention, and the like, which are required if we are to fashion narratives of self-understanding for ourselves.

This does not yet say how the world came to be "godless" in the first place, nor does it ask how the ethic of "creative subjectivity" can respond to these circumstances. Additional resources are needed before we can address those questions. They include the notions of alienation, reification, and the commodity, all drawn from Marx, that Lukács outlined in *History and Class Consciousness* as part of his analysis of history under capitalism. Recognizing these conditions in the way Lukács does presents a very different picture than the one we might derive from Hegel. Hegel also recognizes "alienation," though as part of a theodicy where it is both a dialectical necessity and a moment that is overcome. Hegel's account begins from the idea that God must exist not just in Himself, but as other than Himself (i.e., as the human world). This "alienation" is overcome in the achievement of Absolute Knowing, as Absolute Spirit.

"Alienation" says that under the conditions of capitalism human beings are separated (alienated) from the products of their labor. Moreover, their own labor power no longer belongs wholly to them. "Reification" describes the condition in which the relations among human beings acquire a thing-like form. "Commodity" describes the ghostly form that objects take on under conditions of capitalist exchange and production. These factors conspire to set a horizon for consciousness that cannot possibly realize the full potential of experience. Some thinkers have described these conditions as "anti-narrative," but we have to be careful not to take that term more literally than is intended. There are of course narratives in the modern world, but they are specifically novelistic narratives, not epic ones. The "anti-narrative" narratives that we sometimes call novels reflect the fact that heroic action is fraught, if not impossible; they frequently shift focus from actions involving characters to the discourse of the narrator (drawing us to look "at" rather than "through" form); and they offer expansive explorations of inward consciousness (emphatically so in novels built around "stream of consciousness") while also making references to external events that respond to a very different sense of what is important in time and history.

Two examples can help demonstrate what these matters mean for novelistic form in more concrete terms: first, the ironization of heroism and authority in *Don Quixote*; second, the problem of linking verbal styles and images to narrative in the realist novel, where the inherent meaning and of things is not available in spite of the fact that they may be described in great detail.

Every reader of Cervantes knows that the figure of Don Quixote is a parody of the knights-errant of the books of chivalry. What may be less apparent is that the relationship between the main character and the narrator is ironic. This is so for two very different but equally important reasons. One is that the narrator treats the protagonist far more seriously than one might expect, leaving it for the reader to conclude that the actions of the faux knight are foolish and hence to conclude that the narrator's words must be taken ironically. Second, the narrator ironizes his own authority – and in the end not just his own authority, but the very sources of authority on which a "true account" of the story of Don Quixote might be based:

> Some claim his family name was Quixada, or Quexada, for there is a certain amount of disagreement among the authors who write of this matter, although reliable conjecture seems to indicate that his name was Quexana. But this does not matter very much to our story; in its telling there is absolutely no deviation from the truth.[17]

Don Quixote proceeds from one adventure to the next, but that narrative is ironized; consequently, we have no reason to believe that it conforms to the essential nature of events. Quite the contrary: we are quite aware that this is simply the form they have been given in the novel. If one of the principal "themes" of *Don Quixote* is the difference between reality and illusion, then the fundamental irony of its form means that that matter cannot be so easily resolved, and certainly not resolved by an appeal to "what we all know" to be true and obvious things.

Second, consider the problem of coherence in the representation of objects by images in the realist novel and beyond. Realism is a historically specific enterprise, the work of novelists who are inevitably aware that realism is a product of conventions. In literature, any "picture" of the real is fashioned out of elements such as narrative voice, point of view, and other generic conventions (including certain kinds of description), as well as details presented as facts and direct truth-claims. It is more than "objectivity," although objects are certainly important to it. Realism is an effect, a quality, not a category of thought. The literary sense of the real is a function of what Roland Barthes called "reality effects."[18] This is a way of lending a roundedness to representations by adding many minute details, some of them seemingly insignificant, but which serve nonetheless to "fill in" representations of reality and to do so with a measure of exactitude that in turn suggests the superabundance of the real itself. They impart a sense (an "effect") of the real to any scene in which they appear. Describing the room occupied by the character Mme. Aubain in "A Simple Heart," for instance, Flaubert writes of "an old piano supported, beneath a barometer, a pyramidal stack of boxes and cartons."[19] These might seem to be trivial details, but they are crucial to the fullness we associate with the quality of the real. Likewise, the food carts and fish stalls that Zola describes at the beginning of *The Belly of Paris* are important collectively rather than individually. Description is one of the most powerful ways to portray the "roundedness" of experience; Lukács identified it as a crucial element of the historical novel. However, it is at bottom just as problematic as the task of finding narrative coherence for the self. What Henry James described as the "passion for things" in Balzac[20] mirrors larger concerns about death and life. As one recent critic remarked, by asking how literature represents objects we learn something about "the way objects and subjects animate one another;"[21] but we also learn about the places where they share a similar sense of vacancy and confront similar problems of coherence.

Consider Balzac's description of the objects gathered in the curiosity shop near the beginning of *The Wild Ass's Skin*.

> Instruments of death, poniards, quaint pistols, weapons with secret springs were hobnobbing with instruments of life: porcelain soup-tureens, Dresden china plates, translucent porcelain cups from China, antique salt-cellars, comfit-dishes from feudal times. An ivory ship was sailing under full canvas on the back of an immovable tortoise. A pneumatic machine was poking out the eye of the Emperor Augustus, who remained majestic and unmoved. Several portraits of French aldermen and Dutch burgomasters, insensible now as during their lifetime, rose above this chaos of antiques and cast a cold and disapproving glance at them. (34)

This particular passage is illustrative because its "objectivity" incorporates a superabundance of seemingly insignificant details. This "superabundance" goes beyond what objectivity requires and perhaps even beyond what "realism" needs: it suggests a desire for plenitude and order that objects seem unable to fulfill, no matter how abundant they may be. What lends these things coherence? What makes them hang together? In this example it is simply the fact that they all happen to be in an antiquities shop, where they rest as historical remnants of disconnected pasts. There is no greater logic to their coherence, which in turn means that they are brought together by virtue of the power of form and style that the novelist imparts to them.

This set of issues becomes still more visible in Flaubert, who famously expressed a wish to write a "book about nothing." In Flaubert, things hang together *principally* by virtue of style and form. Moreover, there is a diversity of styles in Flaubert, which Roland Barthes aptly described as a play of "codes" of language. Flaubert keeps various codes always in play, so that "one never knows if he is responsible for what he writes (if there is a subject behind his language); for the very being of writing … is to keep the question 'Who is speaking?' from ever being answered."[22] In *The temptation of St. Anthony*, for example, the fundamental problem is how to link together the images that the saint conjures up in his mind. The problem was not how to select them or how to explain their content. They are, after all, "visions" of the saint, not objects. And as one critic aptly said, "their meaning derives from their juxtaposition alone."[23]

These matters have consequences for what Lukács called the ethic of "creative subjectivity." "Creative" here does not imply that subjectivity can be made up in any way one might wish. Rather, it implies an obligation – that subjectivity must be created and that one cannot be wholly original in doing so. Don Quixote models himself on the heroes of the romances of chivalry. Madame Bovary is a "female Quixote." It might well seem that Don Quixote could construct a meaningful narrative for himself by moving from adventure to adventure, all the while reframing his failures so that the way to the next adventure remains open. Likewise, it might seem that all Saint Anthony needs to do is to provide the framework of consciousness and imagination for the series of visions he has. I have already said that these projects are ironized by their narrators or authors. Looking at things from the author's side, however, where coherence and form are no less at stake, it means that the "true," extra-narrative subject is part of a dyad, of which the fictional subject is the essential counterpart. This is implicit in Flaubert's claim that "Madame Bovary is myself" ("Madame Bovary, c'est moi").[24] Likewise, it is implicit in the sly autobiographical references that Cervantes incorporates into his novel. Both are fundamentally different from what Montaigne meant in one of the most famous passages of his *Essays* ("I am the matter of my book").[25] The essays are not narrative, and so address the problem of form in a very different way from what we have seen here; and while Montaigne may be ironic from moment to moment, the overarching stance of the subject of his *Essays* does not depend upon irony. As we shall see, Montaigne cultivates a remarkably fluid sense of self.

Consider along these same lines the narrative project of Rousseau's *Confessions*. There is certainly as close a relationship between author and book in Rousseau as there is in Montaigne, and yet *Confessions* adheres to the form of autobiographical narrative that has been associated with that genre ever since the *Confessions* of St. Augustine. Rousseau writes that "the true object of my confessions is to reveal my inner thoughts exactly in all the situations of my life. It is the history of my soul that I have promised to recount, and to write it I have need of no other memories."[26] Here, the validity of the subject – its truth, certainty, and integrity – rest on an act of demonstration, on a telling that is a form of showing (i.e., revealing his inner thoughts). This is not to say that the subject of Rousseau's *Confessions* is any less problematic than the subject of the novel. Rather, it is to suggest that those problems are resolved in a way that relies far more on the demonstration of sincerity rather than on the self-consciousness we associate with irony.

## Suggested Additional Reading


Judith Butler, *Subjects of Desire: Hegelian Reflections in Twentieth-Century France* (New York: Columbia University Press, 1999).

Geoffrey Harpham, *Getting it Right: Language, Literature, and Ethics* (Chicago: University of Chicago Press, 1992).

Peter Jones, *Philosophy and the Novel* (Oxford: Oxford University Press, 1975).

Adam Zachary Newton, *Narrative Ethics* (Cambridge, MA: Harvard University Press, 1995).

James Olney, *Memory and Narrative* (Chicago: University of Chicago Press, 1999).

Martin Price, *Forms of Life: Character and Moral Imagination in the Novel* (New Haven, CT: Yale University Press, 1983).

Hans-Joachim Schulz, *This Hell of Stories: A Hegelian Approach to the Novels of Samuel Beckett* (The Hague: Mouton, 1973).

Allen Speight, *Hegel, Literature, and the Problem of Agency* (Cambridge: Cambridge University Press, 2001).

Charles Taylor, *Sources of the Self* (Cambridge, MA: Harvard University Press, 1989).

## Chapter 12

# Forms and Fragments

It's tempting to associate the idea of form with the ideals of coherence and of a whole. After all, if form involves binding together elements of experience, concepts, imaginings, words, and so forth, then it would seem reasonable to focus on efforts to lend as much coherence and completeness to them as possible. In the last chapter we discussed the situation of the novel as confronting the problem of coherent form. There is more to be said on this subject. Most important is the fact that the novel is not a single form, but is itself comprised of many forms. The very first novel, *Don Quixote*, incorporates or alludes to the full spectrum of generic possibilities that any sophisticated writer of the time might conceivably have been aware of.[1] This heterogeneity supports what Jacques Rancière described as "the ruin of the generic principle" and the "anti-generic principle of the equality of all represented subjects" in the novel (*Mute Speech*, 50).

Traditionally, genres were associated with particular subjects. But the novel is a form of prose fiction not necessarily linked to any particular subject at all. It is a form that could take up virtually any subject whatsoever. The novel became, in Rancière's words, "a false genre, a non-generic genre … the genre of what has no genre: not even a low genre like comedy, with which some have assimilated it. This also means that it is lacking in any determinate fictional nature. … [I]t is the foundation of Don Quixote's 'madness,' that is, his rupture with the requisites of a scene proper to fiction" (*Mute Speech*, 51). What the novel nonetheless does is incorporate many different genres and forms of speech into something that has the shape of a conversation among many voices. This is where the association of the novel with the project of world-making (even as a "world version") is better traded for a different model entirely.

## Bakhtin: Polyphony and the Dialogic Imagination

I turn now to the work of Russian philosopher, literary critic, and semiotician Mikhail Bakhtin. In a series of essays and books on topics ranging from

Dostoevsky and Rabelais to the relationship between the novel and the epic, Bakhtin drew out the consequences of the proposition that all language is fundamentally dialogic in nature. No utterance, however solitary, stands completely alone. In Bakhtin's view this is because each utterance expects and anticipates a response, even if it is not itself a response in any literal sense. Each utterance is also a response to those that precede it. As such, it incorporates some *other* perspective, one that is not necessarily that of the speaker alone. Bakhtin thus saw language as a living dialogue offering exposure to *alterity*. While in *Problems of Dostoevsky's Poetics* Bakhtin seemed to distinguish between "dialogic" and "non-dialogic" utterances, his later works – *The Dialogic Imagination* most important among them – are committed to the view that all language is fundamentally dialogic. Bakhtin was led to solidify these ideas by his engagements with novelists including Cervantes, Dickens, and Dostoevsky. Several key features of Bakhtin's ideas about "dialogism" were in fact drawn out of their work:

1. *Heterglossia* (literally, a diversity of voices) is something that Bakhtin defined as "another's speech in another's language, serving to express authorial intentions but in a refracted way."[2] The multi-voicedness of the novel arises from the fact that it is a space in which the voices of narrator, author, and characters all converge without a clear sense that any one carries more or less authority than any other. The novel is inherently open-ended, such that inconsistencies created by the convergence of voices within it are never resolved in any absolute way. Rather, the novel is capacious enough to allow them to flourish as incommensurable discourses. In this way it demonstrates a view of the world as similarly plural and open-ended. As Michael Holquist observed in his book on Bakhtin's dialogism, "heteroglossia is a way of conceiving the world as made up of a roiling mass of language, each of which has its own distinct formal markers. These features are never *purely* formal, for each has associated with it a set of distinctive values and propositions."[3]
2. Likewise, *polyphony* refers to the shaping and articulation of the truth via multiple voices, in different registers, and from divergent standpoints. "Truth" is not something that can be presented in the form of monological statements about things or states of affairs in the world. Accordingly, it requires the polyphonic form of a genre like the novel in order to be expressed. Dickens, for example, freely incorporates fragments of ballads into the prose speech of his characters. Flaubert's narrators shift in and out of omniscience and "free indirect style," speaking as if in the voice of a character, though without direct quotation. The swirl of interior

monologues and of narrative speculations in Dostoevsky's fiction weighs at least as much as the claims of his narrators or the words that the characters speak to one another. In Dostoevsky's novels "one is dealing not with a *single* author-artist who wrote novels and stories, but with a number of philosophical statements by *several* author-thinkers – Raskolnikov, Myshkin, Stavrogin, Ivan Karamazov, the Grand Inquisitor, and others".[4] The chief characteristic of Dostoevsky's writing lies in its display of "a plurality of unmerged voices and consciousnesses, a genuine polyphony of fully valid voices" (*Problems*, 6).

3. *Carnival.* The English version of Bakhtin's Dostoevsky book contains a chapter on the "carnivalesque" that relates to some of his early work on Rabelais (published as *Rabelais and His World*). In social terms, "carnival" describes the ritual, pre-Lenten celebration in which the practices and institutions of the regular daily world are turned upside-down. At carnival time, institutional strictures are loosened, hierarchies are abandoned, and new and unexpected connections can be made. In the literary sense in which Bakhtin uses it, the "canivalesque" describes the context in which many different individual voices can be heard, can flourish and interact, without responding to the demand for greater order or synthesis. Like the novel, the carnivalesque offers the potential for displaying an otherness or outsideness to *any* single standpoint by making ordinary meanings strange in light of one another.[5] These are also the situations in which dialogue achieves its greatest potential. The notion of carnival was one way for Bakhtin to describe Dostoevsky's polyphonic style: in a polyphonic world each character speaks with a strongly defined voice, but in that world we also witness the influence that each character has upon all the others.

**Dostoevsky and the Polyphonic Novel**

"Dostoevsky is the creator of the polyphonic novel. He created a fundamentally new novelistic genre. Therefore his work does not fit any of the preconceived frameworks or historico-literary schemes that we usually apply to various species of the European novel. In his works a hero appears whose voice is constructed exactly like the voice of the author himself in a novel of the usual type. A character's word about himself is just as fully weighted as the author's word usually is. ... It possesses extraordinary independence in the structure of the work; it sounds, as it were, *alongside* the author's word and in a special way combines both with it and with the full and equally valid voices of other characters" (*Problems*, 7; emphasis in original).

It is the form of the novel, and above all the dialogic novel, that allows this multiplicity to flourish as a whole. The dialogic novel is a form, not a style, and in Bakhtin's view it is a form that had to be invented in order to capture the tensions between the centrifugal impulses of the world around us and the centripetal impulses at work behind our desire to know it. (As we will see later on, Derrida has argued that styles are always irreducibly plural.) The novel is on this account not a representation of a world but a form that allows the diversity of voices at play in the world to be bound loosely together as a whole.

## The Logic of Fragments

There are some surprising links between the form of the novel, the culture of the fragment, and the "idea" of poetry (in the most general and absolute sense of that term) in German Romanticism that are important to note. Schlegel's "Letter about the Novel" can serve as a point of departure, not least because it presents a much earlier version of the ideas we've seen Rancière express: "I detest the novel as far as it wants to be a separate genre."[6] Schlegel admired the novel as "a mixture of storytelling, song, and other forms" ("Letter abuot the Novel," 102). It is the place where forms are mixed and yet retain something of their independent status. The novel did not aspire to become a truly organic whole (an *organon*), or a "total work of art," in the way that the theatre did.

Even more than the novel, however, Schlegel and those around him regarded the fragment as a form that could bring the principle of subjective spirit to light. As such, the fragment plays an important role in philosophy. Indeed, we sometimes forget that the fragment can itself be a philosophical form, not a failure of philosophy or something inherently literary. Many philosophical works are in fact made from various bits or pieces, not constructed with the idea of achieving a greater, overarching coherence of form and thought. Pascal's *Pensées* (*Thoughts*) is one example; *Pensées* is often described as an ensemble of fragments, in which Pascal was aiming toward a book that was never finished. The *Maxims* of La Rochefoucauld are another example. So too are Nietzsche's works *The Gay Science* and the largely aphoristic *Daybreak*. These works had no ambition to be anything more "whole."

### Fragments and Wisdom Literature

The fragment is often the preferred form for what is known as "wisdom literature." This tradition includes the parables of the New Testament, Pascal's *Pensées*, Erasmus' *Adagia*, the *Maxims* of La Rochefoucauld, Schopenhauer's

*Paralipomena* ("omissions," things left out"), the essays of Montaigne and Emerson, along with many works from non-Western traditions such as the *Analects* of Confucius. There are frequent and important connections between the genre of wisdom literature and the philosophical tradition that emphasizes self-knowledge as fundamental to any pursuit of truth and value.

There have been fragments in philosophy for millennia, beginning with many texts that predate Plato and Socrates.[7] But the majority of extant ancient fragments are parts or pieces of a whole. Heraclitus' *Fragments*, for example, are the remaining bits of the longer work *On Nature*. In the romantic period, however, the fragment – and especially the philosophical fragment – came to be something rather more specific, with an independent genealogy and purpose. The romantic fragment was not regarded as a piece of anything else.[8] It does not depend upon a larger whole. "Many works of the ancients have become fragments. Many modern works are fragments as soon as they start," writes Schlegel.[9] The philosophical fragment was of special interest to the German Romantic writers who were associated with the publication of *Athenaeum*, under the direction of the Schlegel brothers (August Wilhelm and Karl Wilhelm Friedrich). In the three-year course of its existence (1798–1800), the journal included letters, essays, poems, and a number of so-called fragments.

The term "fragment" was not an unfamiliar one, especially in German-language circles. The Swiss writer Johann Kaspar Lavater had published a book entitled *Physiognomical Fragments*,[10] and Lessing had edited, translated, and published some fragments by his Enlightenment predecessor, Hermann Samuel Reimarus.[11] The philosophical notebooks of Novalis contain fragments on a vast array of subjects, including the relations between literature and philosophy. Here is one example: "Poetry is the hero of philosophy. Philosophy raises poetry to the status of a principle. It teaches is to recognize the worth of poetry. Philosophy is the *theory of poetry*. It shows us what poetry is, that it is the one and all."[12] The philosophical issue raised by the fragment, outlined by Schelling in *First Outline of a System of the Philosophy of Nature*, was the relationship between our ideas and organic wholes, and also the status of literature in general (called "poetry") in relation to fragments and wholes. One of Schelling's major concerns was with the limits of systematic thinking in relation to the philosophical desire to be systematic. But the fragment is not just the opposite of the whole or the system. The fragment can also be the germ or the nucleus of a system; it can provide the "seeds" of future systems or, in the words of critic Peter Szondi, "the subjective embryo of a developing object."[13]

The organic metaphor ("embryo") persists in a way that suggests that fragments are somehow natural. The implication is that nature is as fragmentary as it is organically whole.

In his introduction to Schlegel's *Fragments*, Rodolphe Gasché explained the logic of fragments as follows:

> A piece struck by incompletion, a detached piece, a piece left over from a broken whole, or even an erratic piece, is structurally linked with the whole or totality of which it would have been, or of which it has been, a part. … Rather than a piece to be understood from the whole of which it would be a remainder, or broken part, the Romantic fragment is a genre by itself, characterized by *a concept of its own*.[14]

Central to the "concept" mentioned here is the isolation and autonomy of the fragment: "A fragment, like a miniature work of art, has to be entirely isolated from the surrounding world and be complete in itself like a porcupine."[15] Paradoxically, the fragment is also a seed, a germ of something to come, a form of ash that promises generation and development, as Schlegel says at one point. In *Athanaeum*, no. 53, Schlegel remarks that "it is equally fatal for a mind to have a system and to have none. It will simply have to decide to combine the two" (24). This means that the fragment, while germ-like, is not, properly speaking, a beginning. This helps capture its philosophical importance: "Viewed subjectively, philosophy, like epic poetry, always begins in medias res" (no. 84, 28).

These notions had a resonant afterlife in Nietzsche's writings and in Derrida's interpretation of them in *Spurs: Traces of Nietzsche's Styles*. In reading Nietzsche, Derrida appealed to the idea of the fragment as a way to resist any attempt to "capture" Nietzsche's true thought. Not unlike his romantic predecessors, Derrida argued that to imagine the fragment as part of a larger whole would undermine its fragmentary status. That would be especially inappropriate when dealing with Nietzsche: to see the fragment as part of a larger whole would in most instances betray the plurality of Nietzsche's thought, which is in turn wholly evident in the plurality of its styles. "If there is going to be style," Derrida writes, "there can only be more than one."[16]

## Form and Destruction

Some of the oldest thinking about form is about the ability to impose order on the world. This is something different from a purely generative power or creative drive. Friedrich Schiller described the "form-drive" in his *Letters on the Aesthetic Education of Man* as the ability to impose conceptual and moral order on the world. "Form" also describes efforts to impose a material or aesthetic order on the world. A philosophical system gives order to our understanding of knowledge, morality, or beauty. A plot lends order to events by identifying the relationships between beginning, middle, and end. Nietzsche refers to a much more basic notion of form in *The Birth of Tragedy*, where he describes it as a "plastic power" associated with Apollo. The countervailing force to the Apollonian, the Dionysian, offers a different version of the artistic impulses that Nietzsche associates with nature itself. Nietzsche regards artistic making as secondary to the archaic Dionysian and Apollonian forces, and these in turn stand in the shadow of some unknown and unknowable power beyond nature. What is "formed" at this most basic level is "man" himself: "The noblest clay, the most costly marble, man, is here kneaded and cut, and to the sound of the chisel strokes of the Dionysian world-artist rings out the cry of the Elusinian mysteries: 'Do you prostrate yourselves, millions? Do you sense your maker, world?'"[17] (*BT*, 37–38). But Nietzsche was equally interested in the need for destruction, viewing it as necessary for any creative form-making at all. Destruction opens the way for something new to emerge out of the chaos: "The raising of an altar requires the breaking of an altar: this is a law – let anyone who can prove me wrong."[18] Chaos can be fecund.

Nietzsche might seem quite radical in saying this, but Descartes proposed a similar, if less risky, version of destruction when he suggested that we might need to erase all our inherited ideas just as an architect might want to raze a building if he found it had been built on faulty foundations: better to tear down and rebuild than to repair. Descartes also recognized that such a plan would need to be carried out prudently, and not in wholesale fashion; he proposed tackling the buildings one by one, and only destroying those that were key to the stability of others: "once the foundations of a building are undermined, anything built on them collapses of its own accord; so I will go straight for the basic principles on which all my former beliefs rested."[19]

## Kierkegaard's Fragments

The relationship between the fragment and the systematic ambition of philosophy is central to Kierkegaard's *Philosophical Fragments* and to the *Concluding Unscientific Postscript*. Kierkegaard's fragments also need to be understood in light of his reliance on multiple, pseudonymous authors and his particular brand of perspectivism, as evidenced prominently in the construction of the book *Either/Or*. All of these works help illustrate what it means for a philosopher to adopt a series of literary strategies as integral to his work.

The named "author" of *Philosophical Fragments* is Johannes Climacus; Kierkegaard poses merely as the editor of the book. The "author" asserts that he propounds no doctrines. He positions himself, instead, as an ironist and a humorist. But as Louis Mackey observed, "his philosophical essays, like well-turned jokes, are to be taken quite seriously."[20] The humorist occupies a standpoint of "provisional detachment" from life, and so is able to treat serious matters without impugning his objectivity. Kierkegaard sometimes placed his pseudonymity in contrast to the direct speech in which Hegel communicated his philosophical system; in contrast to Hegel, Kierkegaard had "no philosophy of his own to offer, only a warning against system (which could hardly be delivered in a systematic form) and a reminder that 'truth is subjectivity, subjectivity is truth.'"[21] This particular resistance to system stems from an ambition that is close to Montaigne's insofar as it relies on an existential principle of subjectivity. Kierkegaard famously wrote that "subjectivity is truth, subjectivity is reality,"[22] but subjectivity is not a single, contradiction-free entity. Accordingly, Kierkegaard's writings are parts that cannot be synthesized into a whole. In characterizing Kierkegaard as "a kind of poet," Mackey put the matter exceptionally well:

> If each stage on life's way represents a radical self-choice from which there is no exit save by way of another equally radical choice of a radically different self, then it follows that there is no necessary continuity in human personality. … *Either/Or* is incomplete and necessarily so. It is unfinished and open-ended in the same way that man is infinite and always exposed to further possibilities. It has not one protagonist, but two, three, who-knows-how-many *personae*. (274; emphasis in original)

Kierkegaard's prose is fundamentally metaphorical, and not just in the local use of figures. Insofar as philosophy aims at unambiguous propositions, univocal terms, and "strict inferences," it must obey the law of non-contradiction. But metaphorical language is fundamentally analogical, which means that it contains elements of diversity within itself: "its terms admit of many senses, and its propositions interact in ways not open to the statements of logical discourse" (Mackey, 260).

This nonetheless leaves us with a question of how to reconcile the idea of a philosophical project with the many fragmentary, humoristic, and metaphorical forms that seem necessary to carry it out. On one level we need to understand that Kierkegaard's statements, however fragmentary, are part of a larger body of work. Mackey writes that they can only be understood within the context of the formal significance of these larger designs, "a significance that discloses itself to a comprehensive literary study but not to a purely logical analysis" (259). By contrast, the opposite procedure will not succeed:

> [T]he literary techniques of Kierkegaard cannot be interpreted as devices for the expression of a content independently intelligible. Every attempt to isolate such a content leads either to the suppression

> of ideas inconsistent with the scholar's image of Kierkegaard, or to the conclusion that Kierkegaard contradicted himself wildly and foolishly. … The unity and consistency of his thought, not at all apparent to logical scrutiny, is a metaphorical unity. (259)

Kierkegaard is a kind of "poet," or perhaps better said, a philosopher who found that the many forms of poetry (broadly construing the term) were more appropriate to his aims than conventional forms of philosophical writing.

## The Essay as Form

One of the closest parallels to the philosophical fragment is the essay, perhaps best exemplified in the *Essays* of Montaigne. What has been said of the fragment could also be said of the essay – that it "designates a presentation that does not intend to be exhaustive and that corresponds to the … idea that the incomplete can, and even must, be published (or to the idea that what is published is never complete)."[23]

Theodor Adorno suggested that the essay aimed at being a critique of systems and of method. In an essay entitled "The Essay as Form," he wrote that "In the realm of thought it is virtually the essay alone that has successfully raised doubts about the absolute privilege of method."[24] The essay sets its own boundaries and discovers its scope in the course of its own development. In so doing it turns away from an interest in establishing and respecting fixed limits – which was a practice that lay at the core of Kant's three critiques, as of many other philosophical projects. Nor does the essay feel obliged to establish every first principle for itself. It instead cultivates an open-endedness as much in the way it begins as in the way it concludes. It is free from any obligation to discover the preconditions for knowledge and to demonstrate conclusive proofs. The essayist understands that the writer's freedom is a freedom not to have to begin from an absolute, presuppositionless starting point. Indeed, the "presuppositions" of the essayist often include the many works that have been inherited from the past. Adorno explains that "the essay … does not let its domain be prescribed for it. Instead of accomplishing something scientifically or creating something artistically, its efforts reflect the leisure of a childlike person who has no qualms about taking inspiration from what others have done before him" (4).

Here, Adorno himself echoes an essay about essays by Georg Lukács ("On the Nature and Form of the Essay"). Lukács wrote:

> [T]he essay is always concerned with something already formed, or at best, with something that has been; it is part of its essence that it does

> not draw something new out of an empty vacuum, but only gives a new order to such things as once lived. And because [the essayist] only orders them, not forming something out of the formless, he is bound to them; he must always speak "the truth" about them, find, that is, the expression for their essence.[25]

In the flexibility of its form, the essay responds to the insight that the essential order of "things in themselves" – if there is one – is not necessarily the same as the order of ideas or of writing. For Adorno, the notion that these different orders might correspond is produced by the mistaken ascription of an "immediacy" to things that are in fact given to us only by some form of mediation, whether through language, images, social institutions, or other forms. The ubiquity of mediation and the ubiquity of form go hand in hand. For Adorno, this fact reaches to include individual experience itself:

> Merely individual experience, which consciousness takes as its point of departure … is itself mediated by the overarching experience of historical humankind. The notion that the latter is mediated and one's own experience unmediated is mere self-deception on the part of an individualistic society and ideology. (10)

We ought also to bear in mind that "essay" originally meant something like an "attempt" or "try." An essay is an approach to some subject, conducted in light of the awareness that there is no one, definitive approach to it. This is certainly the sense that the term "essay" has in one of the most important examples of the form, the *Essays* of Montaigne. The subject of Montaigne's book is the self, which Montaigne portrays as fluid and evolving rather than fixed. Montaigne's *Essays* give us many different, often oblique, approaches to this subject. Charles Taylor, in *Sources of the Self*, makes the connection to questions of form explicit: "We seek self-knowledge, but this can no longer mean just impersonal lore about human nature, as it could for Plato. Each of us has to discover her own form. We are not looking for the universal nature; we each look for our own being."[26] The contrast with Montaigne's successor, Descartes, could not be more striking. "Cartesianism gives us a science of the subject in its general essence; and it proceeds by a critique of first-person self-interpretations" (182).

And yet Montaigne has sometimes been interpreted in ways that go against the grain of his writing. One such approach to Montaigne is to read the essays as a vehicle for moral philosophy – which at some level they certainly are – but here for the kind of moral philosophy aimed at giving definitive advice about how to live. This is not implausible given the fact that Montaigne was a reader of the ancient stoic philosophers and that one of them, Epictetus (55–135 A.D.), himself left a book of advice about how to live comprised of short essays and aphorisms (*The Art of Living*).[27] A recent book takes just this approach to Montaigne but has to convert his *Essays* into a biography of Montaigne in order to do so.[28] To be sure, Montaigne tempts us to think in biographical terms when he says that he is himself the "matter" of his book. But the essays were not written as a pseudo autobiography. Montaigne is the "matter" of the book[29] because the form of the essay corresponds to the fluctuating and unpredictable nature of individual existence. "I study myself more than any other subject. That is my metaphysics, that is my physics," (821); the phrase looks forward to Walt Whitman: "this is no book, / who touches this touches a man."[30]

Maurice Merleau-Ponty put it well when he observed that Montaigne "imagined a book in which for once there would be expressed not only ideas but also the very life which they appear in and which modifies their meaning ... beneath clear ideas and thoughts he finds a spontaneity abounding in opinions, feelings, and unjustifiable acts."[31] Montaigne has no fixed self. The *Essays* themselves were not just written, but *re*written, over a period of many years. The form is in flux just as much as the self is a fluid entity. Montaigne is well aware of this: "Being consists in movement and action," he writes. "We are carried away, like floating objects, now gently, now violently, according as the eater is angry or calm."[32] Then, citing Lucretius' Latin poem "On the Nature of Things" (first century B.C.), he adds "Do we not see all humans unaware / Of what they want, and always searching everywhere, / And changing place, as if to drop the load they bear?" (*Essays*, 240).

A second approach takes the relationship between Montaigne and the *Essays* as a material one, understanding Montaigne's assertion that he is the "matter" of his book in a rather literal fashion. We know of course that the idea of a relationship between self and book must be metaphorical, and yet the *Essays* devote a tremendous amount of attention to the physical self. On one level, Montaigne is reminding us of the fact that human beings are physical creatures, but his point is not that the body gives us the absolute key to an unchanging human essence. Rather, Montaigne is more like Lucretius (whom he cites more than a hundred times over the course of the *Essays*) in believing that all nature, including physical human nature, is itself a realm of change and flux. The place of the body in Montaigne's *Essays* is to remind us of the changeability of human nature, of its susceptibility to forces beyond our conscious control.

As a form, the essay is well suited to the exploration of this changeability. Montaigne was no doubt also drawn to the essay because it was not a form of academic philosophy. (Montaigne himself was trained as a lawyer, not as a philosopher, though there is ample evidence that he read widely in philosophical texts.) The forms of academic philosophy smacked of dogmatism; he called Aristotle the "prince of dogmatists."[33] Montaigne was a thoroughgoing skeptic. And while it might be tempting to look at Montaigne's essay "Of

Experience" as a precursor of empiricism or phenomenology, his work has little to do with either of these branches of modern philosophy. Indeed, the essay "Of Experience" seems to be mostly about things other than what we now understand as "experience." Montaigne is a skeptic, but he is not, however, the kind of skeptic whose world crumbles under the weight of doubt. Merleau-Ponty put this well when he said that Montaigne's skepticism means "that nothing is true, but also that nothing is false" (*Essays*, 198).

"Of Experience" is but one of many texts that could be invoked to illustrate a further feature of the essay as Montaigne deployed it: its centrifugal nature. Whereas Descartes imagined philosophical method as a systematic way of arriving at whatever may be true (and, equally, of understanding what we cannot know with certainty), Montaigne allows himself to be drawn away from any clearly marked path. The root of the word "method" is "way, path," and Montaigne's pathways are quite unpredictable. His essays typically move away from their stated subjects, often alluding to texts from the past, sometimes incorporating strange and unusual examples, and introducing citations taken from a wide range of sometimes obscure classical sources. Montaigne's essays are "attempts" in the way that in its roots "experience" is neighbor to the notion of "experiment"; the laboratory for his experiments on his self was his library. While Montaigne has sometimes been associated with the beginnings of modern introspection, he looks principally to the writings of others as much as to himself. Though they take the *Essays* in a centrifugal direction, those writings are paradoxically one of his keys to self-understanding.

### Intertextuality in the Essays

Montaigne's *Essays* present the reader with a series of paradoxes. On the one hand, Montaigne asserts that he is himself the matter of his book. At the same time, the *Essays* incorporate dozens upon dozens of citations from other authors. The *Essays* are based on the books in Montaigne's own library as much as they are on personal observation or on introspection in the way we would understand it. They oblige the reader to enter into a dense and rich inter-textual web, as Montaigne cites Cicero, Lucretius, Virgil, Lucan, Juvenal, Ovid, and many more.

And at the same time, Montaigne was far from content with the practice of simply commenting on the works of others. His own practice of reading and citation tends to place himself in an oblique relationship to his "sources." By contrast, he has little hope for the practice of piling interpretation upon interpretation, commentary upon commentary, without making some difference as an author:

"It is more of a job to interpret the interpretations than to interpret the things, and there are more books about books than about any other subject: we do nothing but write glosses about each other. The world is swarming with commentaries; of authors there is a great scarcity" (*Essays*, 818).

Given all that has been said thus far, we might well ask what sort of validity the essay can claim. Adorno drew a parallel between Montaigne's essays and the novels of Proust that can help answer the question. The work of Marcel Proust, he said, was an attempt to express "necessary and compelling insights into human beings and social relations that are not readily accommodated within science and scholarship" (*Essays*, 8). These insights are valid, and yet they require a kind of verification that does not align itself with the procedures of science. More strongly stated, they are open to what science cannot gain us access to. We need essays and novels because "scientific scholarship fails to deliver what it promises the mind: *to illuminate its works from the inside*" (8–9; emphasis mine). This is neither a form of verification nor a form of truth that conforms to a demand for objectivity as conventionally understood: "The measure of such objectivity is not the verification of assertions through repeated testing but rather individual human experience, maintained through hope and disillusionment" (8). We might invoke the notion of "edification" to describe this, though with the added insight that the process of edification need not be centered on the subject as a unitary entity and likewise need not proceed through forms that are themselves modeled on wholes.

## Suggestions for Further Reading

Michael André Bernstein, *Bitter Carnival* (Princeton, NJ: Princeton University Press, 1992).

Anthony J. Cascardi, "*Don Quixote* and the Invention of the Novel," In *The Cambridge Companion to Cervantes*, ed. Cascardi (Cambridge: Cambridge University Press, 2002).

Peter Fenves, *Chatter: Language and History in Kierkegaard* (Stanford, CA: Stanford University Press, 1993).

Jonathan Lear, *A Case for Irony* (Cambridge, MA: Harvard University Press, 2011).

Jean-François Lyotard, *Peregrinations: Law, Form, Event* (New York: Columbia University Press, 1988).

Richard Moran, *Authority and Estrangement: An Essay on Self-Knowledge* (Princeton, NJ: Princeton University Press, 2001).

Mark C. Taylor, *Journeys to Selfhood: Hegel and Kierkegaard* (Berkeley: University of California Press, 1980).

Eric Ziolkowski, ed., *The Literary Kierkegaard* (Evanston, IL: Northwestern University Press, 2011).

# *Afterword: Limits*

> What starts philosophy is no more to be known at the outset than how to make an end of it.
>
> Stanley Cavell, *The Claim of Reason*, 3

The topics we've discussed across the previous chapters will have helped to make it clear that the relations between literature and philosophy are not neatly contained by preconceived definitions of what philosophy and literature are. Given all the intersections between them, does it make sense to think of their independent identities as anything more than illusory or vestigial? Perhaps we should always put the terms "literature" and "philosophy" in scare quotes as a way to recognize that while these designations may indicate what each thinks of itself, they are at best provisional names whose boundaries change. To expect otherwise would entangle us in a project of definitions where instead a genealogy, a tracing of relations would be in order.

That genealogy would also have to include the many examples of boundary-crossing that have kept these questions alive for so long. Formal innovation was a way that Nietzsche and Derrida (among others) saw it possible to engage in a critique of metaphysics. For Derrida, the recourse to a new kind writing seemed necessary because he believed it was impossible to step wholly outside of the inheritance that he wanted nonetheless to question. Among his tactics was the bracketing and crossing out of some of the principal terms associated with metaphysics, placing them "under erasure" (*sous rature*). This practice, inherited from Heidegger, was a way to put pressure on inherited philosophical categories while recognizing that the attempt to "overcome" them completely was bound to fail. Nietzsche's genealogical approach, especially in the way it was adopted by Michel Foucault, tackles a similar issue.[1] Rather than first pondering principles and the nature of essences, the genealogist's practice is one of critical questioning; the point, as Rorty puts it, is to ask "whether these great ideas really came from the good background they never tired of claiming for themselves."[2] Kierkegaard and Wittgenstein were likewise form-breakers, as were the writers of the avant-garde (Stein, Beckett, Brecht, etc.). Form-breaking – sometimes known as iconoclasm – has a long history across both literature and philosophy. But we should be careful to consider what can be expected of it. Adorno observed that the avant-gardes tends to quickly become the next orthodoxy.[3]

Moreover, some of the most ancient questions that literature and philosophy pose for one another continue to have a surprising relevance even as forms change. Derrida's treatment of the *pharmakon* is a re-engagement with Plato. Additionally, some of the oldest forms (e.g., the dialogue) reflect a history of shifting borders that goes back many centuries. The reasons why old forms are not necessarily outmoded when they become old (or are no longer new) are worth considering. This is captured by one sense of what the term *Bildung* means in the context of the human sciences. Gadamer explains that:

> [In *Bildung*] everything that is received is absorbed, but what is absorbed is not like a means that has lost its function. Rather in acquired *Bildung* nothing disappears, but everything is preserved. *Bildung* is a genuine historical idea, and because of this historical character of "preservation" is important for understanding in the human sciences.[4]

"Preservation" is important, yet Gadamer may overstate the case. We cannot keep *everything*. Preservation also needs to allow for what Emerson called "reform," the discovery that "we must cast away our virtues, or what we have always esteemed such, into the same pit that has consumed our grosser vices."[5] Thoreau's concern was not about reform but about the activation of the past, how to make it available, especially in what we read:

> The heroic books, even if printed in the characters of our mother tongue, will always be in a language dead to degenerate times; and we must laboriously seek the meaning of each word and line, conjecturing a larger sense than common use permits out of what wisdom and valor and generosity we have.[6]

Neither literature nor philosophy is an area in which questions are answered and knowledge established in the way that physical laws are expected to explain phenomena in the natural world. Gadamer made a set of related points in *Truth and Method* when he contrasted the "human sciences" (*Geisteswissenschaften*) with the "natural sciences":

> One has not properly grasped the nature of the human sciences if one measures them by the yardstick of an increasing knowledge of regularity. The experience of the socio-historical world cannot be raised to a science by the inductive procedure of the natural sciences. Whatever "science" may mean here and even if all historical knowledge

> includes the application of general experience to the particular object of investigation, historical research does not endeavor to grasp the concrete phenomenon as an instance of a general rule. The individual case does not serve only to corroborate a regularity from which prediction can be made. Its ideal is rather to understand the phenomenon itself in its unique and historical concreteness. (6)

And yet the project to make philosophy a kind of science has been a guiding force at many stages of its history. Together with the invention of method, Descartes's idea that philosophy should be modeled on mathematics was imagined as laying the foundations for advances in medicine. This was precisely what Heidegger rejected when he said that the result would turn all reflection and inquiry into a "research program." What marks a "research program" for Heidegger is that any possible answers are already framed in the ways in which the questions are posed. The kind of thinking and questioning that the human sciences need (and that we need more generally, according to Heidegger) is closed off as a result. Placing literature and philosophy in dialogue with one another is a way of avoiding the foreclosure of such questions. Working across these domains renders the relevant questions open and available. Heidegger wrote that "thinking is a handicraft."[7] If that is so, then literature is a medium through which it works.

The projects described, singly and together, as "literature and philosophy" are endless projects. This does not just mean that they will go on forever, but rather that they are practiced within a framework where the introduction of a specific "end" would be a betrayal of what they are attempting to do. But one might reasonably ask what the goal of *Bildung* is even if it has no determinable end. One of the answers comes neither from literature nor from philosophy directly, but rather from the in-between zone of activity that we sometimes call "criticism." As Ronán McDonald put it, the critic does not simply "broadcast his own subjective enthusiasms," but tries to persuade his or her readers to assent to judgments that make a claim upon us.[8] It is the project of soliciting assent that matters – and assent not merely to what I might say about a given work, but to what might be said about it by anyone. The work of criticism happens in between the "I" and the "we," by which co-create each other. The "we" is not wholly given in advance, but is constructed as a community by those who will (or will not) assent to a particular set of claims. By the same token, there is pressure on the "I" to articulate its claims and its identity not in stark isolation but in relation to a set of others with which the "I" may be in community. This is an endless process of negotiation; the claims of criticism are not established once and for all but must be continuously (re)negotiated because communities change and because they change communities.

This is, roughly, an interpretation of the Kantian account of what aesthetic judgments (claims of taste) attempt to do. But no judgment begins from a clean slate. One enters any situation – any discourse, discussion, language, society, kinship structure, and so forth – not from the very beginning but at a point where things are already underway. Plato recognized this when he said that the quarrel between literature and philosophy was already an ancient one. More recent thinkers have drawn attention to the social, historical, and ethical contexts in which these matters apply. The desire to answer the question of who I am by staking a claim and living out its consequences will have to grapple with the fact that some identity is already projected for me by others, that I not only call myself by a particular name but *am called*. The proto-novel *Lazarillo de Tormes* knew this as well as any other text one might think of. This anonymous picaresque tale begins (in Spanish, where the phrasing is crucial) "A mí llaman Lázaro de Tormes," meaning "They call me Lázaro de Tormes," rather than with the more idiomatic "Me llamo Lázaro de Tormes" ("I call myself," i.e., "my name is"). The narrator's stated wish is to tell the whole truth of his own story; but he cannot quite do so, because he is named *beforehand*.

Louis Althusser made this the point of his interpretation of ideology and interpellation.[9] He likens interpellation to being "hailed." His examples contrast the answer to a knock at the door ("Who's there?" – "It's me," or "It's Jean") with being hailed by the police ("Hey, you there!"). The thesis applies to instances of rejection and scorn just as well as to those in which one is "called" or summoned affirmatively. When Rousseau begins his *Reveries*, wandering around Paris alone, he wishes to take the opportunity to ask himself who he is, independent of what others might have to say about him: "I, detached as I am from them and from the whole world, what am I?"[10] But he is wandering about in reflection only because he has been cast out. And so whatever identity he may discover in the solitude of his walks will be predisposed by circumstances that were not of his making: "So now I am alone in the world, with no brother, neighbor, or friend, nor any company left me but my own. The most sociable and loving of men has with one accord been cast out by all the rest" (27).

These matters pose dilemmas, ethical and otherwise. There is a powerful and understandable desire to tell one's own story, both for the truth one may wish to claim over it and for its role in the project of self-creation. Adriana Cavarero writes that:

> [W]e perceive ourselves and others as unique beings whose identity is narratable in a life-story. Each one of us knows that who we meet always has a unique story [*storia*]. And this is true even if we meet them for the first time without knowing their story at all. … Every human being,

> without even wanting to know it, is aware of being a *narratable self* – immersed in the spontaneous auto-narrative of memory.[11]

But how, then, do I speak to those who are outside my story, and how do I respond to those who may have anticipated a very different story for me than the one I wish to tell? For Wittgenstein, the limits of my language are the limits of my world; what cannot be said must be left in silence, or is nonsense. But what happens when my "world" is constructed by the language of others; this can result in a strangeness, where the limits of my world seem to be set by a language that is not wholly mine. Moreover, that "other" language may well present itself with the force of socially accepted norms. But they were put in place before I arrived, and they name me in ways I might not wish to acknowledge.

The persistence of preexisting structures of language, practices, social context, and so forth would seem to place severe limits on freedom and substantially to reduce the possibilities of autonomous ethical subjectivity. It is important to see why this need not be the case and to understand what the alternatives are. I propose the example of Kafka to help understand what it might mean to exist creatively within a language and a world that have been constructed in advance, by others, and therefore *not* to be at home in one's language. Kafka, a Prague Jew, faced a demand to write in German; this produced what Deleuze and Guattari describe as "the feeling of an irreducible distance from their primitive Czech territoriality."[12] Kafka wrote as if in an artificial "paper language," but in this he transmits a sense of inner exile without ever having to say "exile" explicitly. Yet no language is natural. We are all first born into a foreign land. Wittgenstein recounts how St. Augustine describes the learning of human language "as if the child came into a strange country and did not understand the language of that country; that is, as if it already had a language, only not this one."[13]

The "I" needs a language and a story, but would seem to have no intelligible story it can tell apart from existing norms and their corresponding conventions, whether these be linguistic, ethical, social, or otherwise. That is the dilemma, but the conclusion to be drawn is neither that the "I" is wholly constrained by preexisting norms and can act only to reproduce them, nor that the "I" must strive to be (or can be) wholly self-creating. Judith Butler put this well in saying that "norms are there, at an exterior distance, and the task is to find a way of appropriating them, taking them on, establishing a living relation to them. … [A] subject encounters moral norms and must find his way with them."[14] The norms that preexist us have always ("always already") been there, but they can be and are rearticulated and reinterpreted, sometimes with very different inflections, in each particular moment. Of course, one cannot rearticulate an entire language or social structure all at once, but one can say new things within it – things that may well contribute to restructuring the possibilities of meaningful discourse and action.

It should not go unremarked that all these views presuppose the "human" as their framework. But as Derrida remarked, we do not know the human if we do not also know the *limits* of the human:

> As with every bottomless gaze, as with the eye of the other, the gaze called "animal" offers to my sight the abyssal limit of the human: the inhuman or the ahuman, the ends of man, that is to say, the bordercrossing from which vantage man dares to announce himself to himself, thereby calling himself by the name that he believes he gives to himself.[15]

One of his reference points is a passage from Montaigne's essays: "When I play with my cat, who knows if I am not a pastime to her more than she is to me" (333). Whatever else it might mean to consider the limits of the human, it seems clear that literature is as much a part of the enterprise as it is part of the project of imagining the human itself – hardly to the exclusion of philosophy, but rather as integral to it.

**Wittgenstein and Kafka on the Limits of Language:**

Wittgenstein said that if a lion could speak we could not understand him. But in Kafka's *Metamorphoses*, Gregor Samsa is transformed into a bug, and speaks. The problem is not that his family does not hear him, but that they are so absorbed in their own affairs (money, debts, etc.) that the family cannot understand him when they do speak.

That project has been underway for centuries. Literature has long been involved in in making strange what we know about ourselves from *within* philosophy. In *Meditations* and *Discourse on Method*, Descartes introduced the most radical form of doubt he could possibly imagine: the figure of the absolute deceiver, masquerading as someone whose role was to disguise a world that is false and to present it to us as ours – indeed, as the very world we see and know. The "evil genius" is in the business of making reality a fiction, but he is a creature of the philosopher. This fictional figure plays a crucial role in sustaining the philosopher's pursuit of truth to whatever depth might be required or tolerated. Philosophy is not opposed to literature in the way that a discourse of truth is "opposed" to a discourse of fiction. On the contrary, literature is a discourse that philosophy relies upon in some of its core pursuits. The fictional "evil genius" provides the necessary strangeness that philosophy requires in order to question and revise what it takes as known (i.e., in order to come to know it again, in a better way).

The same could be said for what Wittgenstein does in the course of *Philosophical Investigations*, when ordinary language is made strange by the questioning voice that appears on virtually every page of that book (e.g., "What does it mean to know what a game is? What does it mean, to know it and not be able to say it?"[16]). "Making strange" could also be said of the role that Socrates plays in many of Plato's dialogues, which is to ask a series of incremental questions and thereby to cast doubt upon whatever has just been agreed to. Is Socrates articulating a series of genuine and open questions? Is he using these questions to mask a demand for assent to things he already knows are true? We may not know the final answer, but we do know that in Plato's dialogues he is a figure whose pursuit of wisdom cannot be separated from the literary means by which he makes accepted truths seem doubtful and strange. At the very end of *The Claim of Reason*, Stanley Cavell asked "Can philosophy become literature and still know itself?"[17] The answer might well be that philosophy has always been part literature, and literature always partly philosophical, and that to erase all their differences would be to deprive ourselves of whatever light they can shed on each other from positions that are always partly strange to one another.

# *Glossary of Keywords*

**Aesthetics:** Aesthetics is the branch of philosophy that deals with such things as the beautiful, the sublime, judgments of taste, and the creative power of genius. These matters may apply to nature as well as to works of art.

**Affects:** Like the passions, the affects describe the emotional qualities of experience. They are states of mind and body that include such basic things as pleasure, pain, sorrow, and desire. Because they involve both mind and body, they are not well explained by thinking that regards the mind and the body as separate and distinct entities.

**Appearances:** The realm of appearances (or the "appearing world") was thought by Plato and those who followed him to be the manifestation of timeless Ideas or Forms. The realm of appearances is subject to the forces of time and change and to the distortions of perception. In that regard it was deemed false. Opponents of Plato such as Nietzsche sought to overturn these notions and to re-establish the value of the appearing world, in part by declaring the realm of Ideas as false.

***Archē*, Archaeology:** The Greek term *archē* refers to beginning or origin. It can also mean the root or first principle of something. Archaeology is a much more recent term referring to inquiry into the origins of various forms of human practice, including various kinds of discourse (e.g., scientific, literary, philosophical).

***Bildung*:** *Bildung* carries within it a root (*Bild*) that refers to "image" or "form" (also meaning "picture"). It literally means "formation," in the sense of the education and cultural formation that take place in history and through the institutions of society. Literature can portray *Bildung*, but it is also an element in the formative process. *Bildung* may also refer to the process by which an individual undertakes his or her own formation. In a related context, *Bildung* can mean "cultivation."

***Bildungsroman*:** The term *Bildungsroman* refers to the novel of formation or development. It typically involves a coming-of-age story that pits the development of a sensitive soul against social forces. The growth of the protagonist in a *Bildungsroman* happens through the process of lived experience, which may include coming to recognize that some tensions between the individual and society may be irreducible.

**Catharsis:** Few topics have been debated as much as the meaning of this term. Aristotle uses it in the *Poetics* to describe the effects of tragedy as purging, cleansing, or clarifying the emotions of pity and fear. This draws on the medical associations suggested by the etymology of the word (from the Greek *katharsis*, meaning cleansing, purging).

**Categorical imperative:** This is the fundamental principle of morality in Kant's philosophy. It refers to the kind of obligation ("ought") which admits no exceptions and which must be adhered to by any and every one as a matter of being human. Kant's moral project was to relate human freedom to the categorical imperative.

**Constructivism:** In philosophy, constructivism implies that human beings make knowledge (e.g., from experience) rather than discover it as it exists independently. Constructivism stands opposed to foundationalism. Social constructivism holds that the construction of knowledge is dependent on the institutions and interactions of society, and that the "givens" of the natural world play a relatively small role in it.

**Contingency:** In the contexts relevant here, contingency refers to the belief that the relations among persons and things, and indeed things themselves are not *necessarily* one way or another, but are dependent on language, history, and human practices, all of which may change.

**Correspondence theory of truth:** The correspondence theory of truth says that beliefs and statements are true when they correspond accurately to things or states of affairs. By contrast, it is deemed false to say or believe differently from how things actually are. The notion has a long history, and reaches back to Plato and Aristotle. In the modern era, the correspondence theory of truth involves thinking that our mental representations of things must correspond to the way things actually are if we are to have valid knowledge of them.

**Deconstruction:** The work of deconstruction revolves around uncovering the polar (binary) oppositions that structure language, thought, and social institutions. Deconstruction does not propose that these dualities can be overcome. But it does suggest that one term in any binary relationship tends to be privileged, and becomes dominant in relation to the other. Western metaphysics is structured by a series of binary oppositions that privilege presence over absence, being over nonbeing, and speech over writing.

**Dialectic:** This term refers to a process for resolving different views about a subject, in which each one undergoes ongoing modification and revision in light of what the other shows. In some accounts, a dialectical process may be open-ended; in others, it moves forward with the expectation (even if only in principle) that there is a final resolution to be achieved.

**Dialogism:** This term, developed by Mikhail Bakhtin, refers to a perspective on language in which every utterance is situated within a larger framework of pre-existing utterances, implicit (or explicit) questions, and responses. Its notional opposite is monologism, though Bakhtin eventually argued that there are no wholly monological utterances.

***Différance*:** This is a term coined by Jacques Derrida as a way of explaining the post-structuralist view that while language is organized around a system of differences (phonological, semantic, etc.) these differences have no center or point of resolution because that center is always deferred. In this regard, *différance* means both "difference" and "deferral."

**Dualism:** While dualism may refer to any conceptual scheme in which two elements are set apart and opposed to one another, the kind of dualism most often at stake in discussions of literature and philosophy is the dualism that originates in Descartes's thinking and separates the mind and the body as distinct entities. For Descartes, the mind was the more essential of the two elements of human nature.

**Edification:** In the contexts relevant to this book, edification offers a perspective on the purpose of philosophy that involves various forms of self-creation, including self-improvement (rather than striving for perfection), self-revision (in response to the contingencies that may befall us), and self-overcoming. Its focus is "what kind of person do I want to become?" rather than "what is the nature of the truth or the good in me?"

**Epistemology:** Epistemology is the philosophy of knowledge, and one of the main traditional branches of philosophy along with ontology and moral philosophy. It deals with questions of what and how we know, with the limits of knowledge, with questions of truth, and with matters of certainty and doubt. The term is derived from the Greek *epistêmê*, meaning knowledge.

**Ethos:** Ethos refers to matters of character in the philosophical sense. In the contexts relevant to this book it should not be confused with the idea of a general moral attitude, as more casual usage might suggest. Rather, ethos is associated with the basis of character, where "character" is the core of one's moral being. It can also extend to refer to the moral identity of a community, a nation, and so forth.

**Foundationalism:** Foundationalism refers to a wide range of philosophical views according to which there are basic principles or elements on which the rest of a system of beliefs relies. The term is closely associated with Descartes, who used the notion of a "foundation" as an architectural metaphor for the underpinnings of philosophical beliefs. The search for foundations is in this sense the search for first principles (i.e. the ones on which all others rest). By contrast, anti-foundationalism denies that such principles exist at all.

**Genealogy:** Genealogy refers to a method that originated in Nietzsche and was carried forward by Michel Foucault, in which seemingly timeless principles and beliefs are shown to have emerged over the course of human history and in conjunction with local practices. For Nietzsche and Foucault, the task of genealogy was to expose these things and, furthermore, to expose the relations of power that hold "timeless" beliefs and principles in place.

**Genius (Taste, Rules):** The notion of genius is associated with romantic literature and philosophy, and particularly with Kant's aesthetics (*Critique of Judgment*). For Kant, the genius has the power to make the rules for art. This original, creative, rule-making power is balanced by taste, since judgments of taste require universal agreement.

**Genre:** The term genre means "kind," but especially in the literary sense refers to kinds of writing. There are overarching genres – the dramatic genres of comedy and tragedy, the prose genres of the novel and the like, and the poetic genres of epic and lyric. But there are also many minor genres, or sub-genres, in the realm of literature. While there is often thought to be some relationship between form and genre, this need not be the case. For example, there can be prose narratives (e.g., novels, histories, autobiographies) but there can also be narrative poems (e.g., epics and ballads).

**Hermeneutics:** Hermeneutics is the theory of interpretation, and especially the interpretation of texts. Traditionally, hermeneutics dealt with the interpretation of biblical and legal texts. Modern hermeneutics focuses on literature and encompasses the entire interpretative process, including modes of communication and the many presuppositions (or pre-understandings) that have a bearing on interpretation.

**Heteroglossia:** Heteroglossia refers to the presence of many languages or different ways of speaking, either within the frame of a single speaker or within a given discursive space (such as the novel). As developed by Mikhail Bakhtin, heteroglossia came to be associated with the quality of multi-voicedness that he also describes as "polyphony." Heteroglossia and polyphony both stand in opposition to monological utterances, which reduce to one the many-voiced universe of speech.

**Hylomorphism:** Hylomorphism refers to a relationship between form and content where content is believed to exist independently of the form that gives shape to it.

**Ideas:** For Plato, Ideas are the essential, eternal, and true nature of things. The realm of Ideas is wholly distinct from the realm of what we see and know in the physical world, which is the realm of appearances.

**Idealism:** In contrast to materialism, idealism refers to the set of beliefs according to which everything that exists is ultimately some form of consciousness or "spirit," that it is fundamentally mental, or mentally constructed.

**Ideology:** An ideology is the framework of unspoken beliefs, assumptions, and orientations that underlie social structures, discourses, and practices. Among some thinkers, ideology implies a set of systematic distortions that are held in place by various types of power that remain concealed.

**Imagination:** Imagination describes a power of the mind by which we form mental pictures of things or of states of affairs in the world. Imagination is different from perception (which is based on sensory input) and describes the ability to form images of things that may be real but are not present, or that may not be real at all. Not surprisingly, the imagination has played an important role in theories of art and aesthetics. For the romantics, imagination was associated with the creative powers of the genius. The imagination also plays a role in theories of moral understanding insofar as it allows us to put ourselves in the place of others. This in turn can help explain the role that literature can play in moral philosophy.

**Incommensurability:** When two things are different but can nonetheless be compared on the same scale, they are commensurable. When they are different but cannot be compared on the same scale, they are incommensurable.

Incommensurability proposes that such differences derive from the different frames within which beliefs arise.

**Intertextuality:** Intertextuality describes the belief that writing refers as much to other writing (if not *only* to other writing) as it does to anything that is outside writing (the text).

**Logical positivism:** This philosophical movement was formed from a mixture of empiricism (the belief that knowledge originates in the senses) with mathematical and linguistic logic. Logical positivism has close affinities with logical empiricism. The adherence of both to empiricism and to logic helps explain why logical positivism approaches philosophy as a kind of science.

**Logocentrism:** This term became widespread through the influence of Jacques Derrida. It refers to the tendency in all of Western metaphysics to place the logos (word, speech) at the very center of all things. Words can be spoken or written, although logocentrism privileges speech over writing.

**Logos:** This is one of the most basic and yet most difficult to translate terms from ancient Greek philosophy, in part because of its shifting meanings. It means at once "speech" and "reason," but also refers to an underlying principle of knowledge and order.

**Materialism:** Materialism in philosophy refers to the belief that everything that exists is ultimately some form of matter. Some thinkers inclined toward materialism would include energy as well. Materialism is hence opposed to the idea of a disembodied consciousness that cannot in the end be reduced to some form of matter.

**Metaphysics:** In philosophy, metaphysics is the study of the fundamental nature of things, thought to involve that which transcends the physical world (e.g., forms, ideas, and categories of the mind). Metaphysics may also involve inquiry into the conditions of the possibility of things (i.e., those conditions that are necessary for things to come into being at all).

**Mimesis:** Mimesis means imitation. For Plato it meant something like "copy," in the way that an artist or a craftsperson might make a copy of something. For Aristotle, it meant something much more physical, so that tragedy is said to involve the "imitation of an action."

**Mythos:** Mythos means story, tale, plot. It is the term that Aristotle uses to describe the plot of tragedy.

**Nihilism:** Nihilism is one of the more casually interpreted and overworked terms in philosophical discourse. Sometimes associated with the view that nothing matters, and extended from there to encompass the view that life itself is meaningless, nihilism is at the core a view about value. Its basic sense is that there is nothing of value, hence that there is no such thing as value in itself. While there may be no such thing as value, there may still be values, which we may choose for ourselves and may pursue as forcefully as we are able. In a further, expanded sense, nihilism implies that there is no real difference between *this* and *that* other than what we ourselves create. If we were to follow this train of thought to its logical conclusion, then any thinking that does not respect the essences of things is either a form of nihilism or will quickly lead to it.

**Ocularcentrism:** This refers to the tendency to privilege sight in determining our relationship to the world, and not only to value seeing more highly than the other senses (e.g., hearing, touch), but to do so in a way that constructs our relationship to the world around a set of metaphors that imply the stance of an observing subject looking at an external, object world.

**Ontology:** Ontology is the branch of philosophy that deals with questions of being. It addresses questions such as whether being has priority over non-being (or vice-versa), whether presence has priority over absence, and whether entities are fundamentally simple or complex. Its roots lie in the combination of *ontos* (being) and *logos* (science, knowledge).

**Passions:** The root of the term passion is the Greek *pathē*, which means suffering in the sense of "undergoing." In modern usage, passions refer to states of mind or being that are principally emotional. For Aristotle, passion is a state or category of being, just as action is. More generally, passions are the emotions *by which* the mind is moved (i.e., emotions that affect the mind, hence their kinship with "affects").

**Perspectivism**: Perspectivism offers one of many ways of thinking about truth and morality that rely on visual metaphors. Perspectivism holds that all truth is valid only from a particular point of view. Because there is no such thing as an all-encompassing perspective, nor any position that transcends perspectives altogether, perspectivism holds that all truth is dependent upon the particular frame within which it occurs.

**Phenomenology**: Phenomenology devotes itself to systematic reflection on subjective experience, or "consciousness" broadly understood. Phenomenology creates the basis for understanding the various elements of subjective experience, including judgment, emotions, and perception. Phenomenology takes a philosophical approach to these matters, which also lend themselves to treatment by various sciences, including cognitive psychology and neurology.

**Pluralism:** Pluralism accepts that there may be multiple, incommensurable ways of conceiving the world, and that none of them is entitled to claim priority over the others. Pluralists do not strive to reconcile these differences, but are instead committing to allowing them to flourish.

***Poiēsis:*** This is the ancient Greek term for "making," broadly understood. Its affinity with the modern term "poetry" can be misleading, since *poiēsis* was not limited to the making of anything necessarily literary. Its counterpart is praxis (doing).

**Post-structuralism:** Structuralism is a way of thinking in linguistics and certain branches of anthropology that understands relations of any type as being organized around a basic set of significant differences (raw/cooked; voiced/unvoiced) in the way that sign systems are organized. Post-structuralism holds, among other things, that these differences revolve around an empty center. Additionally, post-structuralism refuses to accept the belief that any structured set of oppositions excludes any middle term between them.

**Pragmatism**: Pragmatism aims to assess claims of truth, hypotheses about the real, and the nature of actions in the moral domain in relation to their practical consequences. In *Pragmatism* (1907), William James wrote: "To attain perfect clearness in our thoughts of an object … we need only consider what conceivable effects of a practical kind the object may involve." Pragmatism exerts a deflationary force on metaphysical approaches to questions of truth and value. It seeks to overcome rather than to refute them.

**Praxis:** This term means "practice" as the regular doing of something (as opposed to the sense in which "practice" refers to rehearsal, as of a play). It stands in contrast to theory. Although praxis requires action, it differs from action because praxis involves regular action.

**Propositional knowledge:** Propositional knowledge refers to "knowing that" such and such is the case, rather than knowledge of how to do something (praxis or *technê*) or the kind of knowledge that suggests acquaintance. It is generally expressed by sentences of the type "q knows that p," where "p" is an utterance that has the form of a proposition. Propositions are simply *statements that* something is the case.

**Reason:** Reason is the ability to think coherently and with logic appropriate to the things under consideration. Reason is broader than logic because, as Kant and others have argued, logic is about the formal rules of thought themselves. To reason about something means to apply the rules of thought appropriate to it. Because there are many different things to which we can apply the powers of reason, there are distinctions that can be made between various types of reason according to their uses (e.g., theoretical reason, speculative reason, practical reason). Whether or not reason is in itself sufficient to motivate action is a question best addressed in the context of the relationship between reason and rhetoric.

**Redescription:** This term originates in the work of recent pragmatist philosophers, especially Richard Rorty. It reflects the belief that things in themselves do not have essences (indeed that there are no "things in themselves"), and that the vocabularies we use to describe them can be changed.

**Rhetoric:** Rhetoric is the art of persuasion. To that very broad definition we need to add that it is typically the art of persuasion using the means that language provides. These may include figures of speech, examples, and argument. The appeals that characterize classical rhetoric are the grounds of persuasion: appeals to character (*ethos*), to reason (*logos*), and to feeling (*pathos*). The distinction between rhetoric and philosophy became important when Plato tried to characterize the uses of rhetoric by the Sophists as inferior and suspicious forms of discourse. Plato argued that rhetoric makes no distinction between what is true or good and what is not. Hence, rhetoric could be the art of persuading us to believe or do things that have no assurance of truth or goodness about them. Another reason for the disparagement of rhetoric lies in the suggestion that it involves mere adornment. Aristotle, by contrast, regarded rhetoric as essential to politics. He describes it as the counterpart to dialectic (rational argument) in the sense that rhetoric involves the art of making demonstrations in accordance with the persuadable aspect of each subject it treats.

**Representation:** When trying to understand how the mind knows things in the world, one answer is that it makes internal representations of them.

Representation is thus a key notion in correspondence theories of the truth. According to this theory, we know something when we make an accurate representation of it in the mind or in language. While there is no single view of what mental representations themselves are, they can be regarded as the form of things as they are known by the mind. Heidegger pointed out that representation was the general approach of the subject toward the object-world and implied a kind of framing that transforms the world into a kind of picture.

**Sophists, sophistry:** The Sophists were thinkers both before Plato and contemporaneous with him, whose work he characterized as deceptive and inferior on a number of grounds. The Sophists used the art of rhetoric (persuasion) and dialectic (argument), but according to Plato they were not necessarily concerned with the truth. As rhetoricians, they would speak simply to win an argument or a contest; at the same time, they would take money for teaching rhetorical skills. Some of the Sophists (Gorgias, Thrasymachus) appear as characters in Plato's dialogues. An entire dialogue (*Sophist*) deals with this subject.

**Speech acts:** Originating in the work of J. L. Austin, the term "speech acts" refers to instances in which saying something changes something else in a direct and efficacious way (e.g., "You are under arrest"). Speech acts occur when words are used to do things, typically in a performative fashion. Austin calls performatives "illocutionary" acts. By contrast, "constative" utterances simply describe things.

**Style:** Every work has a style, which we can loosely associate with its particular manner of speaking (or writing). Whereas questions of genre are questions about *kinds* of works, style suggests both the manner that is common to certain works (e.g., baroque style) and the particular manner of an individual work. In a stronger view, this particularity extends to the individual person. Style is philosophically meaningful when it is traceable to the demonstrations and expressions that an individual makes, and when the individual explicitly or implicitly claims responsibility for those acts. In this regard, style can be a guide to questions of moral character and can provide a link to aspects of moral character that cannot be accounted for by theories of the rational will or of pure practical reason.

**Subject, subjectivity:** The notion of the subject refers to the first-person standpoint as it underlies the relationship of human consciousness to itself and to the body, as well as to the world and to others in it. Heidegger pointed out that the term has etymological roots in the Latin *subiectum* and the Greek *hypokeimenon*. In the development of modern philosophy, the position of the subject (subjectivity) came to be regarded as primary. It is from the position of the subject that the world appears objectively. This subject/object dualism has also become the condition that materialist and idealist thinkers have tried to overcome.

***Technê:*** This is the Greek term meaning "craft," usually contrasted with *epistêmê* (knowledge). Though *technê* eventually came to resemble "practice" as it stands in contrast to theory, it initially meant a kind of art in the sense of "craft." *Technê* incorporates a particular kind of knowing – "knowing how" rather than "knowing that," or having "propositional" knowledge.

**Virtue:** The term virtue translates, via its Latin root, to the Greek word for excellence of character, *arētē*. This kind of excellence was necessarily exhibited in action. Over time, the term "virtue" acquired a much more fixed sense and became associated with certain character qualities. Especially in the Christian tradition's re-interpretation of Aristotle's thinking on the subject, which draws also on the Bible, there arose the notion of a finite set of virtues, including such things as courage, temperance, faith, hope, and love.

# *Notes*

## Introduction

1 This is Cavell eschewing a definition of "perfectionism" in *Conditions Handsome and Unhandsome*, (Chicago: University of Chicago Press, 1990), p. 4.
2 "Discourse" can be a fraught term; I use it simply to describe any loosely bounded sphere of language and of the human practices that language enables.
3 Bernard Williams, *Truth and Truthfulness* (Princeton, NJ: Princeton University Press, 2002), pp. 61–62.

## 1 The "Ancient Quarrel"

1 Following convention, I cite Plato's *Republic* listing book number and page references to the Henrucis Stephanus edition (Geneva, 1578) and in modern translation, here *Republic*, trans. Desmond Lee (London: Penguin, 2003), VII, 515c–516a.
2 The phrase is from Stanley Rosen, *Hermeneutics as Politics* (Oxford: Oxford University Press, 1987), p. 62.
3 Vernant, *Myth and Thought among the Greeks*, pp. 116–117.
4 Heraclitus, *Fragments*, trans. Brooks Haxton (London: Penguin Books, 2001), no. 129, p. 91.
5 Martin Heidegger, *Parmenides*, trans. Andre Schuwer and Richard Rojcewic (Bloomington: Indiana University Press, 1998), pp. xiv, 149.
6 The correspondence theory itself has deep roots in the ancient notion that something – usually a proposition, representation, or idea – can and ought to conform adequately and accurately to the way things are, either to things or states of affairs in the world, or to truths about things such as the good that may lie beyond the world.
7 Friedrich Nietzsche, *Human, All Too Human*, trans. R. J. Hollingdale (Cambridge: Cambridge University Press, 1986), sec. 16, p. 20.
8 Friedrich Nietzsche, *The Birth of Tragedy*, trans. Walter Kaufmann (New York: Vintage Books, 1967), p. 23. Hereafter referred to in citations at *BT*.
9 Jean-Paul Sartre, *Being and Nothingness*, trans. Hazel E. Barnes (New York: Washington Square Books, 1956), p. 5. Emphasis in original.

10 Søren Kierkegaard, *The Concept of Irony, with Constant Reference to Socrates*, trans. Lee Capel (Bloomington: Indiana University Press, 1965), p. 63.
11 Plato, "Ion," In *Early Socratic Dialogues*, trans. Trevor J. Saunders (London: Penguin, 1987), p. 542b. In *The Fire and the Sun* (New York: Oxford University Press, 1977), Iris Murdoch argues that the target is not Homer but the rhapsode.
12 One of the most interesting recent discussions of the question of poetry and kinds of knowledge is Raymond Geuss, "Poetry and Knowledge," In *Outside Ethics* (Princeton, NJ: Princeton University Press, 2005), pp. 184–205.
13 Glenn Most, "What Ancient Quarrel between Philosophy and Poetry?" In *Plato and the Poets* (Leiden: Brill, 2011).
14 David O'Connor, "Rewriting the Poets in Plato's Characters," In *The Cambridge Companion to Plato's Republic*, p. 55.
15 O'Connor, "Rewriting the Poets," p. 73.
16 Friedrich Hölderlin, "Bread and Wine," In *Friedrich Hölderlin: Poems & Fragments*, trans. M. Hamburger (London: Anvil Press, 2004), p. 267.
17 Iris Murdoch, *The Fire and the Sun*, p. 41.
18 Slavoj Žižek, *The Parallax View* (Cambridge, MA: MIT Press, 2006), pp. 161–162. Emphasis in original.
19 Friedrich Nietzsche, *The Will to Power*, trans. Walter Kaufmann and R. J. Hollingdale (New York: Vintage Books, 1968), sec. 481, p. 267.
20 G. W. F. Hegel, *Phenomenology of Spirit*, trans. A. V. Miller (Oxford: Oxford University Press, 1977), p. 9.
21 Friedrich Nietzsche, *The Gay Science*, trans. Walter Kaufmann (New York: Vintage Books, 1974), sec. 110, p. 169.
22 The one exception that scholars are able to agree upon here is the so-called Seventh Letter.
23 In proposing that the novel has its roots in Plato's dialogues, Nietzsche echoes views put forward by Friedrich Schlegel in the *Athanaeum* fragments. For further discussion and references, see Chapter 12. Emphasis in original.
24 Plato, *Symposium*, trans. Walter Hamilton (Harmondsworth: Penguin, 1951), 214e, p. 100.

## 2 Action, Imitations, Conventions of Make-Believe

1 A. E. Taylor, *Aristotle* (1919; rpt. New York: Dover, 1955), p. 12. None of Aristotle's original works have survived, although some passages appear in direct quotations by others; what we know as Aristotle's "works" are the manuscripts of lecture notes transcribed by his pupils.
2 See Halliwell, *Aristotle's Poetics*, pp. 12–13.
3 I cite Aristotle's works according to page numbers from the Immanuel Bekker edition, *Aristotelis Opera edidit Academia Regia Borussica* (Berlin: Deutsche Akademie der Wissenschaften zu Berlin, 1831–1870) and modern editions, here *Poetics*, ed. Gerald Else (Ann Arbor: University of Michigan Press, 1970), 1460b, p. 67.

4 This is one of the basic principles that deconstruction sought to challenge in questioning the presuppositions from which Western metaphysics begins.
5 See Taylor, *Aristotle*, pp. 35–36.
6 Philip Sidney, *A Defence of Poetry*, ed. J. A. van Dorsten (Oxford: Oxford University Press, 1975), p. 36.
7 Aristotle, *Rhetoric*, trans. H.C. Lawson-Tancred (London: Penguin, 1991), 1455b, p. 77.
8 Jane Austen, *Pride and Prejudice*, ed. Patricia Meyer Spacks (Cambridge, MA: Harvard University Press, 2010), p. 29.
9 Joyce Carol Oates, "Afterword" to *I Lock My Door Upon Myself* (Princeton, NJ: Ontario Review Press, 1990), pp. 104, 106–107.
10 Horace, "Ars Poetica," in *Horace: Satires, Epistles and Ars Poetica*, trans. H. R. Fairclough (Cambridge, MA: Harvard University Press, 1970), p. 458. In a similar vein, though in a much more contemporary idiom, Gregory Currie put forward a reading of Anne Brontë's *The Tenant of Wildfell Hall* in which he argues that empathy plays a crucial role in the reader's response to the novel and that few readers would remain engaged with the book otherwise. Gregory Currie, "Anne Brontë and the Uses of Imagination," In *Contemporary Debates in Aesthetics and the Philosophy of Art*, ed. Mathew Kieran (Malden, MA: Blackwell, 2006), p. 219.
11 See Goux, *Oedipus, Philosopher*, trans. Catherine Porter (Stanford, CA: Stanford University Press, 1993).
12 See Heidegger, *What is Called Thinking?* trans. J. Glenn Gray (New York: Harper and Row, 1968).
13 *King Oedipus*, trans. Jascha Kessler, ed. David Slavitt and Palmer Bowie (Philadelphia: University of Pennsylvania Press, 1999), vv. 1691–1692.
14 Stephen Abell, "Stress Tests," *Times Literary Supplement*, 5630 (Feb. 25, 2011), 3.
15 Kendall Walton, *Mimesis as Make-Believe* (Cambridge, MA: Harvard University Press, 1993), p. 11.
16 Stanley Cavell, "The Avoidance of Love," In *Must We Mean What We Say?* (Cambridge: Cambridge University Press, 1969), pp. 267–353. Henceforth referred to in citations as *MWM*.
17 Ludwig Wittgenstein, *Philosophical Investigations*, trans. G. E. M. Anscombe (New York: MacMillan, 1958), pp. 5e, 8e, and passim.

## 3 The Single Observer Standpoint and Its Limits

1 Martin Heidegger, "The Age of the World Picture," In *The Question Concerning Technology and Other Essays*, trans. William Lovitt (New York: Harper and Row, 1977), p. 134.
2 Richard Rorty, *Philosophy and the Mirror of Nature* (Princeton, NJ: Princeton University Press, 1979), p. 45. Henceforth referred to in citations as *PMN*.
3 René Descartes, *Discourse on the Method*, V, In *Philosophical Writings* I, trans. Elizabeth Haldane and G. R. T. Ross (Cambridge: Cambridge University Press, 1975), p. 107.

4 René Descartes, *Meditations on First Philosophy*, I, In *The Philosophical Works of Descartes* II, trans. John Cottingham, Robert Stoothoff, and Dugald Murdoch (Cambridge: Cambridge University Press, 1984), p. 13.
5 Thomas Metzinger, *Being No One: The Self-Model Theory of Subjectivity* (Cambridge, MA: MIT Press, 2004) p. 557.
6 Janet E. Kaufman, Anne F. Herzog, and Jan Heller Levi, eds., *The Collected Poems of Muriel Rukeyser* (Pittsburgh, PA: University of Pittsburgh Press, 2005). For discussion, see Adriana Cavarero, *Relating Narratives*, trans. Paul Kottman (London: Routledge, 1997), pp. 49–54.
7 Aristotle, *Metaphysics*, trans. Richard Hope (Ann Arbor: University of Michigan Press, 1960), 1011b, p. 83.
8 Thomas Aquinas, *Quaestiones Disputatae de Veritate*, trans. Robert W. Mulligan (Chicago: Henry Regnery Compan, 1952), Q.1, A.1–3 (electronic resource at dhspriory.org/Thomas/QDdeVer.htm); cf. Thomas Aquinas, "Summa Theologiae Q.16," In *Summa Theologiae: A Concise Translation*, ed. Timothy McDermott (Westminster, MD: Christian Classics, 1989), p. 48.
9 Nelson Goodman, *Ways of Worldmaking*, (Indianapolis: Hackett, 1978), p. 9.
10 Rorty, *PMN*, p. 144.
11 *Critique of Pure Reason*, trans. Norman Kemp Smith (New York: St. Martin's Press, 1965), p. 17.
12 Alasdair MacIntyre, *After Virtue*, 2nd ed. (Notre Dame, IN: University of Notre Dame Press, 1984), p. 56.

## 4 Contingency, Irony, Edification: Changing the Conversation about Truth

1 Richard Rorty, *Consequences of Pragmatism* (Minneapolis: University of Minnesota Press, 1982), p. xiii.
2 Voltaire, *Philosophical Dictionary*, trans. Theodor Besterman (London: Penguin, 2004), p. 387.
3 Woody Allen, "My Philosophy," In *Getting Even* (New York: Vintage Books, 1978), p. 22.
4 Richard Rorty, *Contingency, Irony, Solidarity* (Cambridge: Cambridge University Press, 1989), p. 101.
5 Marcel Proust, *Remembrances of Things Past*, Vol. 6: *Time Regained*, trans. C. K. Scott Moncrieff, Terence Kilmartin, and Andreas Mayor, revised by D. J. Enright (New York: Modern Library), p. 304.
6 Nietzsche, *Human, All Too Human*, sec. 2, p. 13; emphasis in original.
7 Malcolm Bull, *Anti-Nietzsche* (London: Verso, 2011), p. 32.
8 Rorty is citing Jacques Derrida, *Margins of Philosophy* (Chicago: University of Chicago Press, 1982), p. 27.
9 Rorty, *PMN*, p. 12.
10 William James, *Pragmatism: A New Name for an Old Way of Thinking* (New York: New American Library, 1955), p. 43.

11 Ludwig Wittgenstein, *Philosophical Investigations*, trans. G. E. M. Anscombe (New York: Macmillan, 1958), sec. 38, p. 19e.
12 Charles Taylor, "Language and Human Nature," In *Philosophical Papers* I (Cambridge: Cambridge University Press, 1985), p. 218. Emphasis in original.
13 Hannah Arendt, *The Human Condition* (Chicago: University of Chicago Press, 1958), p. 10.
14 Hannah Arendt, *Lectures on Kant's Political Philosophy*, ed. Ronald Beiner (Chicago: University of Chicago Press, 1982), p. 27.
15 Taylor, "Theories of Meaning," In *Philosophical Papers* I, pp. 259–260. Emphasis in original.
16 Robert Pippin, *Henry James and Modern Moral Life* (Cambridge: Cambridge University Press, 2000), pp. 10–11.
17 Emmanuel Lévinas, *Outside the Subject*, trans. Michael B. Smith (Stanford, CA: Stanford University Press, 1994), p. 115.
18 Emmanuel Lévinas, *Alterity and Transcendence*, trans. Michael B. Smith (New York: Columbia University Press, 1999), p. 76.
19 Stanley Cavell, *Disowning Knowledge in Six Plays of Shakespeare* (Cambridge: Cambridge University Press, 1987), p. 138.
20 William Shakespeare, *Othello: The Moor of Venice*, ed. Michael Neill (Oxford: Oxford University Press, 2006), p. 372, vv. 4–5.

## 5 Values, Contingencies, Conflicts

1 Hilary Putnam, *The Collapse of the Fact-Value Dichotomy and Other Essays* (Cambridge, MA: Harvard University Press, 2002), p. 27.
2 For recent accounts see Bernard Williams, *Ethics and the Limits of Philosophy* (Cambridge, MA: Harvard University Press, 1985) and Harry G. Frankfurt, *The Importance of What We Care About* (1988; rpt. Cambridge: Cambridge University Press, 2005).
3 John Keats, "Letter to Benjamin Bailey, November 22, 1817," in *The Letters of John Keats* I (Cambridge, MA: Harvard University Press, 1958), p. 184. Ralph Waldo Emerson makes a similar pronouncement in "Nature," In *Essays and Lectures*, ed. Joel Porte (New York: Library of America, 1983), p. 36, 83. See also, Iris Murdoch *Metaphysics as a Guide to Morals* (London: Penguin Boks, 1992), p. 430.
4 Simon Critchley, *Things as They Are* (London: Routledge, 2005), p. 23.
5 Ronald Dworkin, *Justice for Hedgehogs* (Cambridge, MA: Harvard University Press, 2011), p. 8.
6 Iris Murdoch, *The Unicorn*, (London: Penguin Books, 1963), p. 100.
7 This is bound up with Aristotle's convictions that (1) what is proper to each thing is naturally most pleasant for it, and (2) that the life according to reason is best for human beings and the key to "happiness" because "reason more than anything else *is* man." *Nicomachean Ethics*, trans. David Ross (Oxford: Oxford University Press, 1980), X.8, 1178a, p. 266. Henceforth referred to in citations as *EN*. Aristotle calls the good the object of a "rational wish," implying both that one could not *rationally*

wish for something contrary to the good, and that the desire for what is other than good does not correspond to reason.

8 Henry James, *The Golden Bowl* (Harmondsworth: Penguin Books, 1982), p. 230.

9 Iris Murdoch, *The Sovereignty of Good* (London: Routledge, 1971), p. 68. Henceforth referred to in citations as *SG*.

10 Martha Nussbaum, *Love's Knowledge* (New York: Oxford University Press, 1990), pp. 7–8. The phrase from James comes from his "Preface" to *The Portrait of a Lady*.

11 Michel Foucault, *Fearless Speech*, ed. Joseph Pearson (New York: Semiotext[e], 2001), p. 97. Judith Butler provides an illuminating discussion of this dimension of Foucault's work in *Giving an Account of Oneself* (New York: Fordham University Press, 2005).

12 Alexander Pope, *Essay on Man*, ed. Mark Pattison (Oxford: Clarendon Press, 1881), I, 289–294, p. 36.

13 Voltaire, *Candide*, ed. Shane Weller (Mineola, NY: Dover, 1993), p.vi.

14 On this self-critical project see Ricardo Quinones, *Erasmus and Voltaire: Why They Still Matter* (Toronto: University of Toronto Press, 2010).

15 Christopher P. Long, "Is there Method in This Madness? Context, Play, and Laughter in Plato's *Symposium* and *Republic*," In *Philosophy in Dialogue: Plato's Many Devices*, ed. Gary Alan Scott (Evanston, IL: Northwestern University Press, 2007), p. 175.

16 Political theorist Carl Schmitt proposed that the power to declare a "state of exception" was constitutive of sovereignty itself. See *Political Theology*, trans. George Schwab (Chicago: University of Chicago Press, 1985).

17 Hegel discusses *Antigone* both in chapter 6 of *Phenomenology of Spirit* (the chapter titled "Geist," or "Spirit") and in *Aesthetics*.

18 Sophocles, *Antigone*, trans. Kelly Cherry (Philadelphia: University of Pennsylvania Press, 1999), vv. 151–163, p. 200.

19 G.W.F. Hegel, *Lectures on Aesthetics*, trans. T. M. Knox (Oxford: Clarendon Press, 1998), II, pp. 1213–1214.

20 Paul Ricoeur, *Oneself as Another*, trans. Kathleen Blamey (Chicago: University of Chicago Press, 1992), p. 248.

21 Plato, "Protagoras," In *Protagoras and Meno*, trans. W. K. C. Guthrie (Harmondsworth: Penguin Books, 1986), 351b, p. 87.

22 Joseph Conrad, *Lord Jim*, ed. Thomas C. Moser (New York: Norton, 1968), p. 18.

23 Pippin, *Henry James and Modern Moral Life*, pp. 11–12.

24 The reference is to Frankfurt's *The Importance of What We Care About*.

25 T. S. Eliot, "Poetry and Propaganda," *Bookman* 70, no. 6 (February 1930), p. 601. Cited in Richard Eldridge, *On Moral Personhood* (Chicago: University of Chicago Press, 1989), p. 21.

## 6 Reason and Autonomy, Imagination and Feeling

1 Stanley Cavell, *In Quest of the Ordinary: Lines of Skepticism and Romanticism* (Chicago: University of Chicago Press, 1988), pp. 229–230.

2 Immanuel Kant, *Foundations of the Metaphysics of Morals*, trans. Lewis White Beck (Indianapolis: Bobbs-Merrill, 1959), p. 67.

3 Jean-Jacques Rousseau, *The Social Contract*, ed. Lester G. Crocker (New York: Washington Square Press, 1967), p. 7.
4 Immanuel Kant, *Critique of Practical Reason*, trans. Lewis White Beck (Indianapolis: Bobbs-Merrill, 1956), p. 32.
5 For further details and discussion, see Richard Eldridge, "The Kantian Moral Criticism of Literature," In *The Persistence of Romanticism: Essays in Philosophy and Literature* (Cambridge: Cambridge University Press, 2001), pp. 71–84.
6 Immanuel Kant, "Introduction" to *Critique of Judgment*, trans. James Creed Meredith (Oxford: Oxford University Press, 1962), p. 14. Henceforth referred to in citations as *CJ*.
7 Mark van Doren, ed., *Selected Poetry of William Wordsworth* (New York: Modern Library, 2002), pp. 652, 660. All Wordsworth citations refer to this volume.
8 Adam Smith, "Of Sympathy," In *Theory of the Moral Sentiments* (Indianapolis: Liberty Press, 1976), I.1, 47, 49. On Adam Smith, Rousseau, and Mandeville, see Charles Griswold, "Smith and Rousseau in Dialogue," In Vivienne Brown and Samuel Fleischaker, eds., *The Philosophy of Adam Smith* (New York: Routledge, 2010), pp. 59–84.
9 Jean-Jacques Rousseau, "Essay on the Origin of Languages," trans. John H. Moran and Alexander Gode (Chicago: University of Chicago Press, 1986), p. 322.
10 Charles Larmore, *The Romantic Legacy* (New York: Columbia University Press, 1996), p. 9.
11 Emerson, "The American Scholar," In *Essays and Lectures*, p. 68.
12 Samuel Taylor Coleridge, *Biographia Literaria*, ed. George Watson (London: J. M. Dent and Sons, 1965), p. 169.

## 7 Forces and the Will

1 Kant was himself well aware of the limitations of reason. In *Critique of Pure Reason* he urges respect for those limits.
2 Edgar Allan Poe, "The Imp of the Perverse," In *The Complete Stories* (New York: Knopf Everyman's Library, 1992), p. 856.
3 Charles Baudelaire, "The Bad Glazier" ("Le Mauvais Vitrier") In *Le Spleen de Paris*, trans. Louise Varese (New York: New Directions, 1947), pp. 12–13.
4 Charles Baudelaire, *The Flowers of Evil*, trans. Richard Howard (Boston, MA: David Godine, 1985), p. 35.
5 Friedrich Nietzsche, *Beyond Good and Evil*, trans. R. J. Hollingdale (Harmondsworth: Penguin, 1979), p. 13. Henceforth referred to in citations as *BGE*.
6 Robert Pippin, *Nietzsche, Psychology, and First Philosophy* (Chicago: University of Chicago Press, 2010), p. 13.
7 See Yirmiyahu Yovel, *Hegel's Preface to Phenomenology of Spirit: Translation and Running Commentary* (Princeton: Princeton University Press, 2005), p. 60.
8 Arthur Schopenhauer, *The World as Will and Representations*, trans. E. F. Payne (New York: Dover, 1969), I.7, pp. 30–31. References are to book, section, and pages. Henceforth referred to in citations as *WWR*.

9 Arthur Schopenhauer, *Prize Essay on the Freedom of the Will*, trans. E. F. J. Payne, ed. Günter Zöller (Cambridge: Cambridge University Press, 1999), pp. 93–94.
10 Friedrich Nietzsche, "Schopenhauer as Educator," In *Untimely Meditations*, trans. R. J. Hollingdale (Cambridge: Cambridge University Press, 1983), p. 152.
11 Friedrich Nietzsche, "On Old and New Law Tables," In *Thus Spoke Zarathustra*, trans. R. J. Hollingdale (Harmondsworth: Penguin, 1982), IV, p. 216.
12 Sandine Byrne, ed., "Man and Superman," Act II, In *George Bernard Shaw's Plays* (New York: Norton, 2002) pp. 158–159, 175.
13 *WWR*, IV.55, p. 189. As Richard Freadman explained, "the empirical self through which the blind, impersonal will moves is an irreducible particular self." *Threads of Life: Autobiography and the Will* (Chicago: University of Chicago Press, 2001), p. 312. There is, in Schopenhauer's words "great difference of individual characters" (*WWR*, I.26, 131).
14 Hugh Roberts, *Shelley and the Chaos of History* (University Park: Pennsylvania State University Press, 1997), p. 385.
15 Donald Reiman and Neil Fraistat, eds., "Julian and Maddalo," In *Shelley's Poetry and Prose* (New York: Norton), vv. 172–173, p. 125.
16 P. B. Shelley, *The Revolt of Islam*, VIII, xxii, 3 (London: John Brooks, 1829), p. 188.
17 P. B. Shelley, "Preface" to *Prometheus Unbound*, In *Shelley's Prose and Poetry*, ed. Donald H. Reiman and Neil Fraistat (New York: Norton, 2002), p. 207.
18 "Preface" to *The Cenci*, In *Shelley's Poetry and Prose*, p. 144.
19 Johann Wolfgang von Goethe, *The Sufferings of Young Werther*, trans. Harry Steinhauer (New York: Norton, 1970), p. 27.
20 Goethe and Lessing share the view that human nature is susceptible to the powers of seduction and of self-deception. Indeed, the Emilia of Lessing's play herself declares that "force is nothing," or rather "Seduction is the only true force." Ernest Bell, ed., "Emilia Galotti" In *The Dramatic Works of Gotthold Ephraim Lessing* (London: George Bell and Sons, 1878), V.vii, p. 223.
21 Friedrich Nietzsche, *Will to Power*, trans. Walter Kaufmann and R. J. Hollingdale (New York: Vintage, 1968), sec. 481, p. 267. Henceforth referred to in citations as *WP*.
22 See Alexander Nehamas, *Nietzsche: Life as Literature* (Cambridge, MA: Harvard University Press, 1985).
23 Martin Heidegger, *Nietzsche: The Will to Power as Art*, trans. David Farrell Krell (New York: Harper and Row, 1991), III–IV, p. 74.

## 8 Opacity

1 Marx, *The Eighteenth Brumaire of Louis Bonaparte*, trans. Daniel de Leon (Chicago: Charles H. Kerr, 1907), p. 9.
2 Paul Ricoeur, *Freud and Philosophy: An Essay on Interpretation*, trans. Denis Savage (New Haven, CT: Yale University Press, 1970).

3 Sigmund Freud, *Beyond the Pleasure Principle*, trans. James Strachey (New York: Norton, 1961), p. 7. Henceforth referred to in citations as *BPP*.
4 Peter Brooks, "Freud's Masterplot," In *Reading for the Plot* (New York: Knopf, 1984), pp. 90–112. Equally important is the essay "Narrative Desire," pp. 37–61.
5 Freud summarizes one dimension of *The Interpretation of Dreams* this way in *Dora: An Analysis of a Case of Hysteria* (New York: Simon and Schuster Touchstone Books, 1977), p. 9.
6 Honoré de Balzac, *The Wild Ass's Skin*, trans. Herbert J. Hunt (Harmondsworth: Penguin Books, 1977), p. 91.
7 This analysis follows Brooks, "Narrative Desire" In *Reading for the Plot*.
8 William Shakespeare, *The Merchant of Venice*, ed. Barbara A. Mowat and Paul Werstine (New York: Simon and Schuster, Folger Shakespeare Library, 2010), III.ii, v. 105, p. 109.
9 William Shakespeare, *King Lear*, ed. Stephen Orgel (New York: Penguin Books, 1999), I.1.62.
10 Ricoeur, *Freud and Philosophy*, p. 311.
11 Freud, "On Dreams" In *The Freud Reader*, ed. Peter Gay (New York: Norton, 1989), p. 149; emphasis in original. Henceforth referred to in citations as *OD*.
12 Slavoj Žižek, "How Did Marx Invent the Symptom," In *Mapping Ideology*, ed. Slavoj Žižek (London: Verso, 1994), p. 29.
13 See his "Analysis of a Phobia in a Five Year Old Boy," In *The Wolfman and other Cases*, (London: Penguin, 2003).
14 Lear, *Love and its Place in Nature*, p. 45.
15 In what follows here, I draw on Lear's *Love and its Place in Nature*.
16 Karl Marx, *Grundrisse*, trans. Martin Nicolaus (London: Penguin Books, 1973), p. 307; emphasis in original.
17 Terry Eagleton, *Marxism and Literary Criticism* (Berkeley: University of California Press, 1976), p. 650.
18 See Fredric Jameson, *The Political Unconscious* (Ithaca, NY: Cornell University Press, 1981), pp. 101–102.
19 Among many other instances, see Jacques Derrida, *Of Grammatology*, trans. Gayatri Spivak (Baltimore, MD: Johns Hopkins University Press, 1974), p. 101. For Derrida, phonologism implies the debasement or exclusion of writing (102). Derrida began his critique of phonocentrism and logocentrism in his very first book, on Husserl's *La Voix et le Phénomène* (translated as *Speech and Phenomena*) and continued the development of this critique over many years and in connection with writers as different as Plato and Rousseau, all as part of a critique of Western metaphysics.
20 Jacques Derrida, "White Mythology," In *Margins of Philosophy*, trans. Alan Bass (Chicago: University of Chicago Press, 1982), p. 232.
21 Sarah Kofman, *Nietzsche and Metaphor*, trans. Duncan Large (Stanford, CA: Stanford University Press, 1993), p. 14.
22 Immanuel Kant, *Foundations of the Metaphysics of Morals*, trans. Lewis White Beck (Indianapolis: Bobbs-Merrill, 1969), p. 21n.

23 J. Hillis Miller, *The Ethics of Reading* (New York: Columbia University Press, 1987), p. 20.
24 Franz Kafka, *Selected Shorter Writings*, trans. Ian Johnston, The Kafka Project. http://www.kafka.org/index.php?id=162,165,0,0,1,0.
25 Maurice Merleau-Ponty, *The Prose of the World*, trans. John O'Neill (Evanston, IL: Northwestern University Press, 1973), pp. 12–13.
26 Lévinas, *Outside the Subject*, p. 93.

## 9 Ubiquitous Form

1 Molière (Jean-Baptiste Poquelin), *Le Bourgeois Gentilhomme* (London: Cambridge University Press, 1952), II.vi, p. 22.
2 This is discussed in Richard Lanham, *Analyzing Prose* (New York: Continuum, 1983), pp. 192–193.
3 The terms "theatricality" and "absorption" have also been proposed (specifically, in relation to Diderot's writings on the theatre) as ways to describe this difference. See Michael Fried, *Absorption and Theatricality: Painting and Beholder in the Age of Diderot* (Berkeley: University of California Press, 1980).
4 Walter Benjamin, *The Origin of German Tragic Drama*, trans. John Osborne (London: Verso, 1977), p. 30.
5 Ludwig Wittgenstein, *Culture and Value*, trans. Peter Winch (Chicago: University of Chicago Press, 1980), p. 24e; emphasis in original.
6 Christopher Shields, "A Fundamental Problem about Hylomorphism" in *The Stanford Encyclopedia of Philosophy* (Spring 2011 Edition), ed. Edward N. Zalta, http://plato.stanford.edu/entries/aristotle-psychology/suppl1.html.
7 See Jacques Derrida, "Form and Meaning: A Note on the Phenomenology of Language," in *Margins of Philosophy*, trans. Alan Bass (Chicago: University of Chicago Press, 1982), pp. 155–173.
8 William Shakespeare, Sonnet 130, v. 1. In *Shakespeare's Sonnets*, ed. Stephen Booth (New Haven: Yale University Press, 1977), p. 112.
9 Martin Heidegger, "The Origin of the Work of Art," In *Poetry, Language, Thought*, trans. Albert Hofstadter (New York: Harper and Row, 1971), p. 45. Henceforth referred to in citations as "OWA."
10 Simon Critchley, *Things Merely Are* (London: Routledge, 2008), p. 57.
11 *OWA*, p. 45.
12 *The Collected Poems of Wallace Stevens* (New York: Vintage Books, 1982), p. 278.
13 On form in Kant, see Rodolphe Gasché, *The Idea of Form: Rethinking Kant's Aesthetics* (Stanford, CA: Stanford University Press, 2003) and Richard Eldridge, "Beauty and Form" In *An Introduction to the Philosophy of Art* (Cambridge: Cambridge University Press, 2003), pp. 47–67.
14 "[B]y 'plot' I here mean the structuring of the events, and by the 'characters' that in accordance with which we say that the persons who are acting have a defined moral

character, and by 'thought' [*dianoia*] all the passages in which they attempt to prove some thesis or set forth an opinion." Aristotle, *Poetics*, 1450a, p. 26.

15 Helen Vendler, *Poets Thinking* (Cambridge, MA: Harvard University Press, 2004).

16 George's original reads: "Kein ding sei wo das Wort gebricht." Cited in Heidegger "The Nature of Language" In *On the Way to Language*, pp. 57–108.

17 William Shakespeare, *Richard II*, ed. John Dover Wilson (Cambridge: Cambridge University Press, 1971), II.i, vv. 40–50, pp. 26–27.

18 "Beauty is one way in which truth occurs as unconcealedness" (Heidegger, *OWA*, p. 56).

19 Vendler, *Poets Thinking*, p. 65.

20 R.W. Franklin, ed., *The Poems of Emily Dickinson* (Cambridge, MA: Belknap Press of Harvard University Press, 1998), vv. 9–12, 17–20, p. 208. I follow the conventional modification of Dickinson's idiosyncratic spelling, changing "It's" to "Its."

21 William Hazlitt, *Characters of Shakespeare's Plays* (London: C. H. Reynell, 1817), pp. 38, 46, 50.

22 Jacques Rancière, *Mute Speech*, trans. James Swenson (New York: Columbia University Press, 2011), p. 63.

23 Gustave Flaubert, letter to Louise Colet, June 25, 1853, In *The Letters of Gustave Flaubert, 1830–1857*, trans. Francis Steegmuller (Cambridge, MA: Belknap Press of Harvard University Press, 1979), p. 189.

24 Samuel Beckett, *Endgame* (New York: Grove Press, 1958), p. 39. See also Stanley Cavell, "Ending the Waiting Game," In *Must We Mean What We Say?* (Cambridge: Cambridge University Press, 1969), especially pp. 120–121.

25 Wittgenstein, *Philosophical Investigations*, sec. 116, p. 48e.

26 Some of the implications for literary studies are developed in: Kenneth Dauber and Walter Jost, eds., *Ordinary Language Criticism* (Evanston, IL: Northwestern University Press, 2003).

27 Richard Eldridge and Bernie Rhie, "Introduction" to *Stanley Cavell and Literary Studies* (New York: Continuum, 2011), pp. 1–2.

28 Cavell, *Must We Mean What We Say?* p. 275.

29 Cavell, *In Quest of the Ordinary*, p. 9.

30 Ibid.

31 Ludwig Wittgenstein, *Tractatus Logico-Philosophicus*, trans. C. K. Ogden (Mineola, NY: Dover, 1999), sec. 5.6, p. 88.

## 10 Linguistic Turns

1 Thomas Hobbes, *Leviathan*, ed. C. B. Macpherson (Harmondsworth: Penguin Books, 1968), p. 105.

2 Wittgenstein, *Tractatus Logico-Philosophicus*, p. 29.

3 This section is indebted to Rorty, *PMN*, especially pp. 257–311 ("Epistemology and Philosophy of Language").

4 Hilary Putnam, "What is Realism?" *Proceedings of the Aristotelian Society*, 1979, pp. 183–184.
5 Thomas Kuhn, *The Structure of Scientific Revolutions* (Chicago: University of Chicago Press, 1962).
6 Gilles Deleuze, in dialogue with Michel Foucault, "Intellectuals and Power," In *Language, Counter-Memory, Practice* (Ithaca, NY: Cornell University Press, 1977), pp. 206, 208.
7 Stanley Cavell, *The Claim of Reason: Wittgenstein, Skepticism, Morality and Tragedy* (Oxford: Oxford University Press, 1979), p. 11.
8 J. L. Austin, *How to Do Things with Words* (Cambridge, MA: Harvard University Press, 1975), p. 1.
9 Henry Staten, *Wittgenstein and Derrida* (Lincoln: University of Nebraska Press, 1984), p. 118.
10 Jacques Derrida, *Limited, Inc.* (Evanston, IL: Northwestern University Press, 1988), p. 208; emphasis in original.
11 Emerson, "Self-Reliance," In *Essays and Lectures*, p. 270.
12 Cavell, "Being Odd, Getting Even (Descartes, Emerson, Poe)," In *In Quest of the* Ordinary, p. 109.
13 Judith Butler, *Gender Trouble* (New York: Routledge, 1990), p. 140.
14 Alexander Nehamas, *Nietzsche: Life as Literature* (Cambridge, MA: Harvard University Press, 1985), p. 173.
15 Michel Haar, "Nietzsche and Metaphysical Language," In *The New Nietzsche*, ed. David Allison (New York: Delta, 1977), pp. 17–18.

## 11 Form, Narrative, Novel

1 J. David Velleman, *The Possibility of Practical Reasoning* (rpt. Ann Arbor: University of Michigan Library, 2000), p. 162.
2 Louis Mink, "History and Fiction as Modes of Comprehension," In *Historical Understanding* (Ithaca, NY: Cornell University Press, 1987), p. 50; see also "Narrative Form as a Cognitive Instrument," pp. 42–60.
3 MacIntyre, *After Virtue*, 2nd ed.; Wilhelm Dilthey, "The Construction of the Historical World in Human Studies," In *Collected Writings*, ed. H. P. Rickman (Cambridge: Cambridge University Press, 1976), p. 238
4 Hegel, *Phenomenology of Spirit*, sec. 2, p. 2.
5 Hegel, "Preface" to *Phenomenology of Spirit*, p. 11.
6 Ilya Kliger, *The Narrative Shape of Truth: Veridiction in Modern European Literature* (University Park: Pennsylvania State University Press, 2011), p. 19. Kliger draws directly on Jean Hippolyte, *Genesis and Structure of Hegel's Phenomenology of Spirit*, trans. Samuel Cherniak and John Heckman (Evanston, IL: Northwestern University Press, 1974), p. 25.
7 Hegel, "Preface" to *Philosophy of Right*, trans. T. M. Knox (Oxford: Oxford University Press, 1980), p. 10.

8 See Yovel, *Hegel's Preface*, pp. 14–16.
9 Ricoeur, *Oneself as Another*, p. 119.
10 Aristotle, *EN*, 5.1.1129a, p. 106.
11 Italo Calvino, *t zero*, trans. William Weaver (New York: Harcourt Brace, Jovanovich, 1970), p. 75.
12 Eldridge, *On Moral Personhood*, pp. 11–12.
13 Fernando Pessoa, *Book of Disquiet*, trans. Richarad Zenith (London: Penguin Books, 2001), p. 9.
14 Jay Bernstein, *The Philosophy of the Novel: Lukács, Marxism and the Dialectics of Form* (Minneapolis: University of Minnesota Press, 1994), p. 191.
15 Georg Lukács, *The Theory of the Novel*, trans. Anna Bostock (Cambridge, MA: MIT Press, 1971).
16 I draw here on Martin Heidegger, *Being and Time*, trans. John Macquarrie and Edward Robinson (New York: Harper and Row, 1962), sec. 45–47, pp. 274–285.
17 Miguel de Cervantes, *Don Quixote*, trans. Edith Grossman (New York: Harper Collins, 2003), pp. 19–20.
18 Roland Barthes, "The Reality Effect," In *The Rustle of Language*, trans. Richard Howard (Oxford: Basil Blackwell, 1986), pp. 141–148.
19 Cited in ibid., p. 141.
20 Henry James, "Honoré de Balzac," In *Literary Criticism, Volume Two* (New York: Library of America, 1984), p. 48.
21 Bill Brown, *A Sense of Things* (Chicago: University of Chicago Press, 2003), p. 16.
22 Roland Barthes, *S/Z*, trans. Richard Howard (New York: Hill and Wang, 1974), p. 140.
23 Pierre Macherey, *The Object of Literature*, trans. David Macey (Cambridge: Cambridge University Press, 1995), p. 180.
24 Francis Steegmuller, *The Letters of Gustrave Flaubert, 1830–1857* p. 234.
25 Michel de Montaigne, "To the Reader," In *The Complete Essays of Montaigne*, trans. Donald Frame (Stanford, CA: Stanford University Press, 1958), p. 2.
26 Jean-Jacques Rousseau, *Confessions*, trans. J. M. Cohen (London: Penguin, 1953), p. 262.

## 12 Forms and Fragments

1 Georg Lukács pointed to a disorderliness in the novels of Lawrence Sterne in "Richness, Chaos, and Form," In *Soul and Form*, trans. Anna Bostock (Cambridge, MA: MIT Press, 1974), pp. 124–151.
2 Mikhail Bakhtin, "Discourse in the Novel," In *The Dialogic Imagination*, trans. Caryl Emerson and Michael Holquist (Austin: University of Texas Press, 1981), p. 324.
3 Michael Holquist, *Dialogism: Bakhtin and His World* (London: Routledge, 1990), p. 69; emphasis in original.

4 Mikhail Bakhtin, *Problems of Dostoevsky's Poetics*, And ed. Caryl Emerson (Minneapolis: University of Minnesota Press, 1984), p. 5; emphasis in original.
5 I draw on Holquist's excellent discussion of this point in *Dialogism*, pp. 89–90.
6 Schlegel, "Letter about the Novel," In Ernst Behler, ed. *Dialogue on Poetry and Literary Aphorisms*, trans. Behler and Roman Struc (University Park: Pennsylvania State University Press, 1968), p. 101., See also Philippe Lacoue-Labarthe and Jean-Luc Nancy, *The Literary Absolute*, trans. Philip Barnard and Cheryl Lester (Albany: SUNY Press, 1988), p. 97.
7 See Hermann Diels, *The Fragments of the Pre-Socratics* (Berlin: Weidmann, 1903) and also Kathleen Freeman, *Ancilla to the Pre-Socratic Philosophers* (Oxford : Blackwell, 1962).
8 See Jacqueline Lichtenstein, "The Fragment: Elements of a Definition," In *The Fragment: An Incomplete History*, ed. William Tronzo (Los Angeles: Getty Research Institute, 2009), p. 125.
9 August Wilhelm Schlegel, *Athenaeum* no.24, In *Philosophical Fragments*, trans. Peter Firchow (Minneapolis: University of Minnesota Press, 1991), p. 21.
10 The full title is *Physiognomical Fragments for the Advancement of Human Knowledge and Human Life* (*Physiognomische Fragmente zur Beförderung des Menschenkenntniss und Menschenliebe*). It was published in four volumes between 1775 and 1778 (Winerthur: Heinrich Steiners).
11 Gotthold Ephraim Lessing published these as "Fragments by an Anonymous Writer" In *On History and Literature* (1774–1778). See *Lessings Werke*, XV (Berlin: G. Hempel, 1868).
12 Novalis (Georg Philipp Friedrich Freiherr von Hardenberg), "Logological Fragments," II, #41, In *Philosophical Writings*, trans. Margaret Mahony Stoljar (Albany: SUNY Press, 1997), p. 79.
13 Peter Szondi, "Friedrich Schlegel und die Romantische Ironie," cited by Rodolphe Gasché, "Foreword: Ideality in Fragmentation," In *Philosophical Fragments*, p. xii.
14 Gasché, "Foreword," pp. viii-ix; emphasis mine.
15 *Athenaeum*, no. 206, p 45.
16 Jacques Derrida, *Spurs: Traces of Neitzsche's Styles*, trans. Barbara Harlow (Chicago: University of Chicago Press, 1978), p. 139. See also Nehamas, *Nietzsche: Life as Literature*, pp. 14–21.
17 Friedrich Nietzsche, *Genealogy of Morals*, trans. Francis Golffing (Garden City, NY: Doubleday, 1956), sec. 24, p. 228.
18 Freud, "On Dreams," p. 149.
19 Descartes, *Meditations on First Philosophy*, p. 12.
20 Louis Mackey, *Kierkegaard: A Kind of Poet* (Philadelphia: University of Pennsylvania Press, 1971) p. 137.
21 Mackey, *Kierkegaard*, p. 247. The internal quote is from Søren Kierkegaard, *Concluding Unscientific Postscript*, trans. David Swenson and Walter Lowrie (Princeton, NJ: Princeton University Press, 1968), p. 306.
22 Mackey, *Kierkegaard*, p. 247.
23 Lacoue-Labarthe and Nancy, *Literary Absolute*, p. 42.

24 Theodor Adorno, "The Essay as Form," In *Notes to Literature* I, trans. Shierry Weber Nicholsen (New York: Columbia University Press, 1991), p. 9.
25 Lukács, *Soul and Form*, p. 10.
26 Charles Taylor, *Sources of the Self* (Cambridge, MA: Harvard University Press, 1989), p. 181.
27 The book was transcribed by one of his students. Like Socrates, Epictetus himself wrote nothing.
28 Sarah Bakewell, *How to Live or A Life of Montaigne* (New York: Other Press, 2010).
29 Montaigne, "To the Reader," In *Essays*, p. 2
30 Walt Whitman, "So Long," In *Leaves of Grass*, ed. Michael Moon (New York: Norton, 2002), p. 424.
31 Maurice Merleau-Ponty, "Reading Montaigne," In *Signs*, trans. Richard M. McCleary (Evanston, IL: Northwestern University Press, 1964), pp. 199–200.
32 Montaigne, "Of the Affection of Fathers for their Children," In *Essays*, p. 279.
33 Montaigne "Apology for Raymond Sebond," In *Essays*, p. 376.

## Afterword: Limits

1 Michel Foucault, "Nietzsche, Genealogy, History," In *Language, Counter-Memory, Practice*, ed. D. F. Bouchard (Ithaca, NY: Cornell University Press, 1977).
2 The phrase is Peter Sloterdijk's, *The Art of Philosophy*, trans. Karen Margolis (New York: Columbia University Press, 2012), p. 36.
3 This is among the implications of the opening of the first chapter of Adorno's *Aesthetic Theory*.
4 Gadamer, *Truth and Method*, p. 12.
5 Emerson, "Circles," in *Essays and Lectures*, p. 411.
6 Henry David Thoreau, *Walden* (Oxford: Oxford University Press, 1997), p. 92.
7 Martin Heidegger, *What is Called Thinking?* trans. J. Glenn Gray (New York: Harper and Row, 1968), p. 16.
8 Ronán McDonald, *The Death of the Critic* (London: Continuum, 2007), p. 58.
9 Louis Althusser, "Ideology and Ideological State Apparatuses," in *Mapping Ideology*, ed. Slavoj Žižek (London: Verso, 1994), pp. 100–140 (here, p. 130).
10 Jean-Jacques Rousseau, *Reveries of the Solitary Walker*, trans. Peter France (London: Penguin, 1979), p. 27.
11 Adriana Cavarero, *Relating Narratives*, trans. Paul Kottman (London: Routledge, 2000), p. 33. Emphasis in original.
12 Gilles Deleuze and Félix Guattari, *Kafka: Toward a Minor Literature*, trans. Dana Polan (Minneapolis: University of Minnesota Press, 1986), p. 16.
13 Wittgenstein, *Philosophical Investigations*, I, 32, pp. 15e–16e.
14 Butler, *Giving an Account of Oneself*, p. 9.
15 Jacques Derrida, *The Animal that Therefore I Am*, ed. Marie-Louise Mallet, trans. David Wills (New York: Fordham University Press, 2008), p. 12.
16 Wittgenstein, *Philosophical Investigations*, I75, p. 35e.
17 Cavell, *The Claim of Reason*, p. 496.

# Index

For EU product safety concerns, contact us at Calle de José Abascal, 56–1°, 28003 Madrid, Spain or eugpsr@cambridge.org.

www.ingramcontent.com/pod-product-compliance
Ingram Content Group UK Ltd.
Pitfield, Milton Keynes, MK11 3LW, UK
UKHW010043140625
459647UK00012BA/1580